ARGUMENTS
AND
FISTS

ARGUMENTS
AND
FISTS

POLITICAL AGENCY AND JUSTIFICATION
IN LIBERAL THEORY

MIKA LAVAQUE-MANTY

ROUTLEDGE
NEW YORK AND LONDON

Published in 2002 by
Routledge
29 West 35th Street
New York, NY 10001

Published in Great Britain by
Routledge
11 New Fetter Lane
London EC4P 4EE

Design and typography: Jack Donner

10 9 8 7 6 5 4 3 2 1

Library of Congress Cataloging-in-Publication Data

LaVaque-Manty, Mika.
  Arguments and fists : political agency and justification / Mika LaVaque-Manty.
    p. cm.
  Includes bibliographical references and index.
  ISBN 0–415–93198–3 — ISBN 0–415–93199–1 (pbk.)
   1. Liberalism. 2. Agent (Philosophy) I. Title.
  JC574 .L38 2002
  320.51'3—dc21

                                  2001048458

For my parents and my brother

CONTENTS

ACKNOWLEDGMENTS

This book began as a dissertation at the University of Michigan philosophy department sometime in the mid-1990s (the actual beginning lurking in a metaphysical haze) and was finished across the campus in political science, with a three-year detour to the University of Washington in between. Numerous teachers, colleagues, and friends have contributed to the book, some more than they know, and have left me with a pile of debts.

Inspiring teachers got me on this path and, even though they might not recognize their contributions in the book, helped shape it. Peter Breiner, Mark Kann, Ed McCann, and Robin Romans patiently put up with the adolescent enthusiasm of an undergraduate, presumably in hopes of something more mature down the line. I hope I have delivered. In graduate school, I learned much from Ed Curley, Allan Gibbard, Jim Joyce, Louis Loeb, and Jackie Stevens, among others.

Conversations with colleagues and friends over the years have also helped make this book better, often because they sharpened the ideas here, sometimes because they had nothing to do with those ideas. I am grateful to Nadeem Hussain, Margaret Levi, Michael Taylor, T. J. Pempel, Andrea Simpson, Liz Wingrove, and Steve Yablo. Erik Wibbels has helped me develop my thinking in exciting new directions and is a wonderful friend besides. Unusual suspects in these circles, the members of my virtual running community, Northwest Dead Runners—particularly Bryan Beel, Dave Hays, and Kelly Kruell— deserve thanks for helping me aspire to Justinian's old ideal, *mens sana in corpore sano.*

Many people read parts of the book in their various stages. I want to thank Lisa Ellis, Chris Laursen, Glenn Mackin, Katie McShane, and the participants in my graduate seminars, particularly Ben Smith.

Christine Di Stefano, Steve Hanson, Steve Majeski, Jamie Mayerfeld, Claire Rasmussen, and Bernie Yack all read the entire manuscript and offered valuable comments. Kitty Holland read the manuscript for Routledge and helped me understand my own arguments better; I am very happy about her contribution, and the reader should be, too. Eric Nelson and Jeanne Shu at Routledge have been wonderful editors: helpful, encouraging, and efficient.

There are some people whose influence escapes categories. To my dissertation committee—Liz Anderson, Steve Darwall, Don Herzog, David Hills, and Peter Railton—I am deeply grateful. One couldn't have a finer collection of good teachers and inspiring guides. Liz and Don have been with this project from the very beginning, and their role not only in the development of the book but in my intellectual development and career cannot be overestimated. One of the greatest rewards of pursuing this line of work is that I now get to call people like Liz and Don colleagues and friends. Equally important for my identity as a scholar and teacher have been the examples set by Sally Haslanger and Barbara Herman, both of whom I will always think of as role models.

My greatest debts, however, I owe to my family. Danielle LaVaque-Manty, the better political theorist in the family, read the manuscript more times than anybody, improved its—and my—ideas, and generally made me a better writer, scholar, and person. The long-term support and inspiration from my mother and father, Raili and Jorma Mänty, and my brother, Otto Mänty, are the sine qua non for everything. I dedicate this book to them.

Ann Arbor, October 2001

Part I

A Critique
of Political Agency

AGENCY AND POLITICS— PROBLEMS FOR LIBERAL THEORY?

Carl Schmitt's Challenge

Liberalism, liberal theory, and "the liberal state" have been the free-floating foils for a great deal of contemporary political theory, and the adjective "liberal" is often synonymous with "theoretically weak," "politically unsavory," or both. Liberalism is said to be particularly toothless when it comes to political action. First, it is theoretically weak: Critics charge that liberals favor weak-kneed reformism and parliamentarianism over radical and revolutionary modes of political action only as an afterthought, simply because liberal theory offers such ineffectual resources for thinking about action. This leads to more trouble: On the one hand, the only real model of agency liberal theory has to offer is the *Homo economicus*, for whom politics is merely one of the instruments that makes one's pursuit of one's selfish interests possible. If, on the other hand, liberals think about some actual norms to guide political action, they hold forth on abstract principles such as "public reason," which really means that politics, for a liberal, is all talk and no action.

There are many places where one can find this kind of anti-liberalism; it's a recurring theme in political thought since at least Marx's "On the Jewish Question" or the German Ideology. The early twentieth-century German legal theorist Carl Schmitt offers a good case.

In Schmitt's view, the fundamental principle of liberalism is that "truth can be found through an unrestrained clash of opinion and that competition will produce harmony."[1] There are many ways in which one could quibble about this principle (I will, later), but as an intuitive idea, it is fair enough. It invokes familiar notions of the "marketplace of ideas," "the fact of pluralism," "tolerating the opposing views," and similar liberal slogans. Schmitt's view is that this principle gets liberalism in trouble. The central charge is that the liberal commitment to open discussion is practically untenable and that general liberal principles undermine, rather than facilitate, politics.

Schmitt is not alone in thinking that liberalism is all talk and no action and that such a theory is a mockery of politics. Politics is about making decisions and getting things done, in his view. He approvingly quotes Leon Trotsky's remark to Karl Kautsky: "the awareness of relative truths never gives one the courage to use force and to spill blood."[2] And in his discussion of the anti-liberal Catholic political philosophers de Maistre and Donoso Cortés, he offers a scathing parody of the liberal commitment to public reasoning:

> To suspend the decision at the crucial point by denying that there was at all something to be decided upon must have appeared to them to be a strange pantheistic confusion. Liberalism, with its contradictions and compromises, existed for Donoso Cortés only in that short interim period in which it was possible to answer the question "Christ or Barabbas?" with a proposal to adjourn or appoint a commision of investigation.[3]

It is an anti-liberal staple to charge that the liberal's putative respect of others' perspectives and the consequent need for dialogue result in "cowardly intellectualism": endless discussions and unwillingness of any single party to commit to any sort of action.[4] Responding to this challenge forms the core of this book. In the following chapters, I offer a model of liberal political agency that doesn't turn liberals into either cowardly intellectuals or purely selfish interest-maximizers.

Enter *Herr Professor*

Still, in contrast to the impressive *dramatis personae* of classical political thought— the Prince, the Working Class, the Party, even the more ethereal Invisible Hand and Cunning of History—the character I want to defend as a metaphor for political agency does cut an anemic figure. Immanuel Kant's *Gelehrte*, literally a "learned person" but more freely a "scholar," does evoke images of the fluffheaded professor who writes brilliant treatises but can't fill a book order form or tie his shoelaces. It may be true, a skeptic could say, that politics often *looks* like a committee meeting of social cripples helplessly trying to get things done, but why, for heaven's sake, make this figure a *model* for what it *should* mean to engage in political action? And why, in particular, would that constitute a response to the Schmittian challenge?

Why indeed? Because the metaphor captures important liberal notions about persons and their social relations as well as liberal *ideals* about the norms that should govern those relations. Scholars, ideally, are *individuals* who engage other members of the community of scholars on *open* terms: They must be willing to *justify* their mode of engagement. The engagement thus always has a component that might be called communicative. Further, membership in the community of scholars doesn't wrap the entire person in some comprehensive package—however much the lives of some of our colleagues might suggest that—but is just one aspect of any given person's identity. For Kant, soldiers and clergymen, even monarchs, can also be scholars. At the same time, it is *one* aspect of who the person is. Finally, the scholar metaphor highlights the fact that liberal politics is, as I'll argue, a project of *inquiry* into what relationships of governance and authority should be.

But Schmitt reminds liberals that politics doesn't just take place in the liberal "marketplace of ideas," which the image of a scholar might suggest. Whether political actors should dirty their hands, as B-minus Machiavellians urge, they do. They do so with a regularity that many, reasonably, see as an inevitability. Wherever we look, politics seems to have involved, at least at the extremes, violence and dissimulation, and even routinely it is a site of unreflective passions, heated rhetoric, and sneaky manipulation. Politics seems far from the reasoned scholarly conversation.

Rather than ignore these empirical facts, the Kantian image of the scholar I offer helps make sense of them. It informs the two central theses of this book. The first is analytic, a liberal understanding of political agency: All political action is *necessarily* communicative. On pain of ambiguity or incoherence, for action to count as *political* it must invoke claims to legitimate authority. Despite appearances, this is an analytic claim: I argue that it does capture most action we take to be political—even dissimulation and violence—and also usefully illuminates fuzzy borderlines between political and nonpolitical action.

The second thesis is more explicitly normative. It is an account of what makes something *legitimate liberal* political action. There the scholar, committed to the open contestation and justification of her and others' engagement, marches onto the stage. Those commitments aren't always easy—we are, as Montesquieu observes in Chapter 3, often guided by fickle passions and not just by the calm calculus of reason. Anyone who has ever attended a faculty meeting, say, or an academic conference knows that the world of scholars is no more immune from "distorting" influences to the putative ideals of reasoned inquiry than any other. An account that takes the scholar metaphor seriously must, therefore, be attentive to the influences of emotions, rhetoric, and manipulation. Mine will do that. Conventional wisdom about Kant's exacting, "rigorist" ethics notwithstanding, I argue that the Kantian model can account for a range of emotionally charged politics. This requires some loosening of Kant's demands for the institution of "public reason"; I do, however, retain the spirit. However grudgingly—and she often is—the liberal political actor respects all other agents enough to admit that they have a right to demand a justification of her political engagement. And while this engagement won't encompass the liberal's entire personhood, it has an effect on who the agent is, whether she wants it or not. Out of this emerges a justification for the supposedly weak-kneed reformism of liberal politics, a justification that doesn't, as critics might claim, constrain politics into the soporific realm of elections and interest groups. At the same time, as I show, this model is still rich enough to embrace a very wide range of actual political action, not merely nicely civilized—or cowardly—discourse.

Some Throat Clearing, or Metatheoretical Considerations

What does it mean to offer a *liberal* account of political action? More specifically, what is the connection between explicitly normative theory—liberal theory in this case—and analysis? As the two theses in the previous section suggest, it means two things. First, the analysis must be meaningful to actual persons. This may seem trivial, vacuous, or both, but it isn't. Consider three examples unrelated to liberal theory. Marx's concept of "class," beyond its value as a category in social inquiry, has had a strong effect on how many people see the world and themselves in that world. Especially in the nineteenth century, its radical potential came from the way it allowed industrial workers to articulate a perhaps more inchoate sense of dissatisfaction in politically powerful ways. Or take a similar example from closer to home: Betty Friedan's 1964 concept of "feminine mystique" offered thousands of frustrated women a new, critical way of looking at gender relations.[5] Finally, think of the uses of psychoanalytic concepts in political and social theorizing. Many of them allow people to make sense of the world in ways that can be empowering or conflict resolving. In each case, the meaningfulness is at least partly independent of any claims to truth or even empirical accuracy; psychoanalytic theory is on particularly shaky empirical grounds. Yet all have been powerful.

The same is true here, and the account this book offers attempts to offer people ways of making sense of puzzles and conflicts about what it means to be a liberal citizen or a political actor in general in loosely liberal-democratic societies. Partly because of that, I consider many cases from the real world of contemporary political engagement in the chapters that follow.

The "meaningfulness" criterion is related to another altogether more technical consideration. Normative considerations don't directly attempt to explain the world, but they must be grounded to reasonable accounts of the way the world is. We know from our psychological idiosyncrasies that often the accounts with which we render something "meaningful" are little more than wishful thinking or rationalizations. In political theory, to keep reasonable pluralism from deteriorating into relativist competition of ever wilder accounts of making sense of the world, some link to explanatory theories is needed. You can tell me that gravity is a communist conspiracy, but I am a psychopath if I believe you.

The analytic thesis illustrates what liberal theory must *presuppose* of agents to be plausible as a theory. The explicitly normative component spells out what legitimate political action looks like from a liberal perspective. It makes a difference how we understand that "liberal perspective"—is it a feature of a polity or of individuals, for example?—but the idea is straightforward. The former idea, however, calls for elaboration.

The analysis of what a liberal theory must presuppose to be meaningful offers an account that is, on its face, a descriptive one ("descriptive" in contrast to "prescriptive"). However, it is *not* explanatory. I offer no empirical explanation for why people engage in political action in general or why they choose some particular strategy or movement or forge an alliance. Instead, the account follows a Kantian model of argumentation, or what he understood by the idea of a "critique." The model is simple: For x to be possible, we must assume that y is the case. Here, x is something we are committed to, and one of the main goals of theorizing is to identify and describe y. Take, for example, Kant's argument for the existence of God. There is no proof of the existence of God, Kant admits in *Religion within the Limits of Mere Reason*, but for us to make sense of the very fact of life, reason demands that we assume there is a God. It's important to understand the "weakness" of this assumption; it means less that "we assume that the proposition 'God exists' is true" than "we must behave *as if* God existed." The same argumentative model can be found in Kant's solution to the free will/determinism question (we must assume we are autonomous agents) and to the teleology of the human race (we must assume we are making progress), to mention just a few salient examples, but it characterizes his entire approach. The analysis I am offering is, then, a critique of political agency.

The descriptive account in this book provides the y in a formula where normative liberal theory is the x: How are we to conceive of political action if liberal theory is to make sense? As I suggested earlier, the obvious problem with this move is that it becomes difficult to see how the "as if" view could bolster the plausibility of a normative theory. It may be legitimate to deny the account any explanatory power, but if it's divorced from empirical reality it is nothing but wishful thinking or apriorism of the worst kind. There must be some meaningful standard for evaluation that goes beyond "it's good for our theory."

An analytic account like the one I am offering must be *empirically adequate*. The empirical adequacy requirement comes in two flavors: weak and strong. The weak empirical adequacy requirement demands that an account be consistent with empirical reality. This may seem trivial—and no theory I know has articulated a normative goal whose attainment violates the second law of thermodynamics, for example—but it does point to the fact that some kinds of empirical accounts can rule out normative ones. The familiar undergraduate lament "Marxism won't work because it goes against human nature" *could* be a sound claim if there were a generally accepted theory of human nature with which Marxism were in conflict.

Strong empirical adequacy asks for more: It demands that generally accepted explanatory theories support the analytic conception in some way. This doesn't— and couldn't possibly—mean that the empirical theory must *entail* the analytic conception. To put the matter in deliberately inexact terms, all it means is that the empirical theory (1) confirm at least some aspects of the analytic account and (2) not contradict any. There is, in a way, underdetermination of higher-order theory—the analytic account—by lower-order theory, just as philosophers of science have argued that there is underdetermination of theory by facts.

An example: The relatively thick account of political agency this book develops is, I contend, empirically adequate if some version of the theory of weakly bounded rationality turns out to be true.[6] It won't be empirically adequate if a comprehensive rational choice theory is true because my view relies on assumptions that violate some central axioms of comprehensive rational choice theory. (For example, the idea that our preference orderings may depend on the *role* in which we consider ourselves to be violates the axiom of transitivity.) Since there is currently no universally accepted explanatory theory in the social sciences, it remains an open question as to whether my account satisfies the strong empirical adequacy requirement. (Or, to put this in more sociologically conscious terms, it depends on the reader's theoretical commitments whether it does.) I remain agnostic on the question in what follows, although my view is that what I offer is consistent with explanatory theories emerging from the recent conciliatory terrain between modest rational choice and more interpretive social theory. But the main point is that this book is about the role of *reasons* in and the *meaning* of political action, not about the *causes*, psychological and other kinds, of political action.

My use of "normative" and "explanatory" as labels may suggest that the theory in this book relies on the conventional stark contrast between normative and non-normative theorizing, between the "ought" and the "is." It doesn't. In fact, the supposed category error known as the naturalist fallacy that Hume's guillotine is meant to stop—the inference from is to ought—doesn't track any robust categories. As Hilary Putnam suggests, to call something "just" a question of fact fails to see that in most questions normativity goes all the way down.[7] (Are unborn fetuses persons or not? Is *that* a question of fact or not?) Arguably, the injunction against inference from is to ought is well founded in the few cases of noncontroversial is claims (the rule of *modus ponens* doesn't entail that I should eat my spinach). But the reason we should be wary of making thick value claims on the basis of descriptions is that the descriptions just say so much less than the thick value claims, and not that they are somehow value-free.

This does suggest, however, that while there is no sharp boundary, a pragmatic distinction between normative and nonnormative claims and theories is meaningful. It helps track a distinction in the practical goals of inquiry. But that's all it does.

While little hangs on this particular metaphysical commitment, it has implications relevant for this study. First, I won't claim that my theory of political action and political agency is a *true* theory. It is, at best, a good theory: defensible on pragmatic grounds, on grounds such as the empirical adequacy and meaningfulness requirements. This means, further, that I had better pay attention to the empirical world and to the agents to whom the account is to be meaningful. Thought experiments won't do for this kind of project.[8] Much of this book discusses theoretical questions via glances at real-world political agents, their arguments, their modes of engagement, and their putative reasons for engagement. The institution of public reason, I argue, exists in the world, not merely in theory, and a theorist who wants to say something about the institution needs to be mindful of its actual uses. While my account isn't explanatory—about agents' motivations, for example—it is still empirical.[9]

Except for the historical Part II of the book, the real-world political agents under discussion here come mainly from the ranks of environmentalists. This for many reasons: First, environmental politics is often said to challenge our conventional conceptions of political boundaries. In the realm of *strategy*, for example, it involves the politicization and political use of consumer choices and other "lifestyle" politics. Some environmentalists also raise questions about the scope of our political *norms*, about whether and how they ought to apply to nonhuman entities. Second, environmental politics, even in the industrial world, to which my discussion is limited, runs the gamut of political ideas from the radical left through liberalism to the radical right and, in fact, might go beyond the conventional dimensions altogether. (Think of the German Greens' "Neither left nor right, but forward!") Finally, debates and contests among environmentalists offer a particularly useful slice of the institution of public reason, as I show in Chapters 5, 7, and 8. The general arguments of the book are not limited to the environmental politics it discusses, but, at the same time, the book, as a normative by-product, offers insights on specific environmental disputes.

Liberal Theory and Why the *Homo economicus* Won't Do

But why should we take Schmitt's challenge seriously? One could, for example, reject the "cowardly intellectualism" thesis by offering a different spin on the liberal political agent. And what better example than the familiar *Homo economicus,* who may in suitable circumstances be as ruthlessly Machiavellian as Schmitt's own favorites, but who also captures the liberal intuitions about pluralism, competition, negotiation, and compromise? Simply, why not grant Schmitt the idea that liberal "politics" is fundamentally competitive but then resist the further claims that it turns agents into timid nerds? According to the conventional liberal conception, people are interested in their own lives, so why not simply think that they are primarily indifferent toward those with whom they must negotiate their lives and that all that is necessary is to set up mechanisms that work, in the long run, for the good of all?

Even if one wants to insist on a difference between marketlike social practices and politics, there are other models. Given the intimate relations between democratic theory and liberal theory, many liberals take it as an unproblematic given that the liberal political agent is none other than the democratic citizen, whoever she might be. There are contests over how one ought to conceive of democratic citizenship—do citizens of necessity deliberate, or do they just form interest groups, for example?—but, one could argue, that's where the debates are, and it makes little difference for liberal theory how those debates turn out.[10]

Why the image of a scholar is preferable, I hope, emerges over the chapters that follow. To be sure, the *Homo economicus* and the citizen as paradigmatic political actor are possible conceptions of liberal political agency. But the dispute over the fitting metaphor is a substantive one: It isn't only about getting liberal theory "right," in narrow interpretive terms, but, rather, about how one might *want to* conceive of liberal ideals. To anticipate things a little, my claim is that the image of a scholar incorporates liberals' ideas that the others can't. Most importantly, there is the idea of a community: Scholars relate to others *as* scholars, as members of a particular community. In that community, the norms that guide them are no mere boundary constraints on what they can do—like those pesky rules about insider trading and caveat emptor on the market—but are partly *constitutive of* the scholars' identities as scholars. That, I argue, is analogous to politics and is an aspect the other models cannot capture as well.

It follows that liberal theorists can't just sit back and watch how debates about the best conception of the democratic citizen turn out. The different conceptions in democratic theory aren't neutral vis-à-vis liberalism, and to say that the conception of democratic citizen is important for liberal theory is to invite oneself into the debates that now range between the "aggregative," "deliberative," and "agonistic" conceptions of democracy. Different models of democratic legitimacy and democratic citizenship have different relationships to liberalism, both at the level of high theory, as my discussion of Rousseau in Chapter 3 shows, and at practical levels, as we know from a host of concrete cases, from electoral districts to campaign finance to the European Union.

Furthermore, it would simply be a mistake to regard discussions of citizenship as coextensive to discussions of political agency. However we understand the concept of "citizenship" or "democratic citizenship"—and questions of globalization are certainly showing that there is room for debate—being a citizen does not exhaust the ways in which a person can be political. My looser metaphor will do a better job.

It won't be altogether loose. As I said earlier, the question of a fitting metaphor is also a question of how one might want to conceive of liberal ideals. I show in Chapter 5 that the different conceptions have different practical implications, which, in turn, raise questions of normative appeal. The *Homo economicus* best informs *one particular version* of liberal theory, and I suggest ways in which the conception I advocate informs a more appealing liberalism.

This doesn't, however, entail that the substantive debate is about the correct version of liberalism. I want to reject any claim to "the" authentic or correct liberal theory. Rather, it seems more fruitful, both theoretically and practically, to think of liberal theory as a cluster of overlapping but also mutually contentious theories and liberalism as a historical and political *tradition*, not a single, transhistorical set of principles or practices. Liberal theories have competing conceptions of what the most important liberal principles are and how those principles ought to be conceived of and/or justified. Take, just for example, the familiar contest between egalitarian and libertarian versions of liberalism, waged memorably as the Rawls–Nozick debate in the 1970s. Or take the questions on the metaphysical status of liberal principles: Are individual rights based on the *principium primum* of human dignity, some sort of latter-day natural-rights-without-God conception, or is human dignity a pragmatically justified, "constructed" contingent principle?

Or, even closer to home, take Montesquieu and Kant, whom I discuss in Part II of the book. Both are liberals and, further, liberals in ways that affords us a response to Schmitt. This doesn't mean, however, that their doctrines are the same or even fully compatible. I argue that the two are *uneasily* compatible. They help actual persons make some sense of puzzles and conflicts in a loosely liberal polity, but they don't settle all questions. That, I want to emphasize throughout the book, is an inevitable feature of politics.

Furthermore, while I contrast liberalism to varieties of anti-liberalism—partly to acknowledge the fact that many political critiques since the nineteenth century explicitly target liberalism—such a stark distinction can actually obscure important connections. I try in Part II to make this point vivid. Just as much as the liberalisms of Montesquieu and Kant stand in partial tension with one another, each has an equally complex relationship to the thought of Rousseau, despite its anti-liberalism. Exploring the connections, similarities, and differences does help us see why Montesquieu and Kant are liberals and Rousseau isn't, but equally importantly, it highlights the degree to which liberal theory mines resources from outside the putative liberal staples of toleration, pluralism, reason, et cetera.[11]

Of course, some liberals—those, for example, who think that *truth* is an attainable goal for a political theory or those for whom liberal theory owes nothing to the unsavory types outside its mainstream—regard many of these disputes as temporary and soluble. At the end of the day, in their view, it will turn out that a liberal theory x is correct and that the putative liberals of the y variety are merely impostors or at least people who were wrong. (In other words, in that view, some people are *already* wrong and simply don't know it.) That *may* be the case. At the moment, however, it is at least an empirical fact that there is no agreement on one unique comprehensive conception of what liberalism or liberal theory is. The view I advocate here is that it is more than an empirical fact, that liberalism is primarily a historical tradition and thus continually subject to reasonable and substantive disagreements on what its ideals are. The scholar metaphor, which I advocate in this book, captures both this openness *and* also a specific set of liberal ideals that are appealing *now*.

None of this is to suggest that liberalism is an amorphous mush. There are two principles that, taken together, no liberal can reject. All liberals worth their salt believe, first, in some version of the fact of pluralism, that is, that disagreements on what makes life worth living are going to be irreducible or almost irreducible and, second, that this entails that a social order is best legitimated and made sustainable if those who live under that social order get to determine the courses of their own lives.[12] Let's call the first the fact of pluralism principle (FPP)and the second the principle of individualism (PI):

FPP: Disagreements on conceptions of good are irreducible (or almost irreducible).

PI: The best social order is one that regards an individual as the *pro tanto* best judge of the good life for that individual.

Although some other scholars define liberalism in very similar terms, liberals do disagree on the details of both of these conditions.[13] For example, some might emphasize the "*almost* irreducible disagreements" because they think that a liberalism can be a robustly *true* theory, which means that theories inconsistent with it will be false. Therefore, as Isaiah Berlin claimed, liberals can't be consistently committed to a thoroughgoing pluralism but, at best to an empirical one: People won't agree on what makes life worth living, even though there is some one best conception.[14] Second, these conditions aren't necessarily the *core* of every conception of liberalism, but they are, I contend, either an implication or a presupposition of all. They can serve as a benchmark by which liberals can be identified.

One common way to make these benchmark criteria more concrete is to spell out normative ideals, that is, principles that would realize what it means to allow all members of a polity to count. These ideals include such liberal staples as toleration, human rights, the rule of law, and, importantly for the purposes at hand, the principle of public reason (PPR). We can define the principle of public reason tentatively as follows:

PPR: Political norms, institutions, or practices are legitimate when they emerge out of a deliberative process effectively accessible to all members of a polity, at least in principle, and that the reasons offered in justification of those principles are themselves acceptable to all.[15]

This principle stems from the idea is that there is no single obvious a priori truth about the human good—either individual or collective—and that this process is an effective way to arrive at a workable conception of a collective good. The workable conception, the idea goes, is "discovered" through an inquiry into all those different individual perspectives and conceptions of the good. This is one of the ways in which scholarship is a fitting model for liberal politics.

Of course, liberals debate among themselves how robust a collective good may figure as a political goal. Some libertarians want to deny it altogether; others accept "collective good" as an abstract idea denoting, for example, the aggregate welfare of individuals, while denying that individual political actors ought to be *motivated* by a concrete notion of collective or common good. This fact might seem to put pressure on the scholar metaphor: The scholarly community is *premised* on an explicit joint goal of discovering useful knowledge, while the actual motives of political actors vary widely, even if we can describe politics as a collective discovery in the abstract.

This agnosticism about the content of "collective good" is reasonable, and I take the fact that it is an open question as a point of departure. The goal of the following chapters is to establish the aptness of the scholar metaphor *given* the open question, not in order to deny it. I argue that liberal theory admits a far more robust sense of common good than many commonly presuppose, but I don't do it by demanding from political agents an antecedent motivational commitment to some robust common good.

What Next?

The following chapters offer arguments for the theses I have briefly outlined here. They show that there is a coherent and paradox-free conception of political action in liberal theory, but one that still enshrines the principle that political action must be justifiable with publicly accessible reasons to all concerned. That argument, as I suggested at the beginning of this chapter, builds on an analytic conception of politics as essentially communicative. The game plan is as follows:

Chapter 2 completes the groundwork begun in this chapter. It takes up the question of how we should conceive of "the political." It rejects the view that politics is a narrow sphere coextensive with the state, but it also regards as overkill the idea that politics is everywhere where power relations are. Instead, by approaching the question of scope through the *politicization* of an issue, it argues that the political is a procedural notion that refers to contests over legitimate authority. As such, the chapter argues, all political action is expressive or communicative.

Part II of the book represents a historical turn. I focus on how Montesquieu and Rousseau (Chapter 3) and Kant (Chapter 4) treat the question of political action. This for several reasons: Schmitt's and others' critiques notwithstanding, I argue that liberal theory has had ample resources for thinking about political action for a long time. Specifically, by contrasting Montesquieu and Kant against Rousseau, I want to motivate the liberal misgivings about revolutionary politics in favor of seemingly weak-kneed reformism and institutional tinkering. Liberal reformism isn't just an incidental afterthought, but a carefully considered response to impatient claims for a total social overhaul. Picking Montesquieu and Kant as the representative liberals is deliberate, even if they might seem like second-stringers—or no liberals at all—to some. As I suggested earlier, my point is to challenge the common if mutually exclusive stereotypes of liberals as relying on conceptions of human nature that are too vulgar or too perfectionist. While at best a protoliberal, Hobbes is often credited with having fathered the vulgar or low-brow version of liberalism that informs a stripped-down "liberalism of fear," in which we enter into political obligations purely for instrumental reasons, to protect our private pursuits.[16] Although Kant can sometimes be found in the high-brow liberals' corner, the usual suspect is J. S. Mill read through particularly Aristotelian and perfectionist glasses: Human life is meant to be the rational cultivation of higher pleasures. The former view grants humans too little and the latter too much, but there is a reasonable balance that we can get out of Montesquieu and Kant. Montesquieu shows, I argue, that the acknowledgment of human imperfection doesn't force us to adopt the low-brow view; Kant accepts as inevitable that humans will always remain, at best, a hybrid of perfectly rational beings, on the one hand, and animals, on the other. If there is an unrealistically high-brow conception of humans, it is Rousseau's.

In a way, then, the theoretical foundation for liberal political agency this book offers is also an attempt to revitalize continental liberalism and bring it from under the shadow of the dominant Anglophone tradition. Montesquieu and Kant, despite their differences, help complicate the view in which liberalism is always only about the individual. This isn't a study *of* continental liberalism—that would require attention to much more than just Montesquieu and Kant—but it is a reminder that neither, say, Locke nor Mill are the only liberal games in town. Such a reminder also implies that reading continental thinkers like Montesquieu and Kant as republicans and treating republicanism generally *in contrast to* liberalism (as, for example, Jürgen Habermas does) are not particularly productive. That contrast can be sustained by a definitional fiat that fixes liberalism onto the Anglophone variants, which is exactly what I want to resist.[17] Little, in my view, would be gained by insisting on interpreting Montesquieu and Kant as *alternatives to* liberalism, rather than interpreting them as offering *alternative conceptions of* liberalism.

The ultimate concern of the book is, after all, our contemporary world, where "liberal democracy" in some form makes up the parameters of a good deal of politics. So in Part III of the book, I return to today's political world and "test" my Kantian account of liberal political action. In Chapter 5, I study the uses—and normative consequences—of public reason by two related but different kinds of environmental movements, the so-called not-in-my-backyard (NIMBY) movements and the burgeoning environmental justice movement. In Chapter 6, I address the supposed poverty of liberal theory to make sense of political movements and other collective agents in the first place. Chapter 7 takes on complications internal to the Kantian account by considering how it fares with emotions and how it handles the general conceptualization of agents. In Chapter 8, the different strands finally come together in a model of legitimate political engagement.

Why I'm Not Habermas

Readers familiar with recent literature in liberal and democratic theory will recognize much of this discussion as pointing to familiar terrain and specifically to one towering figure, Jürgen Habermas. Questions of public reason, political justification, and justifiability have figured prominently in the so-called Rawls–Habermas debate and related discussions.[18] The analytic claim that politics is fundamentally communicative seems to echo Habermas's theory of communicative action.[19] And my account of the relationship between explanatory and normative social theory sounds like Habermas's views on the "facticity" and "normativity" of political institutions such as laws.[20] In a way, this is no coincidence: It would be curious if there weren't a family resemblance in the contributions by theorists who draw significantly from Kant. Naturally, Habermas's influential work also influences this book. At the same time, as Habermas himself observes on his debate with Rawls, another contemporary Kantian, there can be family quarrels about relatively small but significant details.[21]

Therefore, in the following chapters, I occasionally orient my accounts in relation to Habermas's similar-looking arguments by explaining why what I say is different and even, in some cases, a disagreement. For example, my discussion of the NIMBY movements and the environmental justice movements in Chapter 5 addresses questions central to the Rawls–Habermas debate. The argument implies that insofar as the debate is concerned, Rawls gets the better of it, but mainly I want to suggest that the very debate reasonably can be sidestepped. And despite my analyzing political action as essentially communicative, I refrain from drawing from that analysis the kinds of normative conclusions Habermas wants to draw.

The general and most important point is that this book is motivated by an intuition that not only Habermas's work but also much contemporary political philosophy misses something crucial about politics. The problem isn't always excessive abstraction—after all, many political philosophers do write about very concrete issues—but the aspirations of the theorists. Even in his search for the empirical overlapping consensus around principles of justice, Rawls is concerned about finding something more robust than a "mere" modus vivendi, something more than Hobbes's *convenient* articles of peace.[22] And Habermas, despite his explicitly "postmetaphysical" search for the *pragmatic* presuppositions of discursive practices, regards his approach as a "quasi-transcendental" one that still looks for *generally valid* ones.[23] It is, of course, an open question whether anything that robust can be generated or discovered by a theorist, but the intuition this book tries to illustrate is that there are at least some resources nearer at hand. Simply, if we relax our steadfast—supposedly Kantian—insistence on a fundamental difference between motives and reasons, interests and principles, rhetoric and justification, then we can see that they not only can but do as a matter of fact coexist in actual political practices. Kant himself, I argue in Chapter 4, held such a view.

This intuition is nevertheless difficult to defend with any single argument—since it weakens to some extent our faith in the power of argument—but what I offer in the following chapters should at least help motivate it.

two

THE SCOPE
OF THE POLITICAL

C arl Schmitt thinks that liberals are fundamentally confused about politics: They think politics is talk, not action. And this is just conflict avoidance: "A class that shifts all political activity onto the plane of conversation in the press and in the parliament is not match for social conflict."[1] Conflict, after all, is the core of politics: "The specific political distinction to which political actions and motives can be reduced is that between friend and enemy."[2] The distinction both defines politics and generates an implication from which liberals, in Schmitt's view, cower:

> The political enemy need not be morally evil or aesthetically ugly; he need not appear as an economic competitor, and it may even be advantageous to engage with him in business transactions. But he is, nevertheless, the other, the stranger; and it is sufficient for his nature that he is, in a specially intense way, existentially something different and alien, so that in the extreme case conflicts with him are possible.[3]

In other words, the enemy is someone against whom one is, if the need arises, ready to wage a war. Thus politics is always already pregnant with violence.

Versions of this conception have gained some currency recently among democratic theorists skeptical of liberals' excessively harmonious ideals of deliberation.[4] It also resembles even older Marxist critiques of the liberal conception of politics, which, according to Marxists, circumscribes "politics" in ways that always end up pushing the real questions of power, emancipation, freedom, and equality out of critical attention.

However, before we abandon any liberal conception of the political, it is worth stopping to ask whether Schmitt's definition is a reasonable one. Two responses to Schmitt are available. The first is to reject the possibility of *any* coherent analysis of the concept of the political. The political is, one could say, fundamentally so stipulative that it makes no sense to try to pin down a conception and hope it will do any theoretical work.

Consider: "To love or not love the operas was a serious political attitude," Anchee Min says of the "eight model operas" of the Chinese cultural revolution.[5] The right attitude could help you along nicely; a wrong attitude, if you dared voice it, would get you in trouble. This certainly highlights two important features about politics: First, narrow conceptions in which politics is limited to the domain of elections, public policy, and foreign affairs are limited. Second, what counts as political is not fixed, but, rather, contingent on time and place. So during the cultural revolution, one's professed attitude towards Jiang Qing's operas said a lot about one's politics and made a great difference to one's life prospects. In early nineteenth-century England, to take an example from another place and time, you could tell a lot about a man's politics by what he said and felt about hairdressers.[6] That is true even today, although the particular questions might be different: It is profoundly political to want to share software you have created openly with others, instead of making proprietary claims for it.[7]

Or think about contemporary environmentalism. On the one hand, environmentalism is seen—along with feminism—as highlighting the political character of previously apolitical social actions. Arne Naess, the grand old man of the so-called deep ecology movement, writes:

> All our actions, and all our thoughts, even the most private, are politically relevant. If I use a clipped tea leaf, some sugar, and some boiling water, and I drink the product, I am supporting the tea and sugar prices and more indirectly I interfere in the works and capital conditions of the tea and sugar plantations of the developing countries. In order to heat the water, I may have used wood or electricity or some other kind of energy, and then I take part in the great controversy concerning energy use.[8]

Moreover, since the rapid popularization of "ecological products," material consumption and consumerism have supposedly become a form of positive political action: By buying one's cosmetics from Anita Roddick's Body Shop or by switching to a recycled toilet paper, one can think of oneself as doing something political. At the same time, however, mainstream environmental groups have resisted the politicization of environmentalism. The World Wildlife Fund, for example, has taken pride in its being not a political organization of grassroots activists, but, rather, a "scientific" organization of "insiders," at least according to their own claims.[9]

On the one hand, then, we have claims that make your choice of a breakfast teabag—or shoes, as we'll see later—an exercise of political agency. On the other hand, we have claims according to which flexing an arguably strong political muscle is not a matter of politics. On its face, this suggests a kind of amorphous contingency to the concept of the political: We use it unsystematically, and our uses are necessarily controversial. There will be neither coherence to or agreement about whether something is political or not.

Schmitt's idea that politics is about the friend–enemy distinction and the examples of "nonstandard" sites of the political suggest that a model in which "politics" is coextensive with "the state" or "public affairs" is indeed hopelessly limited. However, that doesn't mean the concept is completely empty. In the following, I offer an analytic account of the concept of the political that captures the many ways things can be political *better* than Schmitt's but that, at the same time, allows for the kind of dynamism those who see the political as fully stipulative point to. I argue later that it is, in fact, an important *necessary condition* for something to be political that it is contingent and always open to a certain degree of redefinition and challenge. By thinking about how matters *become* political, I generate an analytic account that sees the political as pointing to *controversial claims to legitimate authority* and consequently sees political action as essentially expressive.[10] This argument affords us resources against Schmitt's claim about liberals' political confusion.

Although the following broadens the concept of the political beyond state or public affairs, it stops short of endorsing the relatively popular view according to which politics is synonymous with all power relations. That view is overinclusive and ends up begging the question: Some power relations clearly aren't political, and what we need is a way of understanding which are and which aren't. The following argument does that.

So while most people might not unequivocally agree with Arne Naess on the political nature of even small personal consumer choices such as drinking tea, most do think that production, consumption, and waste disposal *can* be political. To be sure, production relations have been squarely within the realm of the political at least since those nineteenth-century social theorists and the emerging labor movements placed them there. In recent decades, environmentalism has both expanded and specified the way in which production figures politically. Modern environmentalism, sometimes also called "preservationism" and contrasted with the earlier "conservationism," which wanted to save some patches of nonhuman wilderness while happily developing or destroying most of it, is equated with the politicization of chemicals, wastes, and energy production, to name a few elements.[11] Rachel Carson's *The Silent Spring*, for example, made pesticides used in agriculture a political issue in 1962.[12] Since then, a steady stream of arguments and rhetoric has attempted to include more and more aspects of social and personal life in the sphere of the environmentally political, to the extent that advertisements can now tell consumers that by buying and wearing certain shoes they can "walk their talk," as we'll see later.

Two sets of questions arise. First, how did Carson and others succeed in politicizing these *macro-level* social phenomena? What sorts of criteria were at work? While most may now agree that air pollution, toxic wastes, and the like are political, it is not immediately obvious why that is so. Second, even when we understand how some macro-level phenomena become political, we don't automatically know why and how individual, *micro-level* consumer and lifestyle choices also get politicized.

Science as a Site of Political Contest: Controversial Claims to Legitimate Authority

The conventional view sees science and politics as two very clearly different things.[13] The former is supposedly value-free, the latter the very battlefield of conflicting values. To be sure, it is a platitude that science *can* be political, influenced by political motivations and such, but at least on a rhetorical level an air of disapproval surrounds such connections: "Lysenkoism" and "Nazi-science" make people shudder. However, in some cases science can even be the very locus of the political, not merely influenced by values, but coextensive with certain kinds of politics. Moreover, I claim that such a development is not necessarily problematic; understanding why will help us understand much about the structure of what makes something political. Here, then, is a short outline of how air, water, food, and trash are made political and how science has become the site of that politicization.

First, air pollution is a *systemic threat* to many people's well-being. It is, as economists like to call it, a negative externality. But this does not mean that a systemic threat by itself is always enough to make something political. Consider a conjecture I was taught as a child about the fall of the Roman Empire. The story was that the pipelines for the distribution of water in Roman cities were made of lead, which caused slow brain deterioration and other forms of poisoning in the population. The historical accuracy of this conjecture aside, my point is that the lead pipes of the Roman water distribution system were not a political issue.

Why not? Simply because no one made them a political issue (or so I assume). Similarly, the mere fact that DDT and other pesticides accumulate in food chains and thus provide a threat to many humans is not political. To be sure, many of us think it should be—and *that* is what provides the missing condition: Someone must *make* it political. Don Herzog has argued that the economists' treatment of some phenomena as externalities in fact depends on prior, noneconomic *political* understandings.[14] My point is similar but takes us even further back: What is needed is some *articulation* of the general threat or, more precisely, an account of the phenomenon *and* a ground on which it can be seen as politically salient. Call these the descriptive and evaluative components. The evaluative component is important: If there were no one else in American society but Rudolph Giuliani who minded dung-covered Virgin Marys, politicizing the "Sensation" art exhibit would have been a nonstarter. Similarly, if no one had thought it troubling that their food might be toxic, Rachel Carson would have had a much harder time politicizing pesticide accumulation.

Modality is one key element in the evaluative component. Following Hume and Kant, we might stress that it must be *possible* for people to do something about an issue for it to even to be a candidate for politicization.[15] This modality—whether something is subject to human action—is an empirical question, and therefore the descriptive component is equally important. And the politicization of an issue can take several forms. It can be a collective enterprise, the collective *discovery* of, say, similar experiences of sex discrimination by women in consciousness-raising groups,[16] or of a chemical that seeps in basements in all houses of a particular neighborhood,[17] or the *realization* by indigenous groups in several countries that each of them find themselves threatened by the practices of one particular mining consortium.[18] Because of the way the threats develop, the politicization of environmental threats often turns on scientific expertise:

[O]nce the signs can be interpreted by "just anybody" it can be too late to intervene: the woods have already been reduced by acidification or fish stocks have been over-fished. Environmental groups stand in for nature by claiming special competence in reading the signs vouchsafed by the natural world and by claiming to possess a stock of background knowledge about nature's needs. These groups can make such claims in an authoritative manner because they can invoke scientific knowledge about nature.[19]

In other words, scientific expertise provides the first necessary component in the politicization, namely the descriptive claim about a general phenomenon, while the evaluative one may vary from appeal to people's self-interest to the claim about the rights and needs of nature.[20] My point is not that the descriptive claim must always be a scientific one. But *some kind* of descriptive claim is necessary.

However, given that the boundary between descriptive and evaluative claims is blurry, as I argued in Chapter 1, the issue gets complicated. For example, the politicization of science itself becomes apparent when we realize that even the descriptive component may be the very locus of controversy. Both de facto interests and epistemic uncertainty can ground the controversy. The evaluative component may seep into the descriptive component, either quite deliberately or unconsciously. One's environmental values may lead one to embellish *deliberately* the allegedly neutral descriptive component, as Greenpeace activists did in 1969 when they claimed nuclear testing in Amchatka would trigger earthquakes and tsunamis.[21] It often also leads those opposed to environmental regulation to downplay the potential harms of toxic waste incineration,[22] mining,[23] sportsfishing,[24] forestry,[25] and so on. But explicit interests need not contaminate the descriptive content. Because of the nature of many of the environmental scientific issues (the difficulty of prediction of long-term effects, lack of data, etc.), there is a profound underdetermination of theories by facts, which simply invites controversy.

This turns science itself into one of central sites of environmental politics:

> The perception of ecological devastation and the consequences of industrial growth ... depend on methodological knowledge, measurement procedures, and rules of accountability and acknowledgement in science and law, and also on the usually defensive information policies of the suspect operations and the cooperating authorities. ... No matter how this happens, it is only rarely possible without crucial assistance from experts, that is, alternative experts, so we are dealing with conflicts that polarize professional rationality. The splitting of professional assessments is the prerequisite for and the agent of ecological conflict and ecological consciousness.[26]

Now what is it exactly that makes science political in this manner? One answer is to say that it is simply the *ideological origin* of these very threats: Modern scientific hubris makes people pollute the air, poison the waters, and destroy the earth.[27] The problem with the claim is that such a view must regard controversies within science as limited or even misguided. In that view, activists who turn environmental issues into scientific controversies suffer from some degree of false consciousness.[28] However, if we don't assume that this is necessarily the way in which science is political, then we still need some account. That science is a site of controversy itself is not enough; there are many nonpolitical public controversies in science as elsewhere. For example, there can be controversies over the validity of a scientific theory that aren't political because everyone agrees what the criteria for authority are but where there simply are two legitimate interpretations of the available evidence. The crucial element is that science, as a sphere of social activity, is one locus of certain legitimate authority, namely of epistemic authority. In contrast, religious institutions, for example, are not generally accepted sources of public epistemic authority: When a priest tells me my lifestyle is going to get me condemned to hell I myself can decide whether to accord epistemic authority to the priest. Science, on the other hand, has generally recognized epistemic authority: Public institutions in general have accorded it the authority and have told me that I should accept it as well.

Once a controversy arises, especially if it is irreducible (because, say, of the inevitable underdetermination of theories by facts), the only way to depoliticize the sphere of activity in which this happens is to do away with the authority it has. This is exactly what John Locke argued for in his *Letter Concerning Toleration* and what happened to religious institutions as a result of the religious strife in early modern Europe.[29] However, for arguably good reasons, societies have generally been loath to do this with the institution of science. Science remains socially vital, and the legitimate controversies between, say, conventional and alternative medicines ought not mean a total deregulation of all medicine. So, assuming that the controversies regarding scientific descriptions of the state of the environment and nature will remain controversies, science will also remain at least a partly political realm. This doesn't mean scientific institutions should be subject to the kind of political control they were in the Soviet Union or during the Chinese cultural revolution. Rather, I mean that scientific authority in the areas in which it is controversial is not automatic, but *itself in need of justification*. As clearly has been the case in environmental matters, science cannot always be relied upon as the arbiter of conflicts. In those cases, science itself becomes political.

Making Your Walk Do Your Talk

A more explicit focus on *agency* is necessary if we want to respond to Schmitt's conception of the political and to his charge that liberals are confused about politics. In this section, I focus on how individual agents figure in the politicization of issues that aren't obviously political to begin with. As we know, the politicization of our everyday environment which Rachel Carson helped start has led to the politicization of most aspects of modern industrial society.[30] Naess's earlier point can then be taken to capture something: If tea production and energy distribution are political issues, then by making myself a cup of hot tea I do connect to something political. But the vague "connecting to something political" is not obviously synonymous with "doing something political," or "doing something with political implications." In this section, I will argue that the salience criterion for a micro-level political act is not a direct causal line, but, rather, depends on what we might loosely call "political semantics."

Consider a passage from the mid-1990s "Real Goods" mail order catalogue:

Walk your talk with Deja Shoes. Made from a variety of reused and recycled materials, over 20 different kinds in all. Environmental footwear—from the tough molded outsoles containing recycled tire rubber to the rugged, water repellent uppers of recycled polypropylene. And all manufactured using non-toxic, water-based adhesives.

Deja Shoes are stylish, comfortable and extra-durable. And they arrive in a shoe box made of 100% recycled cardboard, which is reversible as an attractive gift box.

Environmental stewardship, taking care of the planet now for future generations, is what Deja Shoes is all about. It's at the root of everything the company does. And buying environmental products, like Deja Shoes, makes it all happen. It's your purchase of these products that finally closes the loop and helps conserve resources, habitats and species.

I am interested in taking seriously the suggestion that one is supposed to be doing something political by buying Deja Shoes. That claim needn't, in itself, be controversial: I believe we have at least some intuitions like this. What I am specifically interested in is *what* makes Deja Shoes political, if indeed they are.

Imagine a happy new owner of a pair of Deja Shoes who, in his response to our query about the point of his buying Deja Shoes, says, "It helped slow the waste of natural resources by making previously throw-away products such as tires, diapers, aluminum, etc., reusable. This way it helped future generations. It also helped preserve wildlife habitats because the company donates part of their profits for stuff like that." The point of both of these is to have a *causal impact* on the world. How might this be political?

There are two possibilities. One: The owner of Deja Shoes might be a close relative of the *Homo economicus*. Although he is more broad-minded than his selfish cousin, he still conceives of political action as instrumental action. Or, two, he is, instead, a veritable *Homo sociologicus* and uses his shoes to *express* his identity or a role. The former conception, I argue, is unsatisfactory; the expressive account fares better, even though it doesn't mean politics is just about role playing.

The instrumentalist wants to say that there is a direct causal connection between his individual consumer choices and macro-level political states of affairs. Macro-level political states of affairs are, after all, aggregates of individual actions, so individual choices must be relevant. For example, driving less, he produces fewer greenhouse gases; consuming less, he contributes less to overall production; and consuming "green," he contributes to ecological modes of production.

But this is fallacious. While it may be true that what and how societies consume is a political question at the macro level, it only means that individual consumer choices are *somehow* connected to political questions. It doesn't mean that an individual's actions have the relevant kind of causal connection.

We can distinguish three different ways for how individual actions relate to macro-level states of affairs. (1) There are actions that are inefficacious as individual acts and whose impact is questionable even in a reasonable aggregate.

(2) Some actions are entirely inefficacious as individual actions but causally significant in the aggregate. (3) Some are minimally significant but not entirely inefficacious as individual actions and significant in the aggregate.[31] An individual person's disinvestment of, say, a company stock is an example of (1): Whether an individual person or even many individuals decide to sell their shares in disapproval or the company policy is not going to have a significant causal impact since the shares have to be sold to some other people. Voting in larger than local elections is generally a good example of the second category: My vote is not going make any difference by itself (I ignore the unlikely case of tie-breaker votes), but the aggregate impact is obviously important. Finally, my not driving a car or someone's buying a pair of Deja Shoes are examples of (3). The conceptual difference to the zero marginal impact of voting is that the act continues to have an impact, albeit a small one.

So buying Deja Shoes does make a *small* difference. But we still have no handle for deciding whether that difference is enough to make the action political. In fact, the distinction between kinds of impact only highlights the fact that the political salience of an individual act does not always lie in its causal impact. Voting *is* a political act, even though a single vote has no marginal impact. Moreover, I want to claim that both acts of type (1) and (3) can be political.

What is the difference between voting and buying Deja Shoes that makes the former political and the latter not? The most obvious one is that everyone knows voting is political, whereas not everyone thinks that buying shoes is. If anything, people think that footware procurements are nonpolitical. Of course, people may be wrong. Or maybe there is at least some construction on which we understand buying Deja Shoes as political.

Consider consumer boycotts. Example: Shell Oil has been a popular target of boycotts. In the 1980s it was Shell's involvement in South Africa; in the 1990s it was the corporation's support of the military dictatorship of Nigeria. Say I decide to boycott Shell. In a causal analysis, this is a case of type (3) action: My not pumping at Shell has a tiny effect on the company's profits. But so does the action of my neighbor, who has a discount card with Mobil. If my act is political merely by virtue of its causal impact, then so is my neighbor's. And that can't be, at least not in a world when most people who don't use Shell are like my neighbor and not like me. It doesn't help if I insist that I'm *changing* my fuel consumption habits for political reasons; again, it is likely that *most* such changes are the results of consumers' properly microeconomic reasons: Exxon has a sale.

Maybe something on the background provides the clincher. Back to the shoes: Does it make a difference if we know what our shoe purchaser considers the *alternative uses* for the same money? Maybe he needs shoes and opts for Deja Shoes instead of boots made of endangered rattlesnake skin. Or he doesn't need new shoes, but wants a pair of these hip environmental things, anyway. Or he considers whether to donate the money to Greenpeace instead. The causal impact varies in each case, but not enough to make the purchase anything other than type (3) case. Further, the variance is likely to depend on complicated empirical facts about which we can hardly expect consumers to think all the time.

All this amounts to saying that the act of buying Deja Shoes is ambiguous, and ambiguity is a feature of *meaning*, not of causal relations.[32] Remember, voting, this causally inefficacious act, is unequivocally political because people *understand* it as such.

Thus the expressive account looks more appealing. Imagine that the Deja Shoes buyer is entirely aware of both the ambiguity of his action in causal terms—*he's* buying them for nature, someone else for fashion—and the questionable causal impact. He nevertheless buys them for a political reason, namely to *send a message.* By wearing them, he believes that he sends a message about ecological values, about recycling, about consumption habits, and so on.

This distinction looks much like Max Weber's distinction between *zweckrational,* instrumentally rational, and *wertrational,* value rational.[33] It also evokes Hume's typology of political action into interest-based, principled, and affective.[34] The resemblance is not a coincidence, although Hume, unlike Weber and me, thinks that principled and affective reasons aren't really good ones. The general point is that treating political action as value-rational or affective expressions of attitudes helps us understand what is political about wearing Deja Shoes.

Call an action or an omission that conveys a message an *expressive exercise of agency.* There are several kinds. The person who sports Deja Shoes is, I take it, sending a message about her personal political preferences or values. This *may* be ultimately instrumental, in the sense that the agent is trying to have an effect on other people's preferences, values, and even behavior, but it needn't be. The agent may also be trying to locate herself publicly on a political map: The Deja Shoes mark her out as an environmentalist—or so she hopes. Here, even acts of type (1) can be meaningful: "*I* will not own stock in Shell, even if someone else does." These forms of expressive action are fraught with complications—the threat of seeming hypocrisy among the more obvious ones: If our eco-consumer also drives a sports utility vehicle and dons a fur coat, her credibility or even the meaning of the message can be undermined. Complications notwithstanding, the idea is intelligible.

While attempts at persuasion and identification can be aimed at the relevant political community at large, expressions of *solidarity* are aimed at those with whom one sympathizes.[35] When an agent expresses her solidarity with someone, she is identifying herself *to* that someone: "I am with you." Note that solidarity is an interesting case: Sometimes the expression of solidarity exhausts the agent's options for the exercise of her political agency. Consider: I may identify with an American political campaign, but if I am not a U.S. citizen, I cannot vote, and political prudence about foreign contributions suggests that I refrain from contributing to the campaign materially. It nevertheless seems legitimate for me to express my solidarity with the campaign. And I will have done something political, even if the expression of solidarity exhausts my options.

At this point, we might have the Schmittian on board again. After all, for Schmitt, one important component of politics is to create and maintain political identities with publicly intelligible identifiers.[36] However, solidarity doesn't require one's identification *with* the political goals of those to whom one expresses solidarity: I may be indifferent or critical toward the goal you have, yet think that your claim is legitimate and support you in it as a matter of principle. The late 1980s Wisconsin political battle about Native American fishing rights is an example of this: Many nonnative supporters of the embattled Chippewa disapproved of their traditional spear fishing, yet supported the campaign on justice-based grounds.[37] Similarly, in the late-1990s Washington state controversy over Makah Indians' right to whale, many non-Indians expressed solidarity toward the Makah without endorsing the actual hunt.

None of this is to say that expressive action isn't closely hooked up with causal connections. They intermesh in several ways. First, communication is a causal process, where the mere uptake of a message can be understood through a causal analysis. Second and less trivially, securing the right uptake of the expression depends on all sorts of causal processes on the background. I can send a message with Deja Shoes because of the kinds of causal processes involved in their production, and it would be very difficult for me to send the same message with sweatshop-produced snakeskin boots. The central distinction I am after, however, has to do with the agent's understanding of the action in a causal chain. In the expressive action I am discussing, the agent doesn't conceive of her action in terms that make it an *instrument* for some causal impact. The point of action is not to get something *done,* but to get something *said.*

But why aren't these merely examples of very complex instrumental action? Couldn't we say that the particular choices of action the agent makes reflect her thinking it the best means for the overall end? I want to suggest two reasons why returning to the instrumental picture would be unwise.

First, remember that we are trying to understand what makes an act a political act. We saw that unvarnished causal analysis doesn't get us far. So at least when looking for the criteria of the political, we simply must look somewhere else. Of course, I don't want to deny that expressive and instrumental action often occur together. In fact, consumer boycotts are an example of just this: Recall that they are based on type (3) causal impact, that is, on the aggregate impact of several minimally effective individual actions. The aggregate impact is achieved, if at all, by persuading people to join the boycott. But even then, it is not the causal impact, but the meaning of the act that makes it political. Everyone may understand my Shell boycott as political, yet disagree with me and refuse to join.[38]

In many cases, expressive action is nonreducible to instrumental action. Think of how an agent would respond to changes in the relevant circumstances. If a Shell boycotter discovers that the boycott is in fact having bad consequences—lack of foreign capital destabilizes Nigerian politics in the wrong way, for example—then she may want to change her strategy. Or if the boycott achieves its ends, then its rationale disappears. These facts about the changed state of affairs appear in the agent's deliberative field as a *reason* for some different action. Contrast this to our expressive Deja Shoes wearer. We might discover that the net ecological effect of Deja Shoes is not just marginal, but zero, say, because the ecological costs in transporting are greater than the savings in resources. She might nevertheless say, "It doesn't matter, *that's* not the point. People understand this as environmentalism." In this way, in an appropriate context it might make more environmentalist sense to buy and wear Deja Shoes than donate the money to Greenpeace, or whatever.

Or consider agency as an expression of solidarity: If the solidarity is genuine, it does not end even if the movement one supports is losing. This doesn't mean that expressive agents aren't responsive to facts: If it turned out Deja Shoes were a by-product of napalm production in a mob-owned sweatshop, the agent certainly would have good reasons to change her behavior, and, on pain of hypocrisy, she should. But this is not in the first instance because of what her act *does*, but because of what it *means*.

Do we now have criteria for calling something political? No: I can express solidarity to my school football team or to my alma mater; I can also try to send a message that I'm really cool with a nose ring and a tattoo, or even with Deja Shoes. That an action is expressive doesn't make it political. Secondly, the problem of ambiguity remains. Even when acts are understood to be partly expressive, it might not be obvious *what* is being expressed: A vegetarian might be condemning the treatment of animals in agribusiness or the ecological wastefulness associated with meat production—and these are just two of the political reasons, in addition to ethical or health reasons.[39] Despite all this, clearly the *meaning of actions* is somewhere at the heart of the matter.

The problem is that people don't understand our agent's act of wearing Deja Shoes as political. Solution: Make them understand. Explicitly endow your action with a political meaning. How would one do this?

In this post-Wittgensteinian world, we know that meanings are not private. It will not make it political if I just *think to myself* that the way I hold my pencil expresses my condemnation of capitalist economy. One way or another, this idea needs to be made public. "Look, here, the way I hold my pencil expresses my condemnation of capitalism." But there would be something odd if people were satisfied to think that, from now on, pencil holding in a particular way is *political*. Something more is needed. One strategy that seems appealing is to make an argument. It is doubtful that I could marshal an argument to make my pencil holding intelligible as a condemnation of capitalism (although it and other issues of body comportment might be used to say something about class politics, say, or gender). Arguments that make the shoes we wear political aren't far-fetched at all. A relatively common argument is to establish the small causal connection between individual consumer choices and macro-level states of affairs, and then say something like, "If everyone did this, the exploitation of natural resources would be diminished." If this argument is about consumer choices, it renders not only the *arguer's* consumption political, but mine and others' as well—assuming the argument goes through.

Thus the argument can appeal to something understood to be political and explain why the specific issue at hand is connected in the right way. Even with zero marginal impact, wearing Deja Shoes can be argued to be an instantiation of some "eco-political" principle or value: The idea is that recycling is valuable, whether or not a single instance does anything. The shoes can also be argued to be an expression of a kind of solidarity or identification with a political cause, the combat boots of a green uniform.

Schmitt and liberals might have some grounds for agreement here (at least if we don't insist that liberals must be *Homines economici*): Politics is expressive. But liberals might also insist that the analysis vindicates the very commitment to public communication Schmitt criticizes. If the analysis so far is right, it suggests that reasoning that appeals to social meanings is at the crux of the political. And if that is so, then we get two cornerstones of liberal theory out of seemingly nonnormative premises, simply out of understanding what politics is all about. Far from mere regulative ideals from high-faluting full-compliance theory, public reason and deliberation, it seems, are what *make* something political. From this, it would be a short step to justifying the idea that politics *presupposes*, rather than possibly generates, liberal democracy.

This is too good to be true, and a conclusion like that would be hasty. Expressive action isn't the same as public reason. Think of the T-shirts that say, "It's a black thing. You wouldn't understand."[40] Again, I will assume that there is little question on whether people take this as political. Even if a person can't quite place the message (Is it a black nationalist slogan—or something else?), most socially literate persons in North America today would understand it as saying *something* political. It is obviously directed *outside* the African-American community—to the "you" who wouldn't understand. So it is "public," but it is decidedly not a use of public reason. "You wouldn't understand, so I won't bother."

The slogan is best as a meta-level claim about the authority to make various ground-level claims. Consider the following exchange: "I don't understand Kwanzaa," I, the culturally dense white person, might claim. "It's a black thing. You wouldn't understand," responds my interlocutor (who needn't be African American). "But look," I say, "it's an artificial holiday, invented just recently on the basis of a historical hodge-podge." "It's a black thing. You wouldn't understand." It is an open question who is acting unreasonably in this exchange. My interlocutor is not engaging in the use of public reason, to be sure, but from her perspective, I might as well be telling her what it is like to be a bat. *If* she is right, then I'm not in a position to make any claims about the intelligibility of Kwanzaa. The T-shirt slogan is based on a notion of epistemic privilege that tracks race, but that doesn't mean it is false; it's an open question. To decide on the reasonableness of the exchange, a move to a second-order evaluation of the truth of *that* claim would be necessary. What are the *reasons* for my alleged inability to understand the issue? What are my reasons for the claim that I would understand it, and so be in a position to pass judgment on Kwanzaa? *If* the discussion moves on to the meta level, we'll be talking about something like public reason. But, as we know from many an everyday political interaction, that often doesn't happen.

What makes the issue political is a controversial claim to some type of authority. Here, it is a little less obvious than in the case of science what is the relevant authority about which the controversy arises. The issue, I take it, is not any old claim of epistemic privilege. If a physicist told me, "It's quantum mechanics, you wouldn't understand," I most likely would agree. But given putative ideals of race blindness and the idea that "we are all humans," *race* is not supposed to work the same way. My life experience is different from that of people of other races—or even from that of other individuals, regardless of race—but surely I should be able to understand matters if they are explained to me, particularly if we are talking of people who live in the same culture. To say, then, that something would be unintelligible for a nonblack person "because it's a black thing" is to disagree with either race blindness in general or with the claim that it has been achieved; it is to say that the cultural differences between African Americans and others, at least whites, run much deeper than some people currently say they do.

Now the Schmittian has a retort ready: Liberals are those clueless types who, in the name of universal humanity, insist that they would too understand "the black thing" even if they were all white and who, further, insist that because of this everybody just might as well discuss the matter reasonably. They miss, the Schmittian charge goes, what makes the whole thing political in the first place: the T-shirt slogan's rejection of the liberal principle of "reasonable discussion." So they are confused about what is political about political controversies. And they are at a possible impasse since they can't demand for the potentially conciliatory move on to the second-order discussion because they have no mutually agreed-upon principles with the other side. Hence, the Schmittian declares, are liberals' confusion and their misguided and cowardly intellectualism. Politics is expressive, to be sure, but not in the ways liberals would want.

That it takes the rest of this book to generate a satisfactory rejoinder to the Schmittian should indicate how serious this challenge is. Of course, one liberal response would be to dig in one's heels and still insist on the *Homo economicus*'s conception of the political. But that, as I suggested earlier, just misses the point of politics in another way. Also, as I suggested in Chapter 1, it is too thin to capture liberal ideals we intuitively regard as valuable: There is much to be said for the institution of public reason. And if we want to regard "cowardly intellectualism" merely as a pejorative description of the liberal commitment to political reform-ism, then it needs a defense, not an embarrassed abandonment. Hobbes's theory reminds us that a conception of justice as mutual advantage—the only conception the *Homo economicus* knows—doesn't quite give us the principles most moderns, whether liberal or not, take for granted.

To be sure, the Schmittian challenge does turn on a particular conception of liberalism. For Schmitt, liberalism is a "complete metaphysical system" according to which "truth can be found through unconstrained discussion."[41] It wouldn't be difficult to show that, strictly speaking, the conception mischaracterizes many versions of liberal theory.[42] However, taken more loosely, it does track many a contemporary construal, and it is not a coincidence that recent critics of liberalism have found Schmitt appealing.[43] One way to describe the Schmittian challenge would be to say that the liberal confusion about politics stems from their having an a priori commitment to only one kind of legitimacy.

Take Weber's standard conception of legitimacy as a point of departure. For Weber, a system enjoys legitimacy when it is considered binding.[44] My morning routine—up at 6 A.M., a bagel, coffee, and a run—might be a system, but it is not binding, whereas my clocking in at the factory at 8 A.M. every morning is not just a contingent routine, but a routine that binds me. Of course, this just begs the question: What is necessary for something to be considered binding? And let's not let the social theorist's infuriating passive voice dull our senses: considered *by whom*?

Weber suggests that the legitimacy of an order can be guaranteed in two ways: subjectively or by "the expectation of external effects," that is, by the system's serving some objective interests.[45] In the first case, in other words, people simply regard the relevant system as legitimate. This comes about in three different ways. It may be *affective*, that is, people simply "emotionally surrender" to it, for whatever reason. The victim of a protection racket or a black market may, despite its extortionate effects, come to think of the racket as legitimate, as "the way it works, whether I like it or not." The legitimacy might also be granted because of *religious reasons*: A person might think tithing is a legitimate system because it helps guarantee her salvation. Finally, the legitimacy may rest on *value rationality*: People living under the system believe it, on reflection, to express moral, aesthetic, or political principles.[46]

In the second main case, that is, when the legitimacy of a system follows from its serving some objective interests, the subjective feeling that it is binding isn't necessary. Grumble as they might, we tell children that our making them eat their broccoli is legitimate because it is good for them. Obviously, in these kinds of cases, *someone* must regard the system as serving the objective interests; it simply needn't be those whom the system nevertheless binds.

One way of formulating "controversial claims about legitimate authority" is to frame it as disputes over which of these different modes of legitimacy ought to govern the system in question. The separation of the church and the state, for example, emerged out of a dispute in which a religious legitimation for social institutions lost to other candidates. Now the liberal idea, the Schmittians claim, is to *presuppose* that only one particular value-rational conception is in fact legitimate. Other conceptions are faux legitimacies, mere pretenders. My concession to the Schmittian challenge is to grant that insofar as liberals do indeed presuppose that the value-rational conception of legitimacy sets parameters to political discussion, they are misguided about politics. And my point in the following chapters is to offer a model that does generate a commitment to value-rational legitimacy *as a conclusion* but that respects the actual practices of politics, those controversial claims to legitimate authority, in doing that.

Conclusion

One might object to my conception of the political by saying that it turns everything into politics. Since most human interaction is governed by some norms, it looks as if everything might be or become political. The worry is unwarranted: Only norms relevantly related to *legitimate authority* can be at issue. In many social practices, individual persons are the unproblematic authorities of what to do, which is one way of saying that many social practices are such that controversies over legitimate authority are unlikely to arise. Consider the German Green politicians who courted controversy by entering the Bundestag in sweaters in 1984. In that context, authority over dress rested on norms of etiquette, and the Greens challenged it by implying they, as individuals, should be the authorities of their own sartorial norms. The way we dress at home, or at leisure with our friends, is *not* regulated in a similar way, even if there are conventions: The authority on norms—or normlessness—rests with us. If I wear a suit at home, I'm flaunting convention but not challenging anyone's authority. Sure, there are conventions here as well, but the conventions are not authoritative. There is room for nonpolitical idiosyncrasies in the conception of the political advanced here.

So, what can we say about the people who think they are doing politics with Deja Shoes? *Can* they make their walk do their talk with Deja Shoes? The answer, I take it, is a qualified yes or, perhaps more accurately, the maddening "it depends." It depends on the background beliefs of those among whom they are trying to walk their talk. Those background beliefs are, of course, partly open for the agents to change, and it makes a difference whether they do something about that. If you convince me that footware choices are a matter of politics, I'll interpret people's shoes as political expressions. But the background beliefs are only partly open to changes. Nothing I have said does away with the ambiguities entirely. The background beliefs against which acts are understood can conflict, and it is possible no unequivocal social meaning can be found. Seeing someone with Deja Shoes, I might wonder whether the point is political and might in fact be unable to decide without further clues. That is, I want to claim, a condition with which we must live. The political is not an unambiguous or unchanging social fixture. The ground under political agents is decidedly shifty, and what they do is partly responsible for how it shapes up. But it isn't just up to them.

Political action isn't, then, quite like dancing in chains, to borrow Nietzsche's clever metaphor.[47] The structures that constrain the exercise of meaningful agency aren't completely unyielding once you come to the end of the slack. The boundary for what counts as intelligibly political can be extended beyond the prevailing conceptions as long as one can appeal to some existing understandings. It's more like bungee cords than chains.

What does this mean in practice? The most important constraint is that a person, to count as a political agent, must address herself to the relevant community—those governed by the system of norms in question, what I will call "justificatory community" in Part III—and operate with its background beliefs. This is not trivial. First, even the lone terrorist or eco-saboteur operating in secret needs a context in which his or her act can be understood as political, not as a random act of violence or vandalism. Second, there can be *privately* expressive acts that aren't political. Think of the person who quietly buys Deja Shoes because, in her not unreasonable view, buying any other shoes would amount to doing something wrong, and she is not going to dirty her hands. Her's is arguably an exercise of moral agency, but it is not political.

In what *constitutive* ways, if any, does the political shape persons? What does it enable? The answer is that it turns persons into *sources of claims* about legitimate authority. (Let's be attentive to the word order: This is not the same as my taking you as a *legitimate source* of claims.) This is conceptual, not causal: "Source of claims about authority" is not some reward a person is granted upon successful completion of a properly political act. Doing something political is simply to *be* such a source of claims.

Again, this is far from trivial. According to some conceptions, politics can only take place between equals.[48] This conceptualization offers one possible gloss on that idea: All political agents are equal qua claim-makers. For me to acknowledge your action as political is to grant you a particular status. Further, since political claims are, *per definitionem*, about legitimate authority, that is, about the scope, nature, and modes of justification for the system of norms that governs us, then I have no noncontroversial grounds to claim that *my* status as a claim-maker is higher than yours. When my students ask, "Why should we believe you?" the goodness of my answer, "Because I'm your professor" depends on what they mean with their question. If they are asking because they are wondering about this baby-faced character holding forth in front of the room, my answer should satisfy them. But if they are pedagogical radicals and mean, "Why should we believe professors?" then my answer is no good. That's the very authority the question is challenging. Ergo, politics only takes place among equals.

Note that the account resembles the core components of Jürgen Habermas's theory of discourse ethics, although mine is an analysis of politics while Habermas generates the theory out of an idealization of all communication. It is Habermas's next move, however, that I really want to resist. Using a "quasi-transcendental" argument, he turns this fundamental fact about communication into a normative one: Anybody engaged in communication must, on pain of contradiction, recognize some normative facts about fundamental human equality.[49] The normative content can be thickened further, and on some, only partly facetious, readings of Habermas, the very logic of human communication entails social democracy and federalism for the European Union.[50] My view, in contrast, is that the *conceptual* equality of political claim-makers doesn't entail any thick political norms. This is not because of any great reverence for the is–ought gap on my part. I am not suggesting that Habermas commits the naturalist fallacy—he compellingly avoids it—but, rather, that the minimal equality in communication offers no satisfactory argumentative resources against someone who wants to deny the thicker normative conclusions.

The crux of my disagreement lies in the weight of the "transcendental" aspects in Habermas's view. Insofar as Habermas *also* draws from pragmatist concerns, his argument is compelling. The standard pragmatist argument for why contradictions are bad is not that they offend Plato or gods, but that they make us bump into things: Thoroughgoing skepticism about that wall in front of me will cause a bruise on my forehead. On that, I have no quarrel. However, Habermas also wants to be a transcendental philosopher, and he implies that the kind of contradiction involved in disrespecting your interlocutor is one of those pragmatically problematic ones. Here I disagree. Not all contradictions cause us to bump into things; humans successfully entertain a host of inconsistent beliefs. A further argument is needed to show why communicative contradictions would be problematic. There is nothing wrong with trying to do that, and the Kantian account I offer in Chapter 4 is in fact an example. But the contradiction alone isn't enough. As my argument about the "black thing" slogan showed, nothing automatically opens a discursive forum for such an argument.

In general, I want to reject the idea that the very nature of politics commits people to recognizably liberal-democratic principles (or, for that matter, to *any* specific principles): to the proscription of violence, to reasoned deliberation, to the assumption of human equality. It would be nice if one could say that anyone rejecting nonliberal and nondemocratic modes of political engagement were somehow making a conceptual mistake, but the fundamental nature of politics is that the status of such arguments is in question.

Simply, the fact that politics is essentially expressive doesn't circumscribe *some particular set* of expressive means. Again, since what's at issue are the very norms of legitimate authority, there is no antecedent principle that would limit the available means to some particular set such as rational arguments. Claims can be made in many ways, and all that is required is that they be understood as claims (which, as I showed earlier, includes actions when they are understood to have the right kind of symbolic meaning). No background beliefs about the claim-makers themselves need be held. I may think you are beneath contempt and refuse to acknowledge or take seriously anything you say. But you may have resources beyond the repertoire of my beliefs: You can, for example, put a gun to my head. For example, if Simon Schama's controversial analysis of the French Revolution is correct, it wasn't the persuasive power of argument that got the revolutionaries' demand of *liberté, fraternité, et égalité* taken seriously, but the guns that accompanied those claims.[51] Granted, many are unlikely to regard such a claim as legitimate (although in the Old West they might have), but that's just a counterclaim and on no firmer antecedent ground than the other. Someone's status as a claim-maker doesn't entail anything specific about the criteria whereby the validity of the claims gets judged.

And, of course, you may completely lack the means to bolster your particular claim to authority, in which case, if I don't believe you to be a claim-maker in the first place, the issue simply fails to get off the ground. To suggest that the very nature of politics entails nice liberal-democratic principles presupposes there is an agreement on who counts in the first place. There isn't: Much political action consists of struggles to achieve a minimal standing as a claim-maker. The putative equality of political agents can be the outcome of a battle, after all. (In Chapter 7, I'll show that the issue doesn't get resolved easily even after we commit ourselves to some specific set of principles for how claims to legitimate authority can be made.) At best the equality of political claim-makers is very weak, much like the weak equality of people in the Hobbesian state of nature.

So while my conception of the political rejects Schmitt's—Schmitt's now seems like one special case—there is something to be said for Schmitt's and other critics' impatience with liberalism. It isn't that liberals are really confused about politics; it's simply that their norms for political engagement seem both arbitrary and inefficient. They are arbitrary because they carve out a set of procedural norms— for example, commitment to public reason, nonviolence—and normalize the relations among political agents—that very thin equality qua claim-makers turned into a robust principle—seemingly ex nihilo. To be sure, if it were a fact that everybody took the liberal principles for granted, then there would be no issue. But they don't: People hijack airplanes, blow up buildings, sink whaling ships, spike trees, break laws, scream and yell, and hold others in or beneath contempt. When that is the reality of political action, the Schmittian says, the liberal norms are themselves a disingenuous god-trick. In this view, Rawls's recent move from the fact of pluralism to *reasonable* pluralism is just a euphemism for what Herbert Marcuse more appropriately called "repressive tolerance."[52]

To respond to this critique, I want to take us back to a context where liberalism wasn't the big man on campus. I want to investigate the emergence of the liberal norms for political engagement in eighteenth-century liberal thought. In this context, the norms were not taken for granted—even at the level of high theory, let alone practice—and had to be defended (1) as meaningfully compatible with what people actually did and (2) against other *new* theoretical contenders. Although the Enlightenment was united by its various strands' opposition to absolutism, the proposed alternatives varied widely.[53] It is therefore useful to think about what makes a theory liberal, what separates it from non- or anti-liberal thought, and what consequences it has for political action. In the next two chapters, I undertake this project by considering two liberals, Montesquieu and Kant, in contrast to Rousseau. From Montesquieu, I argue, we get a commitment to *institutional* solutions to political problems. From Kant, we do get an argument for the liberal principles whose *self-evidence* I have been resisting here, but we also get a surprisingly rich appreciation for the way in which they figure in historical contexts. And from Rousseau, we get an influential standard of anti-liberalism against which the two liberals' theories are made intelligible but to which they also are—perhaps troublingly—related.

Part II

PASSIONS AND REASONS

Part II turns to eighteenth-century political thought to search for a justification for the liberal constraints on political action. By contrasting Montesquieu's and Kant's conceptions of politics and political action against Rousseau's, it tries to make sense of what Schmitt calls liberals' "cowardly intellectualism." The central contribution of this part is a robust justification for liberal reformism and for liberals' worry about deliberate radical social transformation. The individual contributions from Montesquieu and Kant are a theory of administrative institutions to accommodate the fact of pluralism and the institution of public reason, respectively. Montesquieu offers us an argument for constitutional liberalism, where political institutions exist to safeguard individuals' peaceful pursuit of their diverse ends. Kant's theory of public reason spells out the way in which individuals engage in politics as *autonomous agents*. The virtue of each account opens up difficulties: Montesquieu's institutionalism seems to create an "autonomy deficit" a liberal should feel leery of, and Kant's view, despite its greater attention to historical contingencies than usually thought, doesn't dispel all worries about its being practically inapplicable. My goal in the remainder of the book is to explore the ways in which the strengths could be complementary and how the tensions could be minimized. They cannot be gotten rid of—the real world is too messy for that—but together they do generate an account of liberal theory of political agency that is politically meaningful and, I try to show, empirically adequate. Montesquieu's and Kant's theories end up being significantly different from Rousseau's while, at the same time, both influencing (in Montesquieu's case) and borrowing (in Kant's) from him. For some, this renders them too for close comfort to illiberal or nonliberal ideas; my point, however, is that the proximity and the debts are no coincidence but are in some ways a crucial feature of at least these liberal theories. One of the points of this book is to stress that they are nevertheless liberal theories and in fact, because of that very complexity, *appealing* liberal theories.

Part I argued that politics is expressive. It also argued that this fact doesn't entail any liberal-democratic commitment to nonviolent politics, public reason, and happy reformism. This part shows some of the ways in which those commitments can emerge—how they emerged in eighteenth-century liberal thought. They are contingent, not universal or necessary, and pragmatic, not metaphysical, as Schmitt charges. This doesn't mean, as I suggested in Chapter 1, that there aren't liberal theorists who regard their principles as necessary, universal, and true. Pragmatic arguments square better with the nature of politics, which is the extent to which this book goes to defend this version of liberalism. Part III is concerned with showing that.

Given the conception of the political I offered in the previous chapter, there are two ways in which we can think of the Enlightenment politically. First, the Enlightenment itself was a diverse set of political projects.[1] It involved controversial claims about the authority of religious institutions, state institutions, scholarly institutions, cultural norms, social hierarchies, even breastfeeding practices. Second, many Enlightenment thinkers were specifically concerned about how social and political change ought to proceed. Change on virtually all fronts was needed; the questions were who would bring it about and how. And although the proscription of normative inferences from descriptive claims was itself a product of an Enlightenment mind, many political thinkers didn't get terribly caught up with worries about the naturalist fallacy. How things ought to be done depended naturally on how things could be done, but the opposite was sometimes also true: Whether and how something could be done depended on how you conceived of what humans ought to be.

While the philosophes and others contemplated these questions, people were engaging in a variety of activities, some inspired by them and some independent. Further, some of those activities seemed quite crazy, some bad, some hopeless, and not always in line with what the writers envisioned. In thinking about social change, Enlightenment writers had to account for those activities, so consideration of social and political change was circumscribed at the one end by the crazy things people were doing and, at the other end, by what people could become.

For these reasons, returning to the eighteenth-century context is useful. It helps us motivate the kinds of principles many now take for granted (in the sense that they don't think about them) but which nevertheless can't be taken for granted—because political actors routinely violate them. Specifically, to understand the development of many liberal commitments, I want to think about an intriguing troika of Enlightenment thinkers: Montesquieu, Rousseau, and Kant. And a troika it is, in the sense that the three are closely connected. Montesquieu offered Rousseau one of his major intellectual influences, and Rousseau similarly Kant. At the same time, Rousseau, the link, is an anti-liberal, while Montesquieu and Kant are liberals (or so I argue). What I want to show is that we can find in classical liberalism robust and perfectly nonmetaphysical accounts of political agency, accounts that are attentive to the contingencies of social life and to the concrete social situations with which politics deals. And in contrasting Montesquieu's and Kant's liberalism to the anti-liberalism of Rousseau, I want to explore what makes liberalism adopt the cautious reformism that it does. Liberal reformism is a principled but, at the same time, pragmatic stance toward the contingencies of political life. It isn't a half-baked afterthought or a symptom of squeamishness.

I do not argue that Montesquieu's and Kant's versions of liberalism are the same. Montesquieu's view of human nature is not particularly sanguine. He doesn't entertain the kind of optimism about the power of reason that Kant makes the centerpiece of his philosophy. For Montesquieu, political order is ensured and sustained by institutional design that curtails the excesses of human folly. For Kant, human reason—exercised as public reason—guides that very institutional design. This uneasy relationship remains, I argue, one of the unsettled and enduring legacies for liberal politics, but one that nevertheless is fruitful.

A few words on what I am *not* doing here: "Presentism," that nasty tendency to project our contemporary views of the world onto history, distorts it and can even render it unintelligible or paradoxical. For example, some people project the contemporary debate between liberalism and communitarianism (or one of its many offshoots, such as the debates about multiculturalism, nationalism, identity politics, and the like) onto discussions of Enlightenment social theorists. To be sure, the projection is tempting and may even seem warranted since many of the arguments in the contemporary debate can be traced to the writings of Rousseau, Hegel, Marx, and the like, on the communitarian side, and to Mill and sundry other liberals in the opposite camp. But the trouble is that while the earlier theorists may in fact have served as the inspiration for the arguments and contemporary participants in the debate, it is far from clear that any of them thought of the issues in the same terms. As Stephen Holmes points out, contemporary communitarians tend to engage in what he calls "antonym substitution," that is, in pointing, say, to the liberal ideal of individualism, they contrast individualism with collective good and not with tyranny, which is what early liberals opposed.[2] For example, while the contemporary tendency is to map Enlightenment republicanism—as if there were no varieties, or differences to the classical communitarianism of Tacitus, or Machiavelli—onto communitarianism, the move is not automatically warranted and only obscures the great differences between republicanism and communitarianism as well as the proximity of liberalism and republicanism. The two aren't always, or even primarily, opposites. Of course, neither are the large majority of liberal and communitarian ideals.

The disadvantage of this backward projection is that it prevents us from appreciating some thinkers and their ideas in sufficient complexity, the illiberal in the liberal, the undemocratic in the democratic, the racist and misogynist in paeans to universal equality. It either forces us to dismiss elements of theories in order to avoid contradiction—since our whiggishness prevents us from countenancing communitarian liberals—or, worse, to dismiss entire theories as contradictory. With complex thinkers, this sometimes results in an ironic tug of war between, say, contemporary liberals and communitarians, with each party claiming a thinker, under a cleaned-up description, theirs. My approach, in contrast, is to keep the complexity in the picture even as I treat Montesquieu and Kant as liberals. The result is that liberalism itself has to be seen as more complex. The payoff of such treatment becomes apparent in Part III.

The next two chapters, then, aren't contributions to the contemporary debate between liberals and communitarians, except by implication: We can learn much that is valuable if we forget the contemporary debate.

three

IF ALL ARE WICKED, HOW CAN THEY CHANGE?

Montesquieu and Rousseau on Humanity and Politics

The Flavors of Montesquieu's Liberalism

When studying the history of philosophy, it is useful to distinguish between exegetical interests in the actual doctrine of a thinker and attention to the philosophical promise in his or her doctrine. In the Anglo-American world, Charles-Louis de Secondat, baron de Montesquieu (1689–1755), has become something of a bit player among canonical political theorists, and there isn't particularly much appreciation either for the promise of his doctrine or its details. This is a little odd: One would have thought, for example, that at the time of a trendy "new institutionalism" in political science, scholars might be interested in the Frenchman whose views on institutional design were cited so prominently in the *Federalist Papers*. It is also unfortunate, since Montesquieu's thought is complicated (because the ideas are hard to pigeonhole), interesting (because he offers a rich analysis of agents and institutions), and relevant (because the analysis is still applicable and illuminates, in particular, liberalism).

Earlier, I wanted to reject a presentist approach to classical political thought because it impoverishes our understanding. A case in point is the question of whether and how Montesquieu is liberal. Because the question is relevant, I want to spend some time thinking about it. It will give us good grounds for caution about the practical applicability of the Kantian model I develop in the following chapter, however appealing the model is. This self-imposed skepticism will, in the end, help us strengthen the Kantian account.

The question of Montesquieu's liberalism is reasonable in the sense that his liberalism isn't obvious, especially in the North American context. After all, he often extols the virtues of republicanism, particularly in their Greek and Roman guises. To someone familiar with late twentieth-century categories, that puts him squarely in the camp of the communitarians, in diametrical opposition to liberalism. But this is just that very presentist mistake we should avoid. A contemporary communitarian or a liberal may, at the end of the day, insist there is an internal incoherence in Montesquieu's thought. I have little to say about such a claim. There is no prima facie internal incoherence, and the burden of proof will be on the contemporary, who will have to find the incoherence in something other than his or her own conceptual categories. *I* argue that what is interesting about Montesquieu is his very uneasiness with liberal values. He *is* an aristocrat worried about popular sovereignty, he *does* think republican virtues provide a necessary ingredient for the cement of society, and, despite the radicalism of his thought, he worries with conservatives about the social costs of social transformation. But the view of this book is that liberalism finds its best justification in cautious, pragmatic considerations, and anyone who thinks like that should be wary of enthusiastic cheerleaders.[1]

There is nevertheless something puzzling about Montesquieu's longing glances at antiquity and about his laments about the modern predicament.[2] He is, of course, not the first or the only one: Machiavelli had done the same before, and Rousseau notoriously would do the same after some decades. Montesquieu does often frame his discussions as a contrast between modernity and antiquity. At the same time, his constructive program bears the marks of liberalism, enough to earn him patron sainthood, to use Nannerl Keohane's phrase.[3] This combination of liberalism and nostalgia is what's initially puzzling about the theory, so let's think about it some more. First, Montesquieu unequivocally subscribes to the two principles that, I argued in Chapter 1, characterize all liberals: He clearly acknowledges the fact of pluralism and thinks that the best way to achieve social order is to accommodate the diversity of interests humans have. (This is obvious in, for instance, the Troglodyte story of the *Persian Letters,* which I discuss at length in this chapter.) In addition, Montesquieu has a laundry list of specific commitments easily recognizable as liberal. They include (1) religious toleration and the separation of religious and political authority, (2) the rule of law, (3) respect for private property, and (4) worry about democratic excesses.[4]

First, on the separation of religious and political authority, consider the following: although Montesquieu grants that *a* religion (not only Christianity) does serve the social function of "render(ing) men into good citizens" along with civil law, "religion, [which is] made to influence heart, should give many counsels and few precepts," that is, strictly binding norms [*The Spirit of Laws* (hereafter SL), XXIV: 7]: "When, for instance, it gives rules, not for what is good, but for what is better; not to direct to what is right, but to what is perfect; *it is expedient that these should be counsels, and not laws*: for perfection can have no relation to the universality of men and things" (SL, XXIV: 7, emphasis mine). In other words, the very notion of perfection only makes sense in reference to a particular conception of perfection. For example, Christianity offers one model, Confucianism another. Perfectionism is, then, a notion internal to a conceptual scheme, and it can't be universal. This could be from Mill's *On Liberty,* and it certainly is more robust than the repressive tolerance of the Locke of the *Letter.*[5] Elsewhere, Montesquieu also suggests that certain religious and political authorities, that is, monarchs and pontiffs, respectively, are properly kept separate except in despotic governments (SL, XXV: 8). The separation is ostensibly a social division of labor, but Montesquieu makes it rather clear which one ought to override in the cases of conflict: The title of chapter 9 of Book XXVI is simply "That Things which ought to be regulated by the Principles of civil Laws can seldom be regulated by those of Religion," and we learn from the chapter that civil laws have "greater extent" than religious ones. Combined with his explicit call for legally enforced religious toleration (SL, XXV: 9), we have a paradigmatic liberal picture.

Or consider the rule of law: Liberty, Montesquieu tells us in the important Book XI of *The Spirit of Laws*, is "a right of doing whatever the laws permit" (SL, XI: 3). In republics—Montesquieu's preferred form of government—the laws bind both those who administer them and other citizens:

> In despotic governments there are no laws; the judge himself is his own rule. There are laws in monarchies; and where these are explicit, the judge conforms to them; where they are otherwise, he endeavors to investigate their spirit. In republics, the very nature of the constitution requires the judges to follow the letter of the law; otherwise the law might be explained to the prejudice of every citizen, in cases where their honor, property, or life is concerned. (SL, VI: 3)

Rule of law by itself does not one a liberal make—just think of Hegel's theory of the state—but Montesquieu's reasoning here is quite liberal. Further, it is related to the recurring critique of aristocratic principles such as the heredity of office.[6] And as the passage suggests, respect of private property is a central component of the rule of law. This is because, for Montesquieu, "the public good always consists in everyone retaining the property which civil laws give him" (SL, XXVI: 15, my translation). That the justification of private property isn't prepolitical, as it is in Locke's paradigmatic case, doesn't make the account nonliberal. Neither does the fact that the value of private property is accounted for in terms of "public good": The point of the entire passage quoted here is that it is incoherent to try to account for public good without the good of individuals (*bien particulier*).[7] As we'll see later in this chapter, this view is very different from Rousseau's. (It doesn't entail, however, that public good is just an *aggregate* of individual good; I return to this in Chapter 5.)

Finally, while Montesquieu favors self-government, he shares liberals' worry about its excesses. This is similar to the worry people would soon come to call the tyranny of the majority, although, again, it is framed in terms and with examples of the classical world. Montesquieu thinks that unchecked political liberty of individuals will lead to petty little tyrannies and eventually to general despotism (SL, VIII: 2).[8] In politics, getting to do anything one wants ultimately undermines the very idea of politics, namely, that there could be legitimate authority.

Sure, liberals aren't the only ones who worry about the tyranny of the majority. Conservatives and aristocrats famously think of it as bad because of the condensation of stupidity when masses are allowed too much political liberty.[9] At times, Montesquieu's rhetoric resembles that, but at other times he does seem to suggest that the reason excessive democratic liberty is a tyranny is that it inhibits the freedom of some specific individuals even before it leads to the overall dissolution of political liberty.[10] I see no great reason to try to reconcile these tensions. They are not theoretical contradictions, but, at least from Montesquieu's perspective, genuine tensions that we can find in real political practices. It is commonsensical that there can be well-functioning democracies and corrupt ones. So while Montesquieu's particular misgivings about excessive liberty may reflect his aristocratic anxieties, it is equally reasonable to suggest that they reflect politics. Being a slightly worried liberal is a perfectly reasonable theoretical position.

What about Montesquieu's nostalgia for classical republicanism? It is just that, nostalgia. Whether or not he "cast in his lot with the Ancients against the Moderns" in his youth and never reversed that, as Keohane claims, it doesn't mean that he regards classical republicanism as viable for his contemporaries or for the future.[11] In Louis Althusser's interpretation, "the age of republics is past" for Montesquieu; republicanism is appropriate only for small states, and those are fast on their way out in the eighteenth century.[12] There are still some heroes of republicanism and thus weak hope for it, but not much. For example, William Penn, one of the few remaining heroes, "a real Lycurgus," just manages to highlight the "dregs and corruptions of modern times" (SL, IV: 6), instead of offering any real hope. (I return to this issue later.)

Moreover, Bernard Yack tells a convincing story about why Montesquieu extols civic virtue and other elements of classical republicanism to advance a liberal agenda. The prominence of republicanism has less to do with the overall excellence of ancient institutions than with their secular nature: They are appealing because they are not Christian.[13] Very little in my analysis at this point hangs on whether Montesquieu's ostensible republicanism is anything more than nostalgia or an advertisement for secular political institutions. The main point is that whatever else Montesquieu might be, he is also a liberal. We can frame the issue as a question: What content would liberalism have if Montesquieu were not a liberal? If the preceding does not enumerate liberal commitments and strategies, then nothing does. That these commitments and strategies look different from, say, Locke's, matters little: The burden of proof is on the Lockean to show that Locke's is the only variety of liberalism.[14] That they come flavored with aristocratic or conservative sentiments or nostalgia for the classical world doesn't make them nonliberal.

Passions as Ideal Types

Montesquieu's liberalism grows out of his empirical observations: His political principles are the ones that can work, given empirical reality. But as Mark Hulliung argues, Montesquieu isn't Machiavellian.[15] If Machiavelli—or at least the Machiavelli credited with "Machiavellianism"—is concerned *solely* with what works and not with the question "works toward what?" Montesquieu wants to keep ends in the picture. It's just that his investigations lead him to conclude that the ends are contingent (which is not the same as Machiavellian relativism). What they should be in the first place and how they can be pursued depend on social and historical conditions.

It turns out that the general problem of bringing about lasting and "just" social order is that people tend to do crazy things. The problem for political inquiry is, first, to understand why people act the way they do and how to respond to it.

Louis Althusser, not surprisingly, reads Montesquieu's solution as a proto-structuralist one: Social order is brought about and maintained (the passive voice is deliberate) *solely* by institutional arrangements.[16] This is because, in Althusser's reading, institutions are responsible for the forces that guide people's behavior. Although Althusser is certainly partly right about Montesquieu's solution—there is that famous division of powers, after all—Montesquieu's goal isn't just the creation of some Althusserian "institutional state apparatus." Humans are agents; their actions are not merely epiphenomena of their historical, geographical, or institutional context.

The logic for Althusser's structuralist reading of Montesquieu is in any case wrong. Montesquieu does argue that how people turn out depends on their context. The notorious "climate theory" of character, according to which climate makes some people lazy and some energetic, not to say anything about intelligence, is just one example. Even more importantly, each of the three ideal-typical political orders—republic, monarchy, and despotism—has an integral signature *principle* attached to it. This principle is, perhaps curiously, a particular *passion*: "There is this difference between the nature and principle of government, that the former is that by which it is constituted, the latter that by which it is made to act. One is its particular structure, and the other the human passions which set it in motion" (SL, III: 1). The passions for a republic, a monarchy, and a despotism are patriotism, honor, and fear, respectively. This close connection between institutional arrangements and human psychology does indeed lend plausibility to a structuralist reading and might even make Montesquieu look like an early relative of Durkheim. However, the structuralist reading is nevertheless mistaken. It is better to explore the connection between institutions and psychology than to read Montesquieu as asserting a simple causality from the former to the latter. Understanding the connection will give us a handle on what Montesquieu thinks about political action in general and why he prefers the liberal principles he does.

First, it is important to realize that Montesquieu's talk of passions is less a psychological theory of the human mind than a *social*-psychological *explanation* for why people do the things they do. In other words, he doesn't claim that a particular psychophysiological apparatus goes well with a particular type of regime. Although he may subscribe to an old faculty-psychological conception of the mind, his language of passions is not concerned about—and so doesn't depend on—the truth of faculty psychology. To say that "*N* did *x* out of patriotism" is simply to offer an *explanans* for a social event, and is shorthand for "*N* did *x* because she loves her country." This is a description of a particular attitude, nothing more. Further, it is obvious from Montesquieu's examples that these attitudes often have robust cognitive content: honor, the passion proper for monarchy, is "the prejudice of every person and rank" (SL, III: 6), that is, the *belief* that persons essentially fit in a particular hierarchy. The contrast here is knowledge, that is, beliefs whose acquisition the person is familiar with (*connoissances*).[17]

To say, then, that passions are what set particular governments in motion is to say that the prevalence of some particular political attitudes make possible the functioning of a particular government. When people have the right kinds of attitudes, they will behave in ways that sustain social order. In the case of despotism, where the signature passion is fear, the relevant behavior is generally omissions rather than actions: People remain politically inactive. The general point is that a particular type of government should try to promote the appropriate passion among the populace. A despot will do his best to keep people afraid, a monarch will foster a sense of honor, and republicans try to make everyone feel patriotic.

Recall that Montesquieu ends up abandoning even his favorite, republicanism, from this trio of ideal types. This is because every attempt to bring about the sociological prevalence of any single passion in modernity will fail. But some fail more than others, for two reasons. First, some sociohistorical contexts simply make some particular sentiment impossible, in Montesquieu's view. Second, some passions end up having more or less internally perverse consequences, even when they can be fostered. In other words, some passions are self-defeating. This second consideration is the reason Althusser's structuralism is wrong-headed: To say that a passion is self-defeating is to say that it butts against conflicting expressions of human agency.

I won't dwell on the first reason, except to point out that there are more and less racist and culturally imperialist ways of taking the point. The general point that the appropriateness of a political system depends on a host of contingent factors is almost trivially true.[18]

The second reason, however, is more interesting for the issues at hand. Fear is the most obviously self-defeating political passion and despotism thus the least stable system over the long run. This stems from the way fear motivates. By tracking a person's interests in harm *avoidance*, it easily comes into conflict with her other, thicker and more positive interests and desires. I very much would like to play on the swingset during recess, but the scary bullies keep me away. (This idea doesn't mean that Montesquieu's account depends on risk aversion. The kinds of fears he clearly has in mind track the interests in remaining alive, healthy, pain-free, and out of jail.) Although Montesquieu does think humans always have interests and desires that come into internal tension and even conflict, this type of conflict is a particularly strong one. When I'm motivated by fear, I say things like "I *would* do x if only it weren't for my fear of y," and y is obviously something I don't want.

But the same issues crop up in the case of the two more interesting political passions, in more interesting but complicated ways. Let's focus on the kinds of passions that both lead to and facilitate genuine political engagement and not just quiet obedience. Montesquieu's discussion of monarchies, aristocracies, and republics will get us further since in each form of regime there are at least some who are politically active. The two kinds of passions relevant for political engagement are love of one's country and honor (SL, III: 6; V: 1). By its definition, honor is not the appropriate political passion in republics since it would be in conflict with their egalitarianism, but in monarchies it may be appropriate. It, as Montesquieu observes, "sets all the parts of the body politic in motion, and by its very action connects them; thus each individual advances the public good, while he only thinks of promoting his own interest (*intérêts particuliers*)" (SL, III: 7). (Very little turns on the subjective nature of "interest" here since its recognition plays such an important political role. As long as you genuinely have that interest of "prejudice of every person and rank," stability demands it be promoted.) Although Montesquieu does not tell us in detail how the body politic is set in motion through this mechanism, the politically activating force of honor comes from its being essentially a *social* interest.

If I want to glorify myself and my honor, I want to do socially visible things since honor is based on social expectations about myself in a certain relationship to others. In other words, I want to demonstrate my honor. Often the position of social superiority to others goes together with an aspiration "to preferments and distinctions" (SL, III: 7), which, in turn, can be obtained through good offices to higher persons or visibly for the common good. That it ultimately is self-interest that keeps the nobility busy is not, in itself, a problem since it generally is, as Montesquieu points out, useful for the public.

However, honor has its drawbacks as a politically motivating passion. First, one's sense of social superiority does not necessarily lead one to engagement in socially useful causes, and it may even be counterproductive because it creates resentment. Consider how Usbek, the protagonist of Montesquieu's *Persian Letters*, contrasts two models of honor. He is writing to his young Persian friend Rica and has just described an arrogant French nobleman who does everything to show his contempt of those below. Usbek's understanding of his own honor is very different:

> We should have been very ill-natured, Rica, to go and inflict hundreds of petty insults on people who came to see us daily to show us their goodwill. They knew quite well that we were above them, and, if they had not, the benefits we provided would have made it clear to them each day. We did not need to do anything to make ourselves respected, so we did everything we could to be agreeable. [*Persian Letters* (hereafter PL), LXXIV: 150][19]

So while Usbek's can be seen as the ideal political employment of honor, the haughty Frenchman with his petty insults is just as likely a product of a sense of honor. This, what one might call a false sense of honor, increases in likelihood the further social status is removed from genuine merit—hence Montesquieu's opposition to the heredity of offices.

The second problem with a sense of honor is that even when it succeeds as political motivation, the results are not always desirable. In particular, because of the rigorousness of the codes of behavior based on honor, conflict resolution is problematic. Since a conflict is often interpreted as an affront to one's honor and, consequently, a challenge to one's entire sense of self, it becomes an all-or-nothing affair. Hence the practice of dueling over seemingly trivial matters.[20] Moreover, as Montesquieu has Usbek observe in the *Letters*, these conflicts of honor can be explosive because they are contagious:

> If a man knew one of the parties, however slightly, he was forced into the quarrel, and had to suffer the consequences personally, as if he himself had had cause for anger. He invariably felt honoured by being chosen and by receiving such a flattering sign of favour; and a man who would have been reluctant to

give someone else five pounds in order to save him from the gallows, him and his whole family as well, would make no bones about going to risk his life for him a thousand times over. (PL, XC: 172)

In other words, the fact that the maintenance of these public attributes gets "privatized" into kinship and other affective networks can be divisive and disruptive.

So while honor is a better political passion than fear, it is not particularly reliable, either, and Montesquieu's preference of the republican "love of one's country" seems reasonable. Love of one's country is, for him, the essential political virtue (SL, V: 2). I want to discuss two particular benefits of this passion.[21] First, it is a politically motivating passion where an individual agent's intentions are consistent or even synonymous with her actions' social effects. Unlike honor, where social usefulness is a by-product of a private interest, love of one's country produces results that the agent intends and wants to produce; or if the results are not socially desirable—due to, say, the influence of something unforeseen—the agent will have an internal (i.e., motivating) reason to alter her strategy. And here lies the importance of this consistency between individual desires and social effects: Montesquieu is less interested in agents' "good faith"—he would not mind, after all, honor as a politically motivating passion if it were reliable—than in having the passion be something that can be checked. As the counterproductive results of dueling are supposed to illustrate, if my political engagement relies on my sense of honor, I might be unmotivated to change my behavior even if the socially untoward consequences of my honor are pointed out to me.[22] What do I care whether social order shakes when *my* honor has been questioned?

The other advantage of love of one's country is that it also keeps *other* private passions, which might be disruptive and dangerous, in check: "The love of our country is conducive to a purity of morals, and the latter is again conducive to the former. The less we are able to satisfy our private passions, the more we abandon ourselves to those of a general nature" (SL, V: 2). In other words, Montesquieu seems to be saying, if you keep people busy doing good deeds for their country and fellow citizens, they won't have time to develop interests that might lead them to engage in private mischief or other forms of disruptive activity. The example that immediately follows the preceding quote seems to confirm this:

How comes it that monks are so fond of their order? It is owing to the very cause that renders the order insupportable. Their rule debars them from all those things by which the ordinary passions are fed; there remains therefore only this passion for the very rule that torments them. The more austere it is, that is, the more it curbs their inclinations, the more force it gives to the only passion left in them. (SL, V: 2)

But this is puzzling. First, the example hardly seems like an illustration of a *desirable* thing, at least for a democracy. It does not seem very liberal. Second, recall, after all, that Montesquieu is no friend of religious institutions: The *Spirit* is an argument for the separation of the Church from politics, and monastic institutions in particular are a frequent object of Montesquieu's ridicule in the

Letters. So why illustrate an advantage in his favorite form of political arrangement with an analogy he should not find agreeable?

One answer is that Montesquieu might want to highlight a possible problem with the republican love of one's country. In other words, the only thing better about the tension between patriotism and private desires in contrast to the tension between fear and thick private interests is that, in the former case, both are positive passions. I want both: *I*, and not the despot's threats, autonomously enforce the motivating force of patriotism. But the tension remains, and I argue later that Montesquieu wants us to remain mindful of that.

First, however, let us consider another answer. Notice that, in the case of both honor and the love of one's country, the passions relevant for political agency are ways of contributing to one's sense of self; they are, as it were, passions of identity building. If I love my country very much, then citizenship or nationality of that country is generally an important part of my self-identification. I may be an American, but if I don't much care for America, I am unlikely to highlight that when describing who I am, but if I do, I am also likely to include being American as an important attribute of myself. Likewise, challenges to my honor are such a grievous insult exactly because they are challenges to who I am; they challenge *me*.

In this sense, the monk analogy is appropriate. Montesquieu is not talking about the unsavory political aspects of monasticism, but about the moral-psychological mechanism at work in it. Part of being a monk is not to have passions for such mundane things as money, sex, and power. If I sincerely want to be a monk, then an element of what defines me as a monk is that I not have those earthly passions. This is not a result of an oppressive monastic regime imposed on me, but follows simply from the definition of what it means to be a monk. Lack of earthly passions is, to put the point in contemporary jargon, a *constitutive* aspect of monkhook. Similarly, then, if I love my country, then I do not want to cultivate in myself passions or sentiments inconsistent with it but, insofar as they keep whispering to me, try to suppress them. If I love America, I cannot consistently spy for its enemies. If I do, I have not understood what "love of America" means.[23]

So Hard to Be Good: Virtues as Promise and Burden

Things get complicated, however, when we realize that these *normative* conceptions of the psychology of monkhook and patriotism don't rule out the possibility of actual psychological lust or avarice among monks and promptings to (unprincipled) tax-cheating or draft-dodging among patriots. This isn't necessarily a problem. There is nothing theoretically incoherent or empirically impossible about the general idea: One needn't be a student of Aristotle or Mencius to grant that self-cultivation with regard to *x* is largely about overcoming some aversions to *x*, and that it can be done. Anyone who has acquired one of those acquired tastes—for caviar, single malt scotch, or salted licorice—has done it. Rather, the problem is that in *some* cases the distance between normative conception and empirical possibility is too wide. In the former case, Montesquieu is certainly not alone in his skepticism about the feasibility of the monastic ideals.

I want to argue that Montesquieu is also, albeit less, skeptical about the empirical feasibility of the *patriotic* ideal in the modern world. We'll get to that point by proceeding in a slightly backwards order.

Recall Montesquieu's liberalism. Why might one find the argument about patriotism a puzzling account for a liberal to put forth? There are two reasons. First, if the monk analogy does not break down, then Montesquieu can be seen to advocate a very monolithic view of the self, a kind of view nonliberals like.[24] The second problematic point arises out of the common claim that liberals presuppose a *presocial identity*. Commonness aside, the claim is mistaken: Some liberals do presuppose presocial identity, others don't. It will be worthwhile to see why Montesquieu doesn't, so I will tackle this second reason first.

Think of a standard liberal social contract theory in its crudest form: People would like to go and do their own things, but they can't because some people's "own things" include stealing from some, killing others, and all kinds of things that make life that constant war of all against all, nasty, brutish, and so on. So they get together to form a social union of some sort (the details do not matter here) that will allow them to continue doing their own things. In some cases, this social union may force some to adjust what they care about somewhat, but, on the whole, people have a pretty good idea what they want to do. In this view, the social union, the state apparatus, a sovereign, whatever, is there primarily to secure people's pursuit of their primary interests. It has merely derivative value, and the extent to which one must attend to it—get together for choosing representatives, say—is a necessary evil but not much fun. Certainly not a valuable activity, nor a particularly desirable source of identity. To put this in terms of liberal catchwords, the *private* realm is the main source of value for persons, while the *public* is there just to support it. The liberal principle of "the self prior to its ends" captures this story.

Those who think that liberals are committed to the idea of presocial identity take this story and the "self prior to its ends" principle to imply the notion of presocial identity. But note that the notion—apart from being well-nigh unintelligible—*need* not in any sense be a part of a liberal doctrine. A liberal theorist can allow that a person's identity is shaped by her social environment; some even use that very conception of self-formation to argue *for* liberalism.[25] We can, first, have an antecedent idea that a diverse social order is desirable (because it is, say, stronger and more sustainable). Now if a person's identity is understood as the unique nexus of her social relations—her "web of group affiliations," to borrow Georg Simmel's phrase[26]—then, in order to make persons more diverse, the multiplication of those group affiliations seems desirable. And that's just one way to gloss the liberal idea of individualism.

Sure enough, those arguments are controversial; some liberals may think of them as a bastardization of liberal ideals. But the argument is internal to liberalism; my point here is that nothing about liberalism forces a liberal theorist to commit herself to a conception of presocial identity. Montesquieu, as I will show, has no such commitment, from which it follows perfectly well that politics can be as good a source of identity formation as anything else.

Think what it would mean to have presocial identity. Two alternative understandings seem most common. One is a certain kind of naturalism or essentialism of what people are like: "The human nature" is inherently and universally selfish, or rational, or violent.[27] How this would justify or even pertain to the supposedly liberal valuation of the "private" over the "public" is not clear since in most human cultures the private has always included social attachments; what is quite clear is that Montesquieu holds no such view. He does remark on humans' "natural" love of liberty and hatred of violence (SL, V: 15), but these sentiments do not override the cultural, historical, and geographic variety in humans. Montesquieu does not seem to think that something worth calling an identity would remain if the contingent cultural attributes were stripped off people. Similar arguments especially about the role of geography in shaping human identity can also be found in the *Spirit*, but the literary format of the *Letters* allows him to make the point much more forcefully.[28] Consider, for example, the only happy pair of people in a book otherwise populated by a miserable lot: Ibben relates to Usbek the story of Apheridon and Astarte, a brother and a sister who have loved each other all their lives and who, in the end, get each other and live happily ever after in a social setting in which all gender norms are confused (PL, LXVII: 136–143). This story is told without a trace of parody; Montesquieu simply wants to illustrate the wide range of possibilities for happy human life and the fact that they can eschew convention.

Yack notes that Montesquieu, along with many other philosophes, runs into a contradiction here. He wants to assert the natural love of liberty and hatred of violence to get a critique of oppressive political institutions off the ground, but he also wants to emphasize the huge variance of human differences across cultures.[29] It is true that a careful examination of the conflict might be in order, and it is certainly true, as we will see later with Rousseau, that if one examines it, one can be led to rather different results. But I want to let Montesquieu off the hook and gloss over this conflict. This is partly because the project here is interpretive: We are interested in seeing where Montesquieu ends up and whether he runs into contradictions on the way should not the stop the interpretive project. But partly it is because we are not dealing with a real contradiction. I will not defend this view here, but merely offer a handwave on how one might dispel the problem.

Consider the contemporary arguments for a certain "weak" essentialism about humans: Despite the huge variance in social practices among human cultures, some *somewhat* abstracted core principles can be identified among them—humans in all cultures prefer life to death, need attachments of some kind, engage in play, and so on.[30] There are, to be sure, questions one can ask of such accounts—how meaningful can this universal core be if it is very abstracted from its local instantiations, for example—but it is an intelligible and generally defensible view. Something like it would get Montesquieu out of the supposed paradox.

However, this still does not show that Montesquieu is not committed to the other way of understanding presocial identity. According to this conception, presocial identity simply means something like the "standard" liberal preference for the private over the public that I described earlier, the view, that is, that people more or less know what they want before establishing political institutions and that they neither desire nor allow for the political institutions to shape their identities further. This would more properly be called pre*political* identity and, as such, is much more intelligible than the almost incoherent concept of presocial identity. But Montesquieu does not even hold this view.

Take the parable of the Troglodytes, which Usbek tells over four of the *Letters*.

It resembles in both rough outline and several details the biblical story told in Samuel's First Book; in fact, Montesquieu's version lacks just one but significant detail: God. That, and Montesquieu's different emphases, make it one of his many irreverent stabs at Christianity. But like almost everything else in the *Letters*, it does much more.

The first generations of Troglodytes were primitive, selfish, and greedy. In an obvious jab at Hobbes's contract theory, Usbek writes that although the Troglodytes entered into an initial contract to elect rulers, they were too selfish to sustain their society (PL, XI: 53). Of the ruins of the "wicked" Troglodytes, however, a new society arose around two "virtuous" families. The principle by which they organized their growing society, namely, that "the individual's self-interest is always to be found in the common interest," led to a happy, virtuous, and yet powerful commonwealth (PL, XII–XIII: 56–61). There are several messages in the story.

First, Montesquieu seems to recognize an inherent problem in the very intelligibility of presocial or even prepolitical identity. The problem is a first cousin to a better known problem trope in contract theories, "the state of nature." Presocial identity can only exist if something like an *actual* state of nature exists. Even if one had existed at some point—a view, as we know, most theorists reject—then presocial identity can have existed only once. If, on the other hand, the state of nature is an abstraction or a hypothetical device, then presocial identity must also be something like an abstraction. And as we've seen earlier and as I think Montesquieu tries to convey with the Troglodyte story as well, such an abstraction does not work: What people are like and what they want is fundamentally connected to the kind of social order in which they live:

> Soon they had the reward of virtuous parents, which is to have children who resemble them. The younger generation which grew up before their eyes increased through happy marriages. As their numbers grew larger, they remained as closely united, and virtue, so far from becoming weaker among the multitude, was on the contrary fortified by a greater number of examples. (PL, XII: 57)

There is no robust presocial identity since people's identities reflect on the social setting into which they are born; "the customs of an enslaved people are a part of their servitude, those of a free people are a part of their liberty" (SL, XIX: 27). And, in a despotic regime, Montesquieu observes, "there are only manners and customs; and if you overturn these you overturn all" (SL, XIX: 12).

One might think, however, that Montesquieu's rejection of presocial identity is not as strong as I have claimed. After all, aren't even the virtuous Troglodytes pursuing self-interested ends? Haven't they just realized that it is better achieved through the pursuit of the common good? Sure enough, Montesquieu does seem to believe that self-interest in the sense of interest in one's personal survival can be found in most human societies. But this is almost trivial; what he has in mind is something mainly biological, something that does not even set humans apart from other animals and which certainly does not amount to anything that can be called identity. Montesquieu, unlike Rousseau (as we'll see soon) does not make much of this, but seems to take it as uncontroversial. It is clear from the beginning of the Troglodyte story that he does not think the self-interest is selfishness in a more developed sense. The snub at Hobbes—or a straw-Hobbes[31]—with the first generation of Troglodytes shows this.

The interesting end of the Troglodyte story returns us to the worry I identified in the monk analogy, namely, to that of one passion becoming the *sole* motivating force in a person's life (and thus a sole nexus of identity). If political passions were like that, Montesquieu's account wouldn't differ very much from Rousseau's and, I contend, it does.

In the end, the Troglodytes' virtue becomes a burden on them. An old, esteemed member of their society whom they want to elect as a ruler laments this desire and warns them against it, paralleling the biblical Samuel. However, where Samuel imagines all the bad things a king will likely do—take your sons, daughters, and flocks; make you slaves—this old man offers a sociological analysis:[32]

> In your present state, without a ruler, it is necessary for you to be virtuous despite yourselves. Otherwise you could not continue to exist, and you would fall into the misfortunes of your first ancestors. But this imposition seems too hard for you. You would prefer to be a subject to a king, and obey his laws, which would be less rigid than your own customs. You know that you would then be able to satisfy your ambitions, accumulate wealth, and live idly in degrading luxury; that, provided you avoided falling into worst crimes, you would have no need of virtue. (PL, XIV: 60–61)

Being nothing but virtuous, and virtuous in a communally oriented way to boot, can prevent the pursuit of other ends, some of which need not be as pernicious as living idly in degrading luxury. Single-minded virtue is burdensome, and for a good reason. At the same time, it is clear in the Troglodyte story that Montesquieu does not relish the idea that monarchy is a solution to the problem. He *wishes* they could continue to govern themselves under the rule of virtue, but even virtue ends up being self-defeating.

Divided Powers, Channeled Passions

The Troglodyte story ends with the old man's lament, even though the problem of the totalizing virtue has not been solved. Fortunately, the Troglodyte story is not the full extent of Montesquieu's political theory. If monarchy or some stronger form of autocracy and collectivism are the only options for political arrangement, then people are faced with a dilemma: If you want freedom, you will have to spend all your time governing, and in the end lose some freedom (to do what you would rather). But if you want to pursue the ends you want, you have to forfeit your freedom (to govern yourself) to whomever you hire to do the governing. Here is where liberalism is a solution.

Let's think about a "psychological" justification for liberalism. Liberalism is a political arrangement that makes possible the development and maintenance of different kinds of passions simultaneously. It is clear, as we saw earlier, that Montesquieu thinks political passions and political virtues are necessary, but their

exercise should not be a full-time job and, most importantly, should not prevent
the exercise at least of some other passions. Recall that it is the preemptive totality
of monasticism that "renders the whole order insupportable." Liberalism, on the
other hand, offers a social arrangement in which the exercise of political virtues
facilitates the exercise of other passions, desires, and interests. Consider, for
example, this in relation to Montesquieu's great liberal-constitutional idea, the
division of political power:

> As there are in this state two visible powers—the legislative and the executive—
> and every citizen has a will of his own, and may at pleasure assert his
> independence, most men have a greater fondness for one of these powers than
> for the other, and the multitude have commonly neither equity nor sense
> enough to show an equal affection to both. (SL, XIX: 27)

This arrangement, in a sense, turns even capricious passions into a force for
stability. Different political organs draw support from different kinds of passions:
Those motivated by a sense of honor can get channeled into institutions in which
positional goods are constitutive of the institution and that reward the grounds of
honor (e.g., courage under fire in the military); patriotism can motivate people
into public service, a sense of justice specifically into those spheres that administer
justice; passions to be popular can motivate people into elected office; and so on.
Thus potentially problematic appeals to certain people's passions are checked by
the people who remain unexcited by the particular appeals of the time: The threats
of ultranationalism are checked by those more indifferent toward their fatherland,
populist frenzy by grouchy misanthropes, overzealous sweeping legal reforms by
the procedural purists in the judiciary. We know, of course, that even this picture
is fraught with risks: Petty will to power and not the sense of public service
motivates many police officers, for example. The idea is nevertheless ingenious.

The extent to which people's nonpolitical private passions may conflict with or
differ from the political passions is not clear in Montesquieu, but it is clear that
he thought they did to some extent, especially in modernity. No Aristotelian,
Montesquieu has a view of the self Alasdair MacIntyre disparagingly calls the
"divided self," but which liberals celebrate.[33] Usbek, for example, is a learned
humanist, cultured and virtuous, but he is also the dictatorial patriarch of a
seraglio and a rapist. Far from endorsing this particular division of the self,
Montesquieu does find it politically problematic. But it is problematic *politically*,
not a case of schizophrenia.

Political virtue, then, is not the same as moral virtue, although the former may
also be moral virtue in some cases (SL, III: 5n). Political virtues are those directed
"towards the public good (*bien général*)" (SL, III: 5n). So, for example, in a
republic, the primary political virtue is that "most simple thing," love of the
republic (SL, V: 2). This is, in Montesquieu's conceptual scheme, also a moral
virtue in that public good comes within the scope of morality. But it also means
that *private* moral virtue is not a political virtue (SL, III: 5n). Just because I am a
dutiful son to my parents or keep my promises to my friends doesn't mean I give
a hoot about the public good. The relation here is not one of the subsumption of
"public" and "private" virtue under moral virtue, but simply of different kinds of

virtues. There are different criteria for what excellence, to use an Aristotelian term, amounts to in different spheres of social activity. The overlap is contingent. At the same time, Montesquieu doesn't go to Machiavellian lengths: That the partial overlap between morality and politics is contingent doesn't mean that the criteria aren't related at all, and the fact that he further distinguishes morality from "revealed truths,"that is, religion (SL, III: 5n), suggests that he means a secular conception of the social function of morality.

This makes it necessary for Montesquieu to point out that when he is talking about "good men" he is using the attribute in a *political* sense; he is not talking about "good men" in the abstract (SL, VI: 6n). There is a connection between morals and political virtue, even though the criteria are different: "all political are not moral vices, and . . . all moral are not political vices" (SL, XIX: 11; see also V: 3). In his infamous taxonomy of the characters of other nationalities, he points out that "women in the Indies" consider it shameful to learn to read (SL, XIX: 9): The ability to read, a moral vice (for Montesquieu is perfectly happy to be a cultural relativist about moral dicta) would still be a political virtue, even for women. And the Spaniards, while noted for their honesty, a great moral virtue, manage to make it politically pernicious to themselves because it is combined with "their indolence" (SL, XIX: 10). And, as we saw earlier, there is Usbek, the rapist who nevertheless represents many political virtues.

The setup is modern and liberal. It doesn't celebrate a hyper-individualist devaluation of the political, but it recognizes the empirical fact that, in the modern world at least, people are too different to care about the public good in the same way. The point is that they can, *consistently with their private passions*, care about the common good in *some* way. And they do. This neither presupposes nor recommends that they care about the public good only as an extension of their private *interests*. Montesquieu's citizens don't engage in political action solely out of self-interest, as James Madison feared and Robert Dahl hoped. Some do, others don't. Insofar as people engage in politics, all do for some reason they *care about*. (I'm using "reason" here advisedly.) Since these reasons are diverse and since they motivate strongly, conflicts can arise. Further, since the other sense of "reason"— reason as calm and dispassionate reasonability—can't be trusted to keep the passions in check, they have to be rendered safe through institutional arrangements. One good set of institutions to do this is that of a liberal republic— not for any grand metaphysical reasons, as Schmitt would insist, but because they take account of these profane passions.

Rousseau's Nonliberal Liberation

It is well known that the Enlightenment didn't produce only liberals. The socio-historical conditions that made liberal principles seem like a best solution to pressing questions to some implied very different answers to others. To get a better sense of what theoretical alternatives to liberalism one could arrive at, given roughly the similar set of antecedent conditions, I want to turn to Jean-Jacques Rousseau. He is an important figure in my little troika: Himself strongly influenced by Montesquieu, he in turn becomes a great inspiration for Kant; yet he rejects Montesquieu's liberalism, while Kant, again, adopts it—or, more specifically, adopts *a* liberal theory, one I discuss in the following chapter. Once we understand what it is that Rousseau doesn't want from Montesquieu and how Kant differs from Rousseau, we will have a much better sense of what makes one liberal and, in particular, how liberals conceive of political agency.

Rousseau's followers are a colorful bunch. There are radical democrats and less radical ones, collectivists—to the point of fascism—nationalists, internationalist Marxists, revolutionaries, and modern conservatives. Schmitt, for example, draws heavily from Rousseau in his illiberal conception of democracy. This diversity in the following stems from the widely varying emphases and interpretations of his work, the only unequivocal position of which might be its misogyny. Despite these interpretive differences, I will not spend much time painting a picture of a particular Rousseau before my discussion of his conception of political agency. Rousseau's illiberalism will emerge from the discussion itself.

Born Free, Everywhere in Chains

Let's begin with some of Rousseau's many debts to Montesquieu. Although the point each wants to make is arguably different, both write favorably of the republics of antiquity. Rousseau also continues Montesquieu's use of anthropology, such as it then was, to bolster his points (although, of course, they weren't alone in this in the eighteenth century). He even takes the claim that people in warmer climates are lazier and less intellectually developed than those closer to the poles directly from Montesquieu.

However, the most important debt and at the same time difference between the two is what they make of human nature. This underlies all of their other differences.

I noted earlier that Montesquieu does not think very much of human nature, lying as it does somewhere below and independent of the layers of culture. He does think that humans naturally love freedom and despise violence, but this is relevant only because these still shine through the layers of acculturation, even in despotic regimes. Given the way Montesquieu talks about them, it seems that these natural sentiments are just the way biological interest in self-preservation and lack of interest in gratuitous violence manifest themselves through layers of acculturation. However, there is no way of getting to these sentiments in their pure form; the best one can hope for from a political theory is to provide a way for taking advantage of them as they are manifested and for cultivating these. So, for example, if historical circumstances have brought it about that in some people these sentiments manifest themselves as ambition and vanity, as public-spiritedness in others, and as financial self-interest in yet others, the best one can do is to arrange matters so that these different subjective interests—passions, Montesquieu might say—can all survive in as peaceful a coexistence as possible.

Rousseau, too, views a certain self-preservation interest and abhorrence of violence as natural human inclinations, but he takes this in an opposite direction from Montesquieu. For Rousseau, these natural attributes are both presocial and prerational: "[C]ontemplating the first and most simple operations of the human soul, I think I can perceive in it two principles prior to reason, one of them deeply interesting us in our own welfare and preservation, and the other exciting a natural repugnance at seeing any other sensible being, and particularly any of our own species, suffer pain or death" [*Discourse on the Origin and Foundations of Inequality among Men* (hereafter D2), 41]. He labels these natural inclinations "self-love" and "compassion," respectively (D2, 66n). This means that humans are "naturally good," not selfish in a wicked sense, as Hobbes had claimed (on this, Montesquieu and Rousseau have a unified front against Hobbes). But Rousseau does agree with Hobbes that humans are "actually wicked," which "a sad and continual experience of them proves beyond doubt" (D2, Appendix,[34] 106). In the original, the word "actually" does not appear, and the sentence reminds us of the famous opening of *The Social Contract*: "Man is born free, and everywhere he is chains." The resemblance is no coincidence since in both cases the sentence captures the fundamental paradox for Rousseau, which his entire political corpus tries to solve: Naturally, humans are *x*, but actually, they are *y*. His solution includes both an explanation of the paradox and a positive program to escape it.

Let us first look at the psychological wing of the explanatory end, that is, of the paradox of natural goodness and actual wickedness. In a very rough outline, the story, told in the second *Discourse*, is this: The natural self-love, mainly a concern for one's self-preservation, develops into pride, vanity, desire for comparisons, et cetera. This leads people to compete with each other, to have power over one another, et cetera. The concrete social results of this are institutions such as property, those used to establish various kinds of hierarchies, for example. The problem with this is not that these circumstances lead to a Hobbesian state of constant war (we will see later that Rousseau actually does not mind war), but that people are bad, although they need not be. (The political counterpart to this state is the state of human inequality and unfreedom.)

This outline of the human degeneration leaves unclear the mechanisms through which it happens. We can get a sense of that by looking at Rousseau's discussion in greater detail.

First, something must explain why any development of the original human psychology takes place at all. After all, the two natural sentiments are prerational, and Rousseau is quite explicit in thinking that, in those respects, humans are *not* much different from other animals. The one feature that does set humans apart as a species and explains the evolution of the sentiments is the *capacity* to develop oneself, that is, for any given individual to develop himself or herself over the course of a life:

> ... the faculty of self-improvement, which, by the help of circumstances, gradually develops all the rest of our faculties, and is inherent in the species as in the individual: whereas a brute is, at the end of a few months, all he will ever be during his whole, life and his species, at the end of a thousand years, exactly what it was the first year of that thousand. (D2, 54)

We need not worry about Rousseau's mistake about the biological evolution of species since what is relevant is the self-improvement that can take place over individual lives. Rousseau calls this faculty of self-improvement "perfectibility" (D2, 54), and although it implies more teleology than he actually would want or can, at this point, have, we can use it as a shorthand.

So, what happens with the two natural faculties is as follows. Take compassion, "the only natural virtue" (D2, 66), first. In its natural, prerational state, it manifests itself in "the tenderness of mothers for their offspring" (D2, 66), and it is like that of any other nonhuman animal who "never passes the dead body of another of its species without disquiet" (D2, 67). Rousseau cites Mandeville's fable, a

> pathetic description of a man who, from a place of confinement, is compelled to behold a wild beast tear a child from the arms of its mother, grinding its tender limbs with its murderous teeth, and tearing its palpitating entrails with its claws. What horrid agitation must not the eye-witness of such a scene experience, although he would not be personally concerned! What anguish would he not suffer at not being able to give any assistance to the fainting mother and the dying infant! (D2, 67)

"Such is," Rousseau exclaims, "the pure emotion of nature, prior to all kinds of reflection!" (D2, 67). Now we should not, at this point, call him to task for what seems to us straightforwardly bad empirical psychology. Although we may cite examples of people witnessing the most horrible cruelties without much interest, or even exhibiting *Schadenfreude*, Rousseau would regard that as evidence for his point that modernity has gotten us even further from those natural sentiments. He does seem to claim at times that these sentiments still manifest themselves in us. They are also quite clear at least in some adolescents who, instead of being the vengeful and cruel beings ignorant philosophers claim they are, may actually, even until the age of twenty, preserve their natural innocence and are "the most generous, best, most loving and most lovable of humans" [*Émile, ou de l'education* (hereafter E), 286]).[35] Whether this is true is, however, less relevant than the central point that the sense of compassion and pity is an innate human inclination.

And as the passage suggests, it serves as the foundation for many other good sentiments. There are two ways in which compassion gets "extended." The first one happens as a result of the play of human cognitive capacities:

> But what is generosity, clemency, or humanity but compassion applied to the weak, to the guilty, or to mankind in general? Even benevolence and friendship are, if we judge rightly, only the effects of compassion, constantly set upon a particular object: for how is it different to wish that another person may not suffer pain and uneasiness and to wish him happy? (D2, 68)

Knowledge, the product of our cognitive capacities, helps humans recognize and "apply" the "appropriate" variant of compassion in particular instances. Even without knowledge compassion would prompt in us instinctual stirrings when encountering some kinds of suffering, but knowledge extends it, first, by creating a more diverse and complicated set of representations of suffering (an animal or a "precognitive" human might not recognize "sophisticated" forms of suffering as such) and, second, by diversifying the responses to those so that, indeed, generosity is applied to weakness, clemency toward the guilty, and so on.

The diversification of the original sentiment is quite broad. In addition to serving as the foundation for what we might, in general, call "selfless, other-regarding positive sentiments," compassion is also at the root of such a complicated emotion as romantic love (E, 277–286; also D2, 70). It is also the ancestor of aesthetic appreciation: "The love of the beautiful is a sentiment as natural to the human heart as the love of the self" [*Letter to M. D'Alembert on the Theater* (hereafter LD), 23]. While this may seem as if Rousseau wanted to introduce yet another natural sentiment to us, it is clear from his related footnote that what he is talking about is compassion, which contains the capacity to appreciate beauty or, as Rousseau is quick to add, the "morally beautiful."

The other way natural compassion is extended is in its development into virtues. This is, of course, related to its extension through cognitive capacities. But where in the first case the extension depended on the representation of increasingly complex objects and concepts "external" to the person, the development into virtues is facilitated by human perfectibility, and it is the *agent* whose attributes the virtues are. In other words, the agent does not just respond to an increasingly complex world with increasingly complex sentiments; the agent herself becomes more complex. First, we should note that the development of virtues cannot follow from rationality. Rousseau, like Montesquieu, is skeptical of the power of reason: "Although it might belong to Socrates and other minds of the like craft to acquire virtue by reason, the human race would long since have ceased to be, had its preservation depended only on the reasonings of the individuals composing it" (D2, 69). And so, from compassion "*alone* flow all . . . social virtues" (D2, 67; my italics). This statement may actually be stronger than Rousseau would want because he has just remarked that self-love also plays a role in the formation of virtue (D2, 66n[36]). I will return to this small puzzle later; now the important point is that reason does not produce virtues.

The development of compassion into more complicated virtues and other generally beneficial sentiments naturally does not explain why humans are now wicked. The interplay of compassion and the other natural sentiment, self-love, as well as the "fortuitous concurrence of many foreign causes that might never arise," together constitute the "different accidents which may have improved the human understanding while depraving the species, and made man wicked while making him sociable" (D2, 74). So let us now focus on self-love, a much more complicated issue in Rousseau and one on which he himself is not always clear.

There are actually *two* kinds of self-love, *amour-de-soi-même* and *amour-propre*. The textbook interpretation of Rousseau sees *amour-de-soi-même* as the instinctual interest in self-preservation and *amour-propre* as the "bad," comparative selfishness that fuels human wickedness. Rousseau himself does sometimes write as if that were his view, but a careful consideration of his discussion shows that this is not the case.[37] In the following, I refer to *amour-de-soi-même* as self-love and leave *amour-propre* untranslated.

Although compassion and self-love are equally natural, Rousseau talks as if self-love were still *the* most fundamental inclination. It is the "natural feeling that leads every animal to look to its own preservation, and which, guided in man by reason and modified by compassion, creates humanity and virtue" (D2, 66n). It is "primitive, innate, precedes all other [passions], and all the others are, in a sense, nothing but its modifications" (E, 275); in short, it is "the only passion natural to the human" (E, 111). Why, or how, is this? N. J. H. Dent suggests that this is because compassion, *pitie*, is not properly speaking a passion for Rousseau: "By a 'passion' Rousseau understands an affective response on our part . . . to the feelings, dispositions, attitudes, traits or another person particularly as these are directed towards us and incorporate and estimate our standing, value or worth . . . and/or an intent to benefit or harm us."[38] From this it follows that "pity or compassion do not clearly count as passions."[39] But as Dent himself notes, Rousseau does not unequivocally hold on to this understanding of the term "passion." Dent's passage points this out quite clearly: Self-love is regarded as a passion, and yet a "natural" human, motivated solely by self-love, would regard "his fellows almost as he regarded animals of different species" and would not engage in any kinds of comparisons with them (D2, 66n).

So while it is far from trivial what Rousseau actually means by passion, it does not help us here. An easier explanation is simply to note that self-love is, indeed, the primary human sentiment, but that it always necessarily engenders the sentiment of compassion more or less immediately. Self-preservation is the primary human interest, and humans—like all other animals—find themselves reasonably defenseless against all kinds of threats. This leads us to immediately extend our self-love to our nurturer who protects us, as well as to learn to recognize fears and suffering in others (E, 275).

But how is *amour-propre* related to self-love? They are different, Rousseau tells us, "both in themselves and in their effects": "*Amour-propre* is a purely relative and factitious feeling, which arises in the state of society, leads each individual to make more of himself than of any other, causes all the mutual damage men inflict one on another, and is the real source of the 'sense of honour,'"(D2, 66n). This does, indeed, suggest that *amour-propre* is behind the negative sentiments that lead to inequality among humans: pride, vanity, selfish greed, *Schadenfreude*, and so on. In other words, it seems that *amour-propre* is "bad" self-love, pure and simple.

But that would be a hasty interpretation. First, it would raise the problem of origin: If we interpret the "difference in themselves" between self-love and *amour-propre* as a difference between two psychological faculties (whatever that would mean), then Rousseau would have had to include it as one of the natural human attributes. But he does not do that; *amour-propre* is an "artificial" sentiment, artificial in the sense that it is occasioned in the state of society. But as we have seen in the case of compassion, the "artificial" sympathetic sentiments that arise in the state of society still attach to, as it were, or stem from the natural inclination. *Amour-propre* has to attach to something natural, if the Rousseauian psychology is to be consistent, and since *amour-propre* is a kind of self-love, why not think it comes from the good kind of self-love?

Indeed. Rousseau certainly suggests as much. Take, for example, one of the passages about self-love I cited earlier, this time in full:"The only passion natural to the human is the love of self [*l'amour de soi-même*], or *amour-propre taken in an extended sense*. This *amour-propre* in itself or relative to us is good and useful . . . it does not become good or bad except through one's application of it and in the relations one gives it" (E, 111; my emphasis). Far from being two different kinds of creatures, *amour-propre* can be seen as some kind of extension of self-love. But what kind of extension? Consider again the case of compassion. Benevolence, generosity, and so on are extensions of compassion, brought about when a person stands in complicated, cognitively represented relations to others. Rousseau suggests that the relationship between self-love and *amour-propre* is the same (see, e.g., E, 306, 317–319). We can take it, then, that *amour-propre* is self-love, the concern for our well-being, as it manifests itself when we stand in sufficiently complex relationships to other humans whom we recognize, through our use of reason, to be beings like us, also interested in *their* well-being. It is a concern for ourselves in relation to others, "as morally significant beings," as Dent puts it.[40] (As we will see in the next chapter, it is no coincidence that this looks a lot like Kant's notion of dignity.)

We can now return to Rousseau's distinction between self-love and *amour-propre* in the second *Discourse* passage cited earlier. His use is not inconsistent between the *Discourse* and *Émile*; he is *not* saying that *amour-propre* is a *necessarily* bad sentiment, but that badness—selfish, vain comparisons to others, greed, and so on—can be *one* of the ways it manifests itself. It can also manifest itself as a kind of nobility, as one's sense of dignity which depends on treating others with respect, helping others, and so on (e.g., E, 317–319)—although Rousseau grants it "only seldom does good without bad" (E, 319). By making a distinction between self-love and *amour-propre* he shows that human badness is not a natural condition, but can only come about in a state of society. This is exactly the point he makes about Émile:

> But to decide whether among the passions that will dominate in his character are humane and kind, or cruel and malignant, whether they will be the passions of beneficence and commiseration, or of envy and covetousness, one needs to know what place he will feel himself to occupy among people, and what sort of obstacles he believes he will have to overcome to get to the place he wants to occupy. (E, 306)

So, while at this point Rousseau has not fully explained why humans are wicked, he has found its origin. Since self-love is "always good," and *amour-propre*, the result of self-love's encounter with society, *can* be bad, he has a theorem: If humans are wicked, it is, in some way, a result of society. And since the first premise of his project is that humans are, indeed, wicked, he knows that society, somehow, is to blame.

The kind of *amour-propre* that characterizes humans in the corrupted, "wicked" state they are, is "inflamed" *amour-propre*. If noninflamed *amour-propre* is my general concern for myself standing in relation to others as a person, inflamed *amour-propre* is my wanting the others to love me, and just me, as I love myself. But how does this come about? Why does *amour-propre* get inflamed, not in just a few sociopaths and narcissists, but in all or at least most cultures? Consider the version of the story as told in the second *Discourse*: "The first man who, having enclosed a piece of ground, bethought himself of saying 'This is mine,' and found people simple enough to believe him, was the real founder of civil society" (D2, 76), is what Rousseau tells us at the beginning of Part II of the *Discourse*. Before this, we have just been given the psychological diagnosis of human inequality that puts the blame on society. This man is no unambiguous hero, that much is clear.

The important question is: What in property brings about the kind of human society that inflames people's *amour-propre*? Rousseau's answer is that the relevant feature of property as an institution is that it attaches something to a human being, to a self.[41] Moreover, this something is clearly recognized as useful, and this, in turn, makes it possible for this founder of civil society to regard himself as having and thus, in a sense, *being* more. Similarly, it makes at least some others, if not all, think of themselves as having, and thus being, something less: "This repeated relevance of various beings to himself, and one to another, would naturally give rise in the human mind to the perceptions of certain relations between them. Thus the relations which we denote by the terms great, small, strong, weak, swift, slow, fearful, bold, and the like . . ." (D2, 77). And thus the possibility of a noninflamed or, as Dent calls it, "equable" *amour-propre*[42] becomes undermined. Since Rousseau's "natural man" has coexisted with one another as more or less equals, their sense of themselves, in relation to others, has been that of having roughly equal standing. The institution of property upsets this balance. After this, the claim for an equal standing, as one's *amour-propre* would lead one to do, from someone with less land, say, would be inappropriate from the point of view of the "richer" landowner, and, in turn, his refusal inappropriate to the poorer.

The psychological effects of inflamed *amour-propre* are odious. I become dependent on others. "But the *amour-propre* which compares is never content and never could be because the sentiment of our preferring others requires that others also prefer us to them; something that is impossible" (E, 276–277), since others, equally in the grips of the sentiment toward themselves, won't. This can be seen in societal effects. Truly talented people, for example, will sacrifice their talents in their quest for appreciation:

> Every artist loves applause. The praise of his contemporaries is the most valuable part of his recompense. What then will he do to obtain it, if he have the misfortune to be born among a people, and at a time, when men of learning, who have become fashionable, have enabled frivolous youth to set the tone. . . . Let the famous Voltaire tell us how many fine, powerful, masculine passages he has sacrified to our false delicacy, and how much that is great and noble, that spirit of gallantry, which delights in what is frivolous and petty, has cost him. [*Discourse on Arts and Sciences* (hereafter D1), 18]

And people in general not only accept but maintain institutions of inequality. "The civilized man," Rousseau says,

> pays his court to men in power, whom he hates, and to the wealthy, whom he despises; he stops at nothing to have the hour of serving them; he is not ashamed to value himself on his own meanness and their protection; and, proud of his slavery, he speaks with disdain of those, who have not the honour of sharing it. . . . [S]ocial man lives constantly outside himself, and only knows how to live in the opinion of others, so that he seems to receive the consciousness of his own existence merely from the judgment of others concerning him. (D2, 104)

Leaving Animality Behind

After this lengthy diagnosis, it is time for prescriptions. Most important in Rousseau's diagnosis is that humans are not naturally bad and that even the corruption of *amour-propre* into inflamed *amour-propre*, while almost universal, is not *necessary* by any logic of the original human nature since it is also a product of contingent external facts. So there is hope. The question is how to translate the hope into something more concrete.

One way immediately suggests itself. Since humans are naturally good, one could try to capture humans more or less as they are naturally. This is, to an extent, possible: The fact that careful education can push back the onset of Émile's development into a "moral being" is evidence for this. But as a political program, it is not feasible on a large scale. Even with Émile, the best that could be achieved was a delay, not a prevention of self-love turning into *amour-propre*. Moreover, romantic as Rousseau may seem, he is not *so* romantic as to think that a total abandonment of civilization would be feasible as a political project. His Golden Age nostalgia is nostalgic exactly because we can't go back. Since going backward is not an option, the only other option is to head in the very opposite direction: forward, and far. And, as the case of Émile shows, education is a very powerful tool.

One way to characterize the modern condition of human wickedness is something like an "incomplete dehumanization." Rousseau is quite clear that the emergence of society and its attendant psychological effects mean human alienation from its natural state, that is, from what humans naturally are—or were. In that sense, we can talk about dehumanization. The problem, however, is that it is not complete: Inflamed *amour-propre* is still a sentiment that stems from psychology more appropriate to the nondehumanized human, to the human that had to be concerned for his own welfare since nothing else did that. In a state of society, this is neither necessary nor desirable. (I will get to the relevance of this distinction shortly.) So, even though society is to blame for the sad state of humanity, there is no way of getting rid of it. Further, the problem can be seen as a problem exacerbated by the kinds of humans who populate society: They are like *parvenus* who, despite having ostensibly made it to *haute societé*, still behave in ways that belie their vulgar past. In short, then, dehumanization, despite its nasty sound to us, is not all that bad; what is bad is that it is not complete.

This points the way to Rousseau's positive political program. The goal is to get rid of those remnants of humanity, understood in the natural sense, even in their modified forms. This is not in order to establish social order or peace—that may well reign in the "miserable" state of society we or Rousseau live in. Rather, as Yack observes, this program is to ensure human freedom and goodness.[43] Remember, people are wicked and dependent: They lack freedom, and *that* is the problem. Their liberation lies in their abandonment of the remnants of natural humanity—self-interest, compassion—and in a total commitment to the society. Unlike Montesquieu, who argued that self-interest is found in collective interest, Rousseau argues that *liberation* is found in collective interest and in the abandonment of self-interest.

Our recalcitrant self-interested selves will be an obstacle to political trans-formation, that Rousseau knows well enough. First of all, liberation is no rose garden. The constantly warring state of Sparta is Rousseau's model for ideal society, and he is quite explicit that a truly free state would still have to choose between sacrificing freedom for peace and remaining free while suffering constant war [*Considérations sur le Gouvernement de Pologne* (hereafter GP), 393] because all those envious unfree states would be continually attacking a truly free state. In his famous phrase, some people "will be forced to be free" [*The Social Contract* (hereafter SC), 177]. Education, the tool found so useful in *Émile*, will be one of the primary means of political transformation. But neither brainwashing—for the Rousseauian education can amount to that—nor other forms of paternalism can, in the end, be what political action is about. The project is, after all, the liberation of people, and while some indeed will have to be forced to be free, obtaining liberation can only be legitimate when it is the outcome of individuals' exercise of agency. This is what Rousseau's justificatory project, *The Social Contract*, is concerned with.

Rousseau's justification is, as is well known, contractarian. The particular kind of contract differs, however, from those of Hobbes and Locke. For example:

> These clauses [of the contract], properly understood, may be reduced to one—the total alienation of each associate, together with all his rights, to the whole community; for, in the first place, as each gives himself absolutely, the conditions are the same for all; and, this being so, no one has any interest in making them burdensome to others. (SC, 174)

In this arrangement, "no associate has anything more to demand" (SC, 174), and, since everyone receives *equally* the totality of everyone's rights, one's freedom does not diminish. Quite the contrary, one's earlier individual freedom is made qualitatively better: It has become *autonomy*. Rousseau calls this agreement the "general will" to distinguish it from a mere majoritarian decision: "The constant will of all the members of the State is the general will; by virtue of it they are citizens and free" (SC, Bk. IV, ch. 2, 250; see also Bk. I, ch. 5 and Bk. II, chs. 2–3). This idea also grounds Schmitt's conception of democracy, and when we think about the theoretical affinity of the two theorists, their illiberalism begins to take shape (even though Schmitt also accuses of Rousseau flirting incoherently with liberal ideals).[44]

The illiberal element lies in the fact that, for Rousseau, political agency is fundamentally about choosing to alienate oneself from one's self-interest and subjecting oneself under the general will of the collective entity that includes one. While this total alienation of myself from my interests is what is political, Rousseau does not think that this alienation necessarily constitutes human selves in their entirety:

> In fact, each individual, as a man, may have a particular will contrary or dissimilar to the general will which he has as a citizen. His particular interest may speak to him quite differently from the common interest: his absolute and naturally independent existence may make him look upon what he owes to the common cause as a gratuitous contribution, the loss of which will do less harm to others than the payment of it is burdensome to himself. . . . (SC, 177)

We might want to insist that Rousseau must be talking about two kinds of cases: of the person whose personal interests, whatever they are, do not coincide with what she nevertheless subscribes to *and* abides by as a political agent, and of the hypocrite freerider. For liberals, allowing for the possibility of the former kind of citizens is an important element of liberalism (as we saw earlier in the discussion of Montesquieu). However, that Rousseau does not make this distinction and flatly points out how these people will have to be compelled suggests that this psychological possibility is not desirable, but a situation that ideally, in the end, will not occur. A fragmented self is just an unintentional freerider for him. A unified self is the political goal, and the paradigm of political agent is the Spartan mother who thanks the gods upon hearing that her sons have been killed in a battle: "Here is the citizen" (E, 39).[45]

What Is to Be Done?

I want to conclude this chapter by considering what we have learned about Montesquieu and Rousseau by thinking about their attitudes about political transformation, particularly revolution. In a way, neither is a revolutionary since Rousseau is quite averse to thinking of his social transformation as being brought about through a radical overthrow of the plagued modernity.[46] But he is no liberal reformist, either—neither a liberal nor a reformist. His diagnosis of the social ills of humankind do not allow him to be: There is no hope in humans' *current* condition to change it for the better. There is hope in human nature, to be sure, but the layers of culture cannot be peeled off, and the natural goodness of humanity just cannot be tapped into. There is hope in the other direction, too, in completing our incomplete dehumanization, having us shed all of our instinctual self-interest and thus become both good and free. This direction is conceivable, so conceivable, in fact, that it can both be theorized about, and one can find societies in history that exemplify at least some aspects of it. But this ideal state, although Rousseau does not spell this out, is so different from where society currently is that "getting there" would be, in itself, a revolution. In this, we can call him a revolutionary: Whether or not he calls for one, he *needs* one. And while one might argue that the Jacobin attempt to ground the revolutionary Terror on the *Social Contract* was, at best, a bastardization of Rousseau, people weren't wrong to seek inspiration for the French Revolution in Rousseau's work.

This is despite Rousseau's quite explicit rejection of revolution. It was a mistake, "the Frenchman" of the *Dialogues* says of one of Rousseau's alter egos, "J. J.," when "people stubbornly insisted on seeing a promoter of upheavals and disturbances in the one man in the world who maintains the truest respect for the laws and national constitutions, and who has the greatest aversion to revolutions and conspirators of every kind" [*Rousseau, Judge of Jean-Jacques: Dialogues* (hereafter D), 213]. Also, in the July 26, 1767, letter to Mirabeau, he claims that "I don't see anything tolerable between the most austere democracy and perfect Hobbesianism: for the conflict between people and laws, which creates a state of continual civil war, is the worst of all political conditions" [*Correspondance III* (hereafter C3), 481].

This rejection of revolution is not just some rhetorical end-of-career backpedaling or squeamishness about social strife, but is theoretically motivated. For a fan of Sparta and forecaster of constant war, revolution is not a problem just because it might be nasty. Continual civil war is undesirable because it is a condition of unfreedom, not because there is turmoil. Rather, Rousseau realizes that his diagnosis of the contemporary human condition does not afford him any agents of the right kind for transformation. People running around with inflamed *amour-propre* might be perfectly skilled in overthrowing regimes, but they lack what they need, ultimately, to unite under the kind of social contract that he envisions. So there is a fundamental theoretical dilemma between Rousseau's diagnosis and prescriptions, one that hinges on agency. In the end, the para-doxical sound of "forcing people to be free" may be indicative of the failure of the Rousseauian program. Kant, as we will see in the next chapter, comes much closer to working out a solution to this dilemma. The solution is an explicitly reformist one.

Contrasting Rousseau to Montesquieu, we can see how Montesquieu's constitutional reformism, too, hinges on how he conceives of agency. Where Rousseau is profoundly dissatisfied in being what he is when he could be more, Montesquieu marvels at how many things humans can be and dares not to claim that there is some particular "more" they could be. Thoroughly agnostic on any thick notion of the good for humans, he has to take them as they are, warts and all, and make the best of it. Irrational and passionate, they cannot be trusted to get the "right" things done, but they certainly will try all kinds of things. The best thing to do, for him, then, is to channel these passions as usefully as possible and in a way that the passions of some will check the passions of others. To get this plan working, no fundamental overhaul is necessary since the requisite passions are there already; all that is necessary is to curb the power of some stick-in-the-mud institutions, such as the church, that cannot appreciate the bewildering diversity of people's conceptions of the good. For this and for similar jobs, Montesquieu need not dream of some miraculous agent of transformation: The agents are the people sufficiently ticked off by the church to do something about it, and the same goes for other institutions as well.

Montesquieu leaves several questions open, however. On the one hand, he does have a sophisticated—and, as we know, rather successful—design for political institutions. On the other, the institutions come as an answer to an insightful analysis of human agency and social relations. What is missing, however, is an account of the middle ground, namely, politics itself. To put it more explicitly, Montesquieu offers a design for legitimate political institutions, but he doesn't offer an account of *legitimation*. It is not that Montesquieu just forgot this; since he regards reason as a weak guide for human action, his theoretical analysis of politics treats it as essentially similar to any other social activity in which humans engage. But given an understanding of politics as controversial *claims* about legitimate authority, we might want to look for a complementary account that leaves room for self-conscious, perhaps even autonomous, claim-making. Surely his account implicitly allows for agent-centered revision of one's passions, and not just external tinkering via institutions, climate, and so on.

To offer such an account and to relate the Montesquieuian program to the liberal institution of public reason, I now turn to the sober liberalism of Kant.

four

LIBERALISM GROWN PALE
AND KÖNIGSBERGIAN

In Kant's case, many would argue, we would be particularly well advised to make the distinction between the exegetical details of the doctrine and its general promise. Even Kantians often treat him like the eccentric uncle of whom you are proud, but who, you nevertheless hope, doesn't open his mouth in polite company. This is because Kant often says things that are embarrassing to those who are in sympathy with his theories in general. The proscription on lying, even to a murderer who comes looking for your friend, is the best-known example, but not the only one ["Uber ein vermeintes Recht aus Menschenliebe zu lügen" (hereafter VRL), VIII: 425–427].[1] Consider: Mothers who kill their illegitimate children cannot be prosecuted [*Rechtslehre* (hereafter RL), VI: 336]. The two ways in which humans use others physically are cannibalism and sex ["Reflexionen"(hereafter R), 7662,[2] XIX: 481]. And you must always obey the authorities who have power over you (RL, V: 372). Odd and embarrassing stuff, indeed, and it seems sensible to explain them away as instances of senility or some other personal idiosyncrasy, as Kant's fear of censors, or at least as Kant's careless misapplications of his own principles.

However, I want to take the quirky Kant seriously. Much as we might want them to be, the embarrassing applications are not dogmatic naps. The exoneration of maternal infanticide and the strict duty of obedience are, I argue, consistent with Kant's theory. (I do not consider the cases of lying or of sexual relations, as they are less relevant for my purposes here and have been discussed at length by Christine Korsgaard and Barbara Herman, respectively.[3]) The payoff from showing this to be the case is a picture of Kant that is richer and more nuanced than stock accounts and perhaps a little surprising as well: In both ethics and politics, Kant turns out to be a historicist. How we solve moral and political problems depends on contingent, historical facts about the world. To be sure, Kant's historicism is not relativist all the way down; the categorical imperative still grounds the apparatus, but at the social level, it does not generate immutable, eternal, universal prescriptions.[4]

This approach is in contrast to those recent political theorists who are not only troubled by the occasional quirk but who feel, despite their sympathies, that the *overall* program runs aground. The textbook case is Habermas. Although a fundamental Kantianism undergirds his theory, its trajectory is nevertheless a pretty clean tangent away from Kant. The early *Structural Transformation of the Public Sphere* is still a deeply Kantian work, but Habermas's later work amounts to both an attempt to find non-Kantian grounds for Kantian moral intuitions and a critique of Kant's excessively "monological" concept of practical reason.[5] The gist of the Habermasian view is that the theory isolates the moral agent from its morally salient, dynamic relations with other agents, which means that it cannot, by itself, generate a pragmatically defensible normative theory. The irony is that, at least on my reading, Kant's historicist view fares *better* than the Habermasian discourse ethics, which tries to squeeze thick norms out of the rather thin normative commitments we have by virtue of all communication.

This isn't to say, however, that my argument is a general defense or an endorsement of Kant's policies. We can certainly still disagree with Kant on whether some of his own readings are the best or only possible interpretations of his theory. It also offers no blanket claim for a total coherence or consistency of Kant's work. Certainly Kant *can* make mistakes, and sometimes he clearly does: Basing the prohibition of suicide on the Formula of the Universal Law, and not on the Formula of Humanity, is a misapplication of the principles.[6] Moreover, there is much in Kant that cannot and should not be defended even on narrow theoretical grounds. His racism and misogyny are the starkest examples, but insofar as they do "theoretical" work for Kant, it is in the early precritical works such as the *Observations on the Feeling of the Beautiful and the Sublime*, and they are happily less central in the critical works. Thus they can be ignored (theoretically) more easily than the specific examples. Many other unsavory examples, I want to stress, *are* necessary for understanding Kant.

The particular aspect of Kant relevant for this book is his political philosophy, which tends to get belittled—again, even by those sympathetic to him—or downplayed even by those whose own interests have to do with loosely Kantian political philosophy.[7] Kant is a sober German liberal, that much is conceded by all, and his famous essay "What Is Enlightenment?" ("Beantwortung zur Frage: Was ist Aufklärung?") eloquently outlines his commitment to values we recognize as liberal. But this liberalism is often seen as relatively weak and not of great theoretical interest. For example, many take the account of public reason advocated in "What Is Enlightenment?" as oddly misguided and ultimately insufficient for what liberalism really needs. Following Onora O'Neill and others, I want to argue that the dismissal of Kant's explicitly political work as misguided and marginal is itself a mistake and that the pale Königsbergian liberalism should be of great interest to liberals, especially against the Schmittian challenge.[8]

One particular feature that emerges out of Kant's political theory is a quite novel conception of the political, namely, a view of politics as two distinct but related spheres of activity. The first is related to Montesquieu's institutional solution: Kant offers a liberal account of the constitutional state. But as we saw in Montesquieu's case, that leaves us without an account of autonomous political action for individuals. The *other* site of the political fills this gap by illustrating how individuals exercise their political agency in a liberal way. This site is none other than the familiar sphere of public reason, but once we understand it in its historicist guise, we will see that it needn't be anything like cowardly intellectualism. Again, as in the case of Montesquieu, we will find a pragmatic, if not pragmatist, theory that presents liberalism as a contingent but appealing political solution to concrete social circumstances.

Important for this project is understanding the influence of Rousseau on Kant's philosophy in general, but, in particular, on his view of agency and on his political philosophy. The argument therefore takes a slightly circuitous route. First, I go through the relatively familiar terrain of Kant's account of agency, but I scatter about some of the Rousseauian bits and pieces we saw in the previous chapter so that, in the end, the terrain will no longer look all that familiar. This helps set the stage for my main focus, the exploration of the stock pieces of Kant's political thought, that is, his notion of the public use of reason and the allegedly "rigorist" prohibition of resistance and revolution. Reading Kant as a theorist with an acute sociological sense of historical development—and underdevelopment—will unearth the real promise of Kant's political philosophy.

Kant's Debts to Rousseau

It is well known that Kant was very influenced by Rousseau, yet it should also be obvious to anyone who compares the two that their political commitments are different. What motivates the differences are the fundamentally different dispositions in Rousseau and Kant: The former is a relentless, sometimes rabid, critic of the liberal Enlightenment, while Kant remains an optimistic *Aufklärer*—"enlightener"—throughout his life. But the dispositional and temperamental differences explain little about the theoretical differences, and one must look for an explanation in the relevant doctrines. We will find that the political contrast between the two is a reflection of how Kant disagrees with Rousseau on the correct account of human agency and human development.

Historical anecdotes tell us of Rousseau's stature in Kant's life. The only decoration in his sparse study was a portrait of Rousseau, and the only time the good *Bürger* of Königsberg could not set their clocks by Kant's daily walks was when he was reading *Émile*.[9] But we need not rely on anecdotes; Kant's own words echo the same fascination. This is most obvious in his handwritten remarks to one of his early works, *Observations on the Feeling of the Beautiful and the Sublime* ["Bemerkungen zu den Beobachtungen über das Gefühl des Schönen und Erhabenen"(hereafter B), XX: 1–192], made in 1764–1765 when he was reading the *Discourses*, *Émile*, and the *Social Contract*. In some cases, Kant simply accepts Rousseau's analysis: "Society causes one to evaluate oneself only relationally. If others are no better than I, I am good; if all are worse than I, then I am perfect" (B, XX: 95) could be directly from the second *Discourse*. And the bulk of the "Remarks" (politely ignored by most scholars) is only too happy to amend Kant's misogyny of the *Observations* with Rousseauian variations.

In most cases, however, Kant's assent is qualified by his unease with what Rousseau has to say. "Rousseau has set me straight," Kant reports, but being set straight doesn't always mean things look better (B, XX: 45): Rousseau's impassioned account of the deleterious, rather than enlightening, effects of reason compels Kant to shed much of his dogmatic optimism. Kant's reaction to Rousseau's troubling persuasiveness is almost schizophrenic: The first impression "a discerning reader" gets of Rousseau, Kant says, is that he is dealing with a sharp-witted yet deeply feeling genius who may be without a rival. But that is followed with another kind of impression when the reader notices that the genius seems to have mixed his sensible thoughts with such odd and nonsensical ideas that one is led to think of the work as just a vulgar joke (B, XX: 43–44). Kant's final impression, however, is that Rousseau is not joking: He is to be taken seriously.[10] Richard Velkley has argued that Rousseau in fact set Kant on the path that culminates in the three *Critiques*.[11] This may be putting it too strongly since the famous wake-up call from dogmatic slumbers had actually come to Kant five years earlier when Johann Georg Hamann introduced him to Hume's doctrine.[12] Rousseau doesn't quite set Kant on his critical path, but he nevertheless stands at a crucial juncture.[13]

While the immediate influence of Rousseau in the "Remarks" makes for a fascinating study, I want to focus on how the influence is visible in the mature Kant, when he has had time to work on the problems presented by Rousseau. Perhaps the most obvious loan and further development of a Rousseauian idea is the categorical imperative, which is seen as reflecting the "general will." The agent who tests the morality of her maxim by imagining whether it could be generalized into a universal law is doing something similar to Rousseau's citizens who generate, each, in *themselves* the authorization for the sovereign of the civil society.[14] This connection between Kant's moral philosophy and Rousseau's political theory will be explored at length later.

The relationship between Kant's explicitly political philosophy and Rousseau's is quite straightforward. He thinks Rousseau's diagnosis is largely right, but the prescriptions are wrong:

> In his essays *On the Influence of the Sciences* and *On the Inequality of Man*, he [Rousseau] shows quite correctly that there is an inevitable conflict between culture and the nature of the human race as a *physical* species each of whose individual members is meant to fulfill his destiny completely. But in his *Émile*, in his *Social Contract*, and other writings, he attempts in turn to solve the more difficult problem of what course culture should take in order to ensure the proper development, in keeping with their destiny, of man's capacities as a *moral* species, so that this destiny will no longer conflict with his character as a natural species. ["Conjectures on the Beginning of Human History" (hereafter CBH), VIII: 116]

In the 1760s "Remarks," Kant had still thought an Émile-like educational program was promising—"Rousseau's education is the only means to help civil society (*bürgerliche Gesellschaft*) flourish" (B, XX: 175)—but by this point, this sort of single-mindedness is gone. Kant disagrees with Rousseau on "what direction culture should take," while still agreeing with him on the need for further human development. Later, I will spell out what these differences are and why they are there.

Finally, there is a relevant difference here between their views on revolution. As we saw in the previous chapter, when thinking about his political ideals,

Rousseau imagines a radically overhauled society, one in which the entire modernity has more or less been left behind and where individual humans have *transcended* their animality, that is, self-interest, compassion for others, and other purely personal attachments. But as we also saw, his explicit rhetoric on revolution is negative. Kant is the exact opposite. He denies the right of rebellion under any circumstances (although he does waffle on the definition) [RL, VI: 325; *Perpetual Peace* (hereafter PP), VIII: 372–373], yet notes that the French revolution "nonetheless finds in the hearts of all spectators (who are not engaged in this game themselves) a wishful participation that borders closely on enthusiasm ... this sympathy, therefore, can have no other cause than a moral predisposition in the human race" [*The Conflict of the Faculties* (hereafter CF), VII: 85].

In the following, I take up and connect all of these themes in a relatively complicated sketch of Kant's political thinking. First, I explore Kant's discussion of humanity in the state of nature, both in terms of anthropology, that is, the development of the physical species, and in terms of his historical "conjectures," which connect the physical species with the development of *moral* humanity. In doing this, I investigate how exactly the Rousseauian ideas about the general will have been transformed in Kant's ethics. I pay, perhaps surprisingly, particular attention to what happens to the important Rousseauian notions of self-love and *amour-propre* since they help us understand the political differences between the two thinkers. Equipped with Kant's historicist understanding of the human condition, we can then make sense of Kant's odd way of making social distinctions between private, public, and personal and the good and the right. This, finally, will give us a sense of how the political is related to the ethical and of what Kant's political agents are like.

Nature and Society

The resemblance between Rousseau's general will and Kant's categorical imperative is obvious. Compare Rousseau's idea that in the general will, each individual expresses her or his individual will, which coincides with that of everyone else, and which binds all, with the "Formula of Universal Law" of Kant's categorical imperative: "Act only according to that maxim by which you can at the same time will that it should become a universal law" [*Foundations of the Metaphysics of Morals* (hereafter G), IV: 421; see also *Critique of Practical Reason* (hereafter CPrR), V: 30]. While there is, of course, an important difference in that Kant is talking about any maxims (what they are will be discussed later), and from the vantage point of the individual (albeit in relation to the rest of humanity), the general will can nevertheless be seen as an actuated, collective exercise of the categorical imperative on the same maxim. The generality implied in the name of each principle is another feature they share. Again, Rousseau: "Thus, just as a particular will cannot stand for the general will, the general will, in turn, changes in nature, when its object is particular, and, as general, cannot pronounce on a man or a fact" (SC, 187). And Kant:

> The hypothetical imperative, therefore, says only that the action is good to some purpose, possible or actual. In the former case, it is a problematic, in the latter

an assertorical, practical principle. The categorical imperative, which declares the action to be of itself objectively necessary without making any reference to any [one] end in view . . . holds as an apodictical practical principle. (G, IV: 414–415)[15]

Finally, both understand their principles through an individual as her own legislator. Rousseau talks about "a law which we prescribe to ourselves" (SC, 178). Kant's "formula of autonomy" expresses the categorical imperative as "the idea of the will of every rational being as a will that legislates universal law" (G, IV: 431). Clearly Kant is not just reformulating Rousseau's idea of the general will in a new way; much substantive philosophical work has gone into the idea of categorical imperative, and Rousseau is just one of the influences here.[16] But the resemblance is not a coincidence.

We can see this if we expand our attention from the two principles themselves into the grounds and conditions for their application. Here we can find both confirmation of the relatedness of the two principles and an explanation of differences, ultimately, between Kant's and Rousseau's moral and political programs. Recall that the road to expressing the general will in Rousseau is long: It is, according to Rousseau, a solution to a particular condition of human society, given human nature. This preparatory work can be found in Kant, too.

As in the Rousseauian world, for Kant, humans are born free, and the inequality in which we find them is "inseparable from culture" and not a condition of the natural state (*status naturalis*) (CBH, VIII: 118n). But where Rousseau focuses on the two prerational sentiments of self-love and compassion, Kant's emphasis is on reason (RL, V: 213). It is not that some such sentiments do not characterize humans (he is explicit on that they do) [*Anthropologie in pragmatischen Hinsicht* (hereafter A), VIII: 251–256], but it is *reason* that separates humans from other animals. Humans are defined as finite creatures with reason, that is, with the capacity to choose their ends: "The capacity to set oneself an end—any end whatsoever—is what characterizes humanity (as distinguished from animality)" [*Doctrine of Virtue* (hereafter DV), VI: 392]. Having provided humans with reason from the start, nature, "in a stepmotherly fashion," has rigged them to try to rise above their animality (CPrR, V: 146). This is because *reason* supplies our freedom: Reason makes it possible to *choose*, to recognize that one's animal inclinations can be obeyed or left disobeyed (RL, V: 214). This is the idea behind Kant's talk of the will as a "kind of causality" (G, IV: 446; CPrR, V: 42–50). Human development is thus, in a way, the pursuit of ever-expanding scope of choices. The ultimately wide scope would be a state where we are no longer bound by the finiteness of being physical animals: "Man was meant to rise, by his own efforts, above the barbarism of his natural abilities" [CBH, VIII: 118n; see also "On the Common Saying: 'This May Be True in Theory, but It Does Not Apply in Practice'" (hereafter TP), VIII: 289]. However, Kant is quite explicit in that our finiteness is a fundamental and inescapable condition: We cannot deny our natural inclinations, but will remain "an ambiguous cross between angels and cattle," as he puts it in his "Reflections on Anthropology" (R, 488, XV: 211; see also CBH, VIII: 118n).[17] Finitely rational wills can't hope to graduate to pure rational wills.

The state of society (*status civilis*) was, then, bound to emerge. Although Kant admits that we can only have conjectures on how it *actually* came about, we can trace some main steps of development [CBH, VIII: 109; also "Idea for a Universal History with a Cosmopolitan Purpose" (hereafter UH), VIII: 2, 30–31].[18] Fundamental in that is that the emergence of society is not as negative as it is for Rousseau. It is true that Kant sometimes writes in the Rousseauian vein as if the emergence of society were something akin to the fall from the garden of Eden, but, in the Kantian secular theology, this inevitability is the first step toward providence: "The means which nature employs to bring about the development of innate capacities is that of antagonism within society, in so far as this antagonism becomes in the long run the cause of a law-governed social order" (UH, VIII: 20). The emergence of society neither could be nor should have been helped, and where Kant sharply disagrees with Rousseau is in Rousseau's fondness for myths of pre-Fall golden ages. He notes that reflections on golden ages are "empty yearning," "symptoms of that weariness of civilised life" (CBH, VIII: 122). Although Rousseau is not mentioned, he is one of the central foils here. As we saw in the previous chapter, Rousseau waxes nostalgic about all sorts of golden ages.

The state of society is nevertheless a state of inequality for Kant—largely for the same reasons it is one for Rousseau. The important thing is that the state of society is, despite its problems, a step away from mere animality and already, to use only a slightly misplaced Humean term, under the circumstances of justice. In other words, humans can become, even be and behave like moral beings even in the nonideal state of society.[19]

One of the standard rigorist interpretations of Kant would hold that there is nothing surprising in noticing that Kant thinks we can behave like moral beings in a nonideal state of society. In that view, Kantian morality *demands* that we *always* behave according to morality, regardless of the circumstances in which we find ourselves. There is certainly textual evidence for viewing Kant as a rigorist of this sort, but the evidence is not conclusive. I want to suggest that Kant's picture of cultural evolution is evidence against rigorism of this sort. This needn't mean that Kant is not a rigorist in some other way: In fact, it does seem quite plausible, as Marcia Baron argues, that he thinks we are never "off the hook" when it comes to morality.[20] And, despite the fact that "rigorism" is generally used as a term of criticism, there may be much to be said for a rigorism of that sort. Although that discussion is not central here, I want to suggest that my interpretation is compatible with that rigorism.[21]

Morality, Maxims, and Self-love

How, then, do humans exhibit themselves as moral beings? By behaving according to morality, of course. But let's be careful here. The standard Kant interpretation would now hold that "behaving morally" means acting according to the categorical imperative. In a loose sense, this is true. But if the view is specified to claim that people, in living their lives and choosing their actions, constantly reason according to the categorical imperative, the view would be mistaken. It would, legitimately, invite all the standard accusations of empty formalism and puritan rigorism that generally are leveled against Kant. But we know now that Kant's people do not walk about coldly, choosing their actions through goal-neutral formulas; they do not abide slavishly by strict and unyielding moral dogma; and they do not, in general, spend all their time deliberating, but, rather, rely in most cases on the moral responses cultivated in them by education.[22]

Moreover, moral behavior need not always involve the categorical imperative to begin with. Let us look at how practical reasoning, according to Kant, is to proceed. We need to keep in mind that this process need not characterize every action, moral or nonmoral, but, rather, is undertaken in cases where, for example, the agent does not antecedently know whether she should do something. The agent has a desire to have some state of affairs be brought about. If we focus solely on the categorical imperative, it seems that the agent should see if her desire conforms to it. She is, in modern terminology, to test her desire through the "CI-procedure," first to see if the concept of the action involves a contradiction when universalized, then to see if her willing it does.[23]

However, Kant thinks that there are tests prior to the CI-procedure. Remember that our animality, as it were, can give us all kinds of desires and inclinations, some of which may not exhibit ourselves as moral beings. So the first thing that we should do when we confront "in our heart" a desire or inclination is to ask whether acting according to the desire would manifest me as a moral being or just as an animal:

> Humanity in his person is the object of the respect which he can demand from every other man, *but which he must also not forfeit.* . . . Since he must regard himself not only as a person generally, but also as a *man*, that is, as a person who has duties his own reason lays upon him, his insignificance as a *human animal* may not infringe upon his consciousness of his dignity as a *rational man*, and he should not disavow the moral self-esteem of such a being. (DV, VI: 435; first emphasis mine)

But how is this done? And why is this prior to the actual CI-test? For certainly we could test whether my desire to, say, run naked in the woods and eat small animals raw could be universalized. The problem, however, is that this would not be a *maxim*, "the subjective principle of volition" (G, IV: 400n), and, Kant wants to say, not intelligible as such for the CI-procedure. So how does something become a maxim?

Maxims include ends: They are agents' notions of doing something *in order to* do something else.[24] They are not just "raw" psychological states, the kinds of inclinations that nature presents in us, but involve an understanding of *why* the agent wants to do something. (The standard contrast between maxims and Hume's *sentiments* is sufficiently illustrative here.) This "proves," as it were, to the agent that her act is an act on the part of a moral being and not as an animal. However, this is *not* because the formulation of the maxim suggests an instrumental rationality (although this is an element), but because the idea of an end conveys the existence of a choice. And, as we saw earlier, choice is an element of us as moral beings.

Interestingly, this can be put in terms of self-love, the concept so central in

Rousseau's work. The "propensity to make the subjective determining grounds of one's choice into an objective determining ground of the will in general can be called self-love" (CPrR, V: 74), Kant says. A page earlier, he notes that all inclinations, "taken together," constitute self-regard, whose benevolent form is self-love (CPrR, V: 73). What he means is, first, that only in relation to the sum total of my inclinations can any single inclination help constitute a maxim. For something to be an "objective" determining ground of my action flags it clearly as not just being a raw psychological state stemming from my animal nature. Simply: It is objective, something that I—and others—can intelligibly take as a *reason* for action, and not merely as a cause.[25] In his third *Critique*, Kant shows that the objectivity, or "intersubjective validity," of concepts that lack an *actual* object is a perfectly intelligible notion.[26] Here, the idea is that an inclination becomes an intersubjectively valid end not because of any feature about itself, but because of its relation to my self-love, that is, my regard of myself as a being that can have ends. (We can appreciate the thickness of this conception by thinking of how little needs to be true of something for it to count as an end in Aristotle.) Thus we can call the test by which we check that my inclinations would lead to actions exhibiting my moral personhood the "self-love test."[27]

The mere self-love test does not make us moral beings, however. In fact, it is somewhat problematic, for the propensity to make the subjective objective is often not limited to mere objectivity, understood as intelligibility, but to go even further: "when it makes itself legislative and an unconditional practical principle, it can be called self-conceit" (CPrR, V: 74). Self-conceit, in other words, is to demand that my—and *only* my—will can count as an unconditional determining ground; it demands "from others respect which it denies them" (DV, VI: 465). To prevent that is where the further tests of the CI-procedure come into play: "The moral law, which alone is truly, i.e., in every respect, objective, completely excludes the influence of self-love from the highest practical principle and *endlessly impairs self-conceit* ("tut dem Eigendünkel ... unendlichen Abbruch"; CPrR, V: 74; translation in italics mine[28]).

It is important to try to understand what Kant means by self-love. There is a temptation to read it in a relatively narrow way as self-*interest*, and Kant does sometimes write in this way (see, e.g., CPrR, V: 25–26). But, I want to suggest, that narrow conception simply cannot handle the more substantive discussion of self-love. We are better off in tracing the connection to Rousseau and to think of self-love as the "good" or neutral *amour-propre* and self-conceit as its inflamed form. In other words, this self-love is *pride*, a relational, social sentiment, not the presocial *amour-de-soi-même*, or self-interest.[29]

Before proceeding, however, some caution is in place; we should not read Kant's discussion as being exactly the same as Rousseau's account of *amour-propre*. First, Kant's two categories of self-regard are cognitive, not psychologically primitive (noncognitive). They are states of mind to which the agent has introspective access and which she can parse, if need be. Rousseau is less clear on the distinction. Second, more interesting to us here, there are two other main differences from Rousseau. First, for Kant, a certain kind of *amour-propre* helps to guide our practical reasoning in the first instance, and thus is required for our continued existence as moral beings. In other words, the pride is pride for the recognition that the maxim in question is part of the complete set of inclinations that make it *mine*. I am proud of being the kind of creature that can have ends of my own choosing.

The second important difference between Kant and Rousseau is that, for Kant, we *always* have available to us a mechanism to check the stirrings of inflamed *amour-propre* or self-conceit: In his critique of Christian Garve, Kant says that "as an honest man, he has in fact *always* found this separation [between selfish desire and duty] in his heart" (TP, VIII: 285, my emphasis). Simply put, we can always use reason to prevent healthy self-regard from turning into self-conceit. This doesn't mean that anyone can do it at any time; Kant entertains no more illusions than Rousseau about the frequency of our use of this check: We don't, now, use it well enough, and much enlightening of the human race is to be done before humans are where they could be. Kant's calling Garve "an honest man" in fact says as much, since the notion of honesty in the eighteenth century connoted a moral cultivation more than simple truth-telling. And so "we are still a long way from the point where we could consider ourselves *morally* mature" (UH, VIII: 26). But the mechanism is nevertheless already available to us, and thus no fundamental Rousseauian program to "complete" our alienation of our animal inclinations is needed. In fact, complete dehumanization will not be possible: Although man was meant to rise above his natural barbarism, he was yet "to take care not to contravene [natural inclinations] even as he rises above them" (CBH, VIII: 118n).

What is interesting here is that this analysis helps us see why Kant seems to accept even immoral action motivated by self-regard under some circumstances. *Conceptually*, inclinations must pass the self-love test before even being eligible for the properly moral test of the CI-procedure. Analogously, in terms of human and personal *development*, people must be able to have a sense of themselves as persons before they can even be candidates of any sort of moral cultivation or enlightenment. Self-regard is the first step on one's way to full rational autonomy. As counterintuitive as it might seem, acting out of pride or out of the avoidance of shame are the first nonheteronomous sources of motivation.

I want to show this by considering a puzzling piece of casuistry in the *Rechtslehre*.[30] In discussing his retributivist theory of punishment, Kant makes a peculiar exception for two kinds of intentional homicide. The state cannot, through legislation, sentence to death a soldier who murders "a fellow soldier in a duel" or a mother who murders her illegitimate child (RL, VI: 336). The cases share the feature that the killing arises, in Kant's view, out of the sense of "honor of one's sex."

> Legislation cannot remove the disgrace of an illegitimate birth any more than it can wipe away the stain of suspicion of cowardice from a subordinate officer who fails to respond to a humiliating affront with a force of his own rising above the fear of death. So it seems that in these two cases people find themselves in the state of nature, and that these acts of *killing*, which would then not even have to be called murder, are certainly punishable but cannot be punished by the supreme power. (RL, VI: 336, Kant's italics)

The logic is this: For soldiers, military honor is based on one's courage to confront death. When offended, the soldier cannot seek satisfaction through means that leave in doubt whether there really is any basis for his sense of honor. If he, say, merely sues the offender for slander, it shows that he does not have the relevant psychological makeup meriting honor as a soldier and, consequently, can't have had his military honor offended in the first place. So insofar as the only way to respond to an offense is to punish the offender oneself, that is, to "take back" one's right to use violence from the state, one is in a state of nature. And thus the killing in a duel takes place outside the state's conceptual jurisdiction.

The case of maternal infanticide is somewhat more complicated. First, the child born out of wedlock is, according to Kant, outside the legitimate protection of the state. This is because marriage is the only political institution through which new persons can legitimately enter political society, and out-of-wedlock babies are thus, in Kant's appalling choice of words, equivalent to "contraband merchandise."[31] And so the state can "ignore [the child's] annihilation." Second, since "no decree can remove the mother's shame when it becomes known that she gave birth without being married," the only means she has to deal with this shameful event reside with her. Kant is not saying that killing the child is the only thing she can do, but that it is *one* of the things she can do. Important is that whatever she does is not as a *citizen*, with political rights and duties, but as a denizen of the state of nature.

Critics tend to focus on the admittedly unfortunate way Kant characterizes the out-of-wedlock baby's legal status, but that obscures the philosophical import of this example. The extralegal status of the child alone does little to make this case interesting; rather, the overlapping *reasons* for the extralegal status *and* the mother's shame are central to the point Kant wants to make. It is not that it is, in principle, wrong to act in order to avoid shame; quite the contrary, it is morally required, as both the idea of the self-love test and Kant's general disapproval of servility suggest [DV, VI: 434–437; *Lectures on Ethics* (hereafter LE), 126–129]. The problem comes from the conditions on which the shame arises or, conversely, from the conditions on which a woman's "honor of her sex" rest. One of them is obviously marriage: An honorable woman only has children when married. The other conditions are other relevant gender norms, ones to which an honorable woman conforms. In both cases, we are dealing with norms: explicitly legal in the first case and, presumably, both legal and social in general.

Now these sorts of norms are historically contingent. Kant is very explicit that it is society's condition that is to blame for creating the conflict between morality (for killing remains wrong) and the legitimate preservation of one's honor and avoidance of shame:

> The categorical imperative of penal justice remains (unlawful killing of another must be punished by death); but the legislation itself (and consequently also the civil constitution), as long as it remains barbarous and undeveloped, is responsible for the discrepancy between the incentives of honor in the people (subjectively) and the measures that are (objectively) suitable for its purpose. (RL, VI: 336–337)

So, far from constituting a revolting *reductio* of Kant's doctrine, this example actually has protofeminist implications: If bearing an illegitimate child is a source of shame, it is a reason to consider changing social conditions and institutions so that it isn't. The fact that Kant probably had in mind something very different from what we might want does not undermine the political potential of his analysis.

The application of principles of morality, then, at least through politics, is stage dependent. Moreover, this case shows that Kant's talk of the eternal and universal validity of the categorical imperative shouldn't always (if ever) be read in the rigorist way, that is, as telling an individual what she *must always* do. Rather, the eternal universality is of a different kind: It provides an unchanging benchmark against which to evaluate existing conditions by testing, among other things, whether the demands of the self-love test and the CI-procedure conflict.

Principles of the Right

Let us turn to Kant's explicitly political writings to see how all this plays itself out in detail. I want to show how the previous analysis helps us make sense of Kant's ideas of public reason and of the limits of political action. I will show what exactly the political role is that public reason is supposed to play, what kind of political action Kant considers illegitimate, and why. My central claim is that his political program is not some piece of fancy utopian metaphysics, but that it results from Kant's keen sense of the exigencies of history.

There are two kinds of political texts: Kant's numerous "occasional" essays on politics, on the one hand, and his *Rechtslehre*, the Doctrine of the Right from the unfinished *Metaphysics of Morals*. The former seem rather light and have often been thought of as lacking in theoretical substance. The latter, on the other hand, is theoretical enough, but seems like slightly stuffy and dull natural law philosophy.

Both views are, I believe, mistaken. Kant's political essays are not lighthearted and nontheoretical, but, for the most part, what Kant says in them is how he understands his theoretical works to relate to politics. Moreover, following J. C. Laursen, I want to claim that they are *in themselves* political, that is, not just works on politics, but political activity.[32] (Why I think this should become clear in what follows.) Second, it is also quite clear, as I try to show, that the *Rechtslehre* should not be taken as the *whole* view on what Kant has to say about politics. The *Rechtslehre* is richer than it seems, but even then it does not exhaust the theoretical promise of his political philosophy.[33] A more complete picture of Kant's politics emerges only when we relate the *Rechtslehre* to his ethical writings, on the one hand, and his "practical" political writings, on the other.

I approach the issue through Kant's seemingly idiosyncratic and inconsistent use of categories and distinctions we associate with demarcating the sphere of the political. Consider first the distinction we find in the *Metaphysics of Morals*, namely, that between right and virtue. Ethicists focus on this distinction as one between the right and the good, an understandable focus particularly for the twentieth-century scholars who spent their careers worrying about deontology and consequentialism. Sympathetic Kant scholars, in turn, have used the *Doctrine of Virtue* to counter the claims (stemming from that previous debate) that Kant is an unreconstructed deontologist with nothing to say about consequences.

I, however, look at the distinction in a much more flat-footed way. Kant is talking about *justice*, understood in a very traditional way, in the *Rechtslehre*. This is almost trivial: One of the meanings of *das Recht* is simply "justice." Given what we know about Kant's obsession with the architectonics of his doctrine, it seems reasonable to superimpose the distinction between perfect and imperfect duties onto the *Metaphysics of Morals*. Perfect duties can be externally regulated, while imperfect duties cannot; the *Rechtslehre* is about perfect duties and the *Doctrine of Virtue* about the imperfect ones.[34] The content of the *Rechtslehre* suggests as much: The discussion is about institutions, primarily about institutions governed by the state through civil laws. In a way, the book is Kant's treatise on politics since politics, is "an applied branch of right [*ausübender Rechtslehre*]" (PP, VIII: 370).

It would be tempting now to suggest that the distinction between the two doctrines is the notorious liberal distinction into public and private. But we must be careful. First, while the *Rechtslehre* does seem to focus on the sphere of society that is generally called the public sphere, the *Doctrine of Virtue* does not fit in the picture as a liberal treatise of the private sphere, say, of what the individual may do in the social sphere not regulated by principles of justice. It is, as Kant says, about "duties of *inner freedom*," while the job of the *Rechtslehre* is to deal with "outer freedom" (DV, V: 407). The exercise of inner freedom alone has to do with what is *ethical*, treated here as roughly synonymous to *virtuous* (so much for pure deontology). There is no indication that inner freedom can or should only be exercised in the "private." Granted, many of the examples of the *Doctrine of Virtue* deal primarily with what we might call people's private lives—but then so does much of the casuistry in the *Rechtslehre*.

What is the difference here? Outer freedom is a person's ability to do or act without hindrance from others (RL, V: 231), while inner freedom is the kind of state discussed earlier, namely, the ability of a person to act according to her own maxims. The "Universal Principle of *Right*," that is, of outer freedom, is thus as follows: "Any action is *right* if it can coexist with everyone's freedom in accordance with a universal law, or if on its maxim the freedom of choice of each can coexist with everyone's freedom in accordance with a universal law" [RLV: 231; cf. also *Critique of Pure Reason* (hereafter CPR), A316/B373]. Right provides, then, the kind of minimal conditions under which "inner freedom" can develop. It is a matter for politics because it *requires* collective or institutional "implementation" in order to be applicable to all people. But there is nothing here that would limit it to some public sphere and would not allow it to reach into the "private" lives of people. And conversely, Kant does not limit the development of the human inner freedom to private relations. The distinction between right and virtue cannot be read as a public/private distinction.

Second, Kant does not *use* that distinction in the *Metaphysics of Morals*. However, he *does* use the distinction elsewhere, in a way that has seemed puzzling to many. In the essay "What Is Enlightenment?" he makes a distinction between "public" and "private" uses of reason. The public [*Öffentlich*] use of reason is "the use which a person makes of it as a scholar before the reading public [*das Publicum*]," while private use is "that which one may make of it in a particular civil post or office entrusted to him" ["Answer to the Question: What Is Enlightenment?" (hereafter WE), VIII: 37]. Private use of reason can be regulated, Kant says, but the public use must be free and unrestricted. He gives three examples: a military officer, who may not criticize his superiors when on duty, but who may do so "as a scholar"; a citizen, who may not refuse to pay his taxes, but is within his rights when, "as a scholar, he publicly expresses his thoughts on the inappropriateness or even the injustice of these levies" (WE, VIII: 37–38); and, finally, the clergyman, who must preach what the church tells him to, but who, again, as a scholar *has a duty* to "communicate to the public all his carefully tested and well-meaning thoughts on that which is erroneous in the symbol and to make suggestions for the better organization of the religious body and church" (WE, VIII: 37–38; emphasis mine).

This is curious in two ways. First, to our liberal sentiments, the call for the freedom of public expression (for that is obviously what "use of reason" amounts to) while allowing for the suppression of private expression seems insufficient. Sure, liberals may grant that, say, military officers can be banned from public criticism of their superiors, but they may still feel that Kant says altogether too little for us to get a serious freedom of expression off the ground. The other curious thing in Kant's account is this conception of the private/public distinction. I will only tackle the second since an answer to it will help dispel some of our misgivings about Kant's liberalism.

The Public Use of Reason

Recall the context. The distinction is made when Kant is answering the question "What Is Enlightenment [*Aufklärung*]?" posed in the *Berlinische Monatsshrift* in December 1783. The question tapped into a widespread, albeit partly secret, debate among the Prussian intelligentsia on the enlightenment of people.[35] The intelligentsia, many of whom were very close to the administration of Frederick the Great, were concerned that despite Frederick's liberal reforms and attempts at the enlightenment of citizens, superstition, prejudice, and intolerance still reigned among people. It would be worth investigating, J. K. W. Möhsen, Frederick's personal physician, had proposed in a meeting of the secret *Mittwochgesellschaft*, a group of intellectuals behind the *Berlinische Monatsshrift*, "Why the enlightenment of our public has as yet not advanced very far, notwithstanding that for more than forty years the freedom to think, to speak, and also to publish would seem to have ruled here more than in other lands, and that the education of our youth has also gradually improved."[36] One particularly widespread debate had been on the role of clergy in the enlightenment, on the *kind* of role institutional religion should play, and on the kinds of ways it could be either modified or expanded. James Schmidt argues that it is this debate that leads Kant to expound, in his essay, on the clergy when talking about his public/private distinction.[37]

Private use of reason is private because anyone outside the relevant institution might not share the relevant premises and, in particular, might not share premises on what counts as the authority to settle disagreements.[38] I might have to obey the state because it exhibits the Universal Principle of Right, but "it cannot be required that this principle of all maxims be itself in turn my maxim, that is, it cannot be required that *I make it the maxim* of my action" (RL, V: 231, Kant's emphasis). So when a tax collector tells me to pay my taxes, I will obey, but if she tells me about her plans for how to reorganize the Internal Revenue Service, I need neither obey nor, more importantly, be convinced by her argument. I might happen to think that taxes are unjust, so we disagree on an fundamental premise. For me to agree on her premise might require me to grant some authority to the idea of state collection of revenues, or at least to the state in general. Public use of reason, on the other hand, is public exactly in the sense that it presumes, for Kant, no other authority than reason itself. It is a forum for debating the merits of the maxims to adopt. It can directly help public policy (see, e.g., PP, VIII: 368; and CF, Part II), but this is just one variant of the main function, namely, to help free humans "from the leading-strings of instinct to the guidance of reason" (CBH, VIII: 115). In this sense, then, Kant's public/private distinction is exactly what liberals routinely understand by it, although with a twist: The public is not "neutral" on the good—it just does not smuggle any preconceived notion of the good into the debate, which is what happens when communication is "private."

Kant's discussion of the clergy confirms this. There cannot be a "public" religion, some ecumenical federation of (Christian) denominations and churches, engaged in enlightenment; that would merely be a widespread use of private reason. And "an age cannot bind itself and ordain to put the succeeding one into such a condition that it cannot extend its (at best very occasional) knowledge, purify itself of errors, and progress in general enlightenment" (WE, VIII: 39). As *scholars*, taking advantage of the public use of reason, such clergymen could be allowed to *argue for* such a proposal, but "to unite in a permanent religious institution which is not to be subject to doubt before the public even in the lifetime of one man, and thereby to make a period of time fruitless in the progress of mankind toward improvement, thus working to the disadvantage of posterity— that is absolutely forbidden" (WE, VIII: 39). The public use of reason may not itself ever become private since that would be the violation of the Universal Principle of Right in that it would require the adoption of a maxim from the people engaging in the communication. Thus the arena on which humankind's progress toward its improvement is fundamentally made can only counsel and not command and is liable to make mistakes as often as it progresses. In the meanwhile, as Kant puts it, "the human race groans under the evils which it inflicts on itself as a result of its own inexperience" (CBH, VIII: 118n).

The ban on public religion is true even for a single sovereign. In the *Anthropology*, Kant warns of the dangers of state use of religion for political purposes. While religion is necessary, according to Kant, for the development of inner discipline of humans (i.e., conscience), this cannot be politically imposed, for when politically motivated use of religion takes precedence over morality (which is based on reason), this "statutory religion becomes an instrument of the executive of a religious despotism," a malady that will lead to a rule by deception (A, VII: 333n; see also WE, VIII: 40). This would be problematic even if the sovereign were correct in its particular use of religion. The point is not that the state is often wrong (this passage from the *Anthropology* is, after all, about Kant's alleged hero Frederick), but that a state which did that would be violating the proper role of the state, as justified by the dictates of reason. As Alexander Altmann points out, Kant saw a clear analogy between this and his rejection of hypothetical imperatives in moral judgments: Principles based on private, nonuniversalizable notions of self-interest lead to moral evil, and so do private notions of the good, say, of the right religion for all, even when they are held by the sovereign.[39] So, for Kant, philosopher kings would be pernicious: "It is not to be expected that kings will philosophise or that philosophers will become kings; nor is it to be desired, however, since the possession of power inevitably corrupts the free judgment of reason" (PP, VIII: 369). In light of earlier statements, I want to read the end of the preceding sentence not as a causal corruption, but as a conceptual kind: Those in power, qua the executive, *cannot* exercise a free judgment of reason.

What we have here, then, is what we could think of as a *dual* conception of the political. *Society* has a political project, namely, the enlightenment of people and their liberation from their "tutelage" and "immaturity" (WE, VIII: 35–36; CBH, VIII: 118n). This project proceeds—ever so slowly—through the use of public reason. However, the conditions for this will not exist without sufficient conditions of safety, for which a state apparatus must exist to enforce the Universal Principle of Right. This is the *state's* political project. It cannot subsume the former, partly for the conceptual reasons to which I have pointed, but also partly because it would pragmatically undermine its ability to perform its function, as Kant points out in *The Conflict of the Faculties*: The state can't engage in philosophical waffling when people come seeking help (see CF, VII: Preface and Part II). In that aspect of the political, Kant's account is reasonably close to the constitutional liberalism of Montesquieu, minor differences notwithstanding. The social dimension of the political and its relationship to the state-centered solution is the liberal complement I set out to seek at the end of the last chapter.

It is important to appreciate the realm in which public reason is exercised as a *political* realm. This puts me in disagreement with Charles Taylor, whose analysis of the same piece of the eighteenth-century social milieu is otherwise very similar to mine. The important difference is that Taylor invokes the familiar Hegelian concept of civil society to talk about the realm of public reason and explicitly treats it as "extrapolitical."[40] The problem is that in evoking the idea of civil society, we, as it were, skip Kant and harken back to the natural law theorists whose idea of the relationship between positive authority and citizens the concept emulates. So, calling the public sphere [*Öffentlichkeit*] "civil society" misses what a novel conception Kant is expressing. And, furthermore, thinking of the public sphere as extrapolitical risks obscuring the tight conceptual and complicated causal connections involved. Of course, in a *historical* analysis the public sphere or civil society may or may not be seen as contingent from the perspective of Frederick's early state building. However, in Kant's forward-looking normative account of his republicanism, the state is *legitimated* only with reference to the existence of the public sphere, which, in turn, is made possible both causally *and* conceptually by the state. Since the conceptual relations hold both ways, the realm of public reason and the state are interdependent, and it makes little sense to think of the former as somehow outside politics.[41]

Resistance and Revolution

Kant does, however, have his own conception of the limits of politics and political action. Notoriously, resistance and revolution are outside these limits. In this section, I want to make sense of this, in two different ways. First, I show how there may actually be an implicit doctrine of resistance in Kant. Second, I suggest why such a doctrine is not explicit. Generalizing from the account, we get a principled but still pragmatic commitment to political reformism as preferable over revolutionary change.

There are many ways in which Kant seems to be no radical: In promoting the unbridled openness of the public use of reason, he puts it ahead of many other liberties. In fact, it is for him the *only* necessary freedom, as is clear from a dictum he approvingly attributes to Frederick himself: "Argue as much as you will, and about what you will, but obey!" (WE, VIII: 37). There are some questions about the sincerity of Kant's use of this exhortation, but obedience to the existing order is nevertheless important for him, whether that existing order is legitimate or not (RL, V: 372). His rejection of the right of rebellion in numerous places also seems to indicate an almost Hobbesian position (see PP, passim; TP, VIII: 298–299; RL, V: 320ff). But against this, we have his enthusiasm about the French Revolution:

> The [French] revolution of a gifted people which we have seen unfolding in our day may succeed or miscarry; it may be filled with misery and atrocities to the point that a sensible man, were he boldly to hope to execute it successfully the second time, would never resolve to make the experiment at such cost—this revolution, I say, nonetheless finds in the hearts of all spectators (who are not engaged in the game themselves)—a wishful participation that borders closely on enthusiasm, the very expression of which is fraught with danger; this sympathy, therefore, can have no other cause than a moral predisposition in the human race. (CF, VII: 85)[42]

He was also a strong supporter of the Americans in their Revolutionary War against the British.[43] To his contemporaries, Kant's positions seemed potentially revolutionary: His friend Johann Erich Biester had been troubled by rumors about Kant's revolutionary tendencies until reading his explicit rejection of rebellions in "Theory and Practice," after which "a stone fell off his heart."[44] Kant "and Kantianism" were also blamed for social and political unrest in the wake of the French Revolution.[45]

Theoretically, too, Kant's position seems at first equivocal. In his seemingly unequivocal exhortation to obey a de facto authority, he adds parenthetically, "in whatever does not conflict with inner morality" (RL, V: 371). He also has an earlier remark (from sometime around 1779–1783) in which, after seemingly denying the right to commit acts of violence against the sovereign, he adds, "except in those cases that could not at all belong belong to a civil order (*in unionem civilem*), e.g., religious compulsion" (R 8051, XIX: 594–595). Werner Haensel sees the former as an instance of the tension that seems to exist between, on the one hand, Kant's notion of moral autonomy, and his notion of the justification for the state, on the other hand.[46] The latter adds to the tension a limit to state authority contemporary liberals take for granted but which is much trickier for Kant, given his emphasis on obedience.

At issue is not just some practically difficult but theoretically simple issue where we have a justified moral stance against a mere de facto authority—for that would automatically license some kind of *right* of resistance. Rather, the problem is that, for Kant, even a de facto authority can be theoretically justified through a hypothetical contract as long as the authority establishes and enforces certain kinds of political institutions that guarantee reasonable social stability (TP, VIII: 299). In the *Rechtslehre*, Kant's talk is primarily of property rights, but there is a reasonable way of reading this as establishing, in general, conditions without which many different forms of social action would not be possible (see also UH, VIII: 23). This means that the tension is theoretical: We have, on the one hand, an account of autonomy that seems to license at least passive resistance in cases where one is told to do something that cannot be morally justified. On the other hand, we have an account of the state that seems to be an empirical precondition for the exercise of one's autonomy at least in some important aspects.

It is important to appreciate the difficulty of this tension. Kant is not, despite surface appearances, making a Hobbesian argument for a de facto authority. That *any* state is preferable to the dissolution of the state (which a revolution would amount to) does not entail that a state cannot be unjust. Quite the contrary, Kant found Hobbes's claim to that effect "horrifying" (TP, VIII: 303–304). He seems tempted, for exactly these sorts of reasons, to endorse the idea of resistance in some cases.

The implicit doctrine, I think, goes as follows:[47] Given his historicism, Kant is aware of the possibility of a radical discrepancy between the universal principles of morality and the degree to or manner in which the state embodies them. This does not always make the state unjust, although it may do that. In general, the state simply is imperfect. Now as we saw earlier, what tells us that the state is imperfect is exactly that discrepancy between the universal moral principles and the principles the state embodies. The state may nevertheless be legitimate, and it is possible that conditions warranting even the consideration of resistance do not arise. But they may; those conditions are, as Kant observed earlier, when the state exceeds its limits *and* demands something that conflicts with a person's "inner morality."

I emphasize the conjunction, but only to call attention to the fact that we are not actually dealing with a contingent conjunction, but with an entailment relation: *Whatever* demand contradicts my inner morality is, by definition, outside the legitimate scope of the state. This follows from what a Kantian moral agent may, even hypothetically, consent to: She may not consent to citizenship in which she forfeits the possibility to exercise her moral agency. Hence Haensel's talk of the possibility of elevating the right to disobey to a Kantian "holy right of humanity."[48] Thus there seems to be a real possibility of a citizen being confronted with demands that she simply *may not* obey.

If the matter were this easy, we should really wonder why Kant did not spell it out. But note that there is an analogy to the impossibility of the individual agent forfeiting her agency at the political level: A state cannot write its own dissolution into its laws. And since the idea of a *right* has to do with outer freedom, that is, with political business, there simply cannot be a right to disobey, let alone to resist in other ways. Making a distinction between *political* and *moral* rights is not available here, tempting as it might seem: In Kant's doctrine, there are no moral rights.[49]

So there is a quandary. But fortunately this resembles a quandary we have seen before, and which Kant solves. Recall Kant's analysis of the dueling soldier and the murderous mother of an illegitimate child. In the kinds of cases at hand, too, people confronted with immoral demands "find themselves in the state of nature," and have, then, just their own reason to rely on as a source of legitimate norms. So qua citizen one may not resist, but qua a denizen of the state of nature one has a duty to do so. And it is worth noting that it is *the state* that puts the agents into the state of nature, not the agents' actions.

In the foregoing, I have been flagging points of difference between Kant and Hobbes, but here we actually arrive at a remarkable similarity. This implied doctrine of resistance resembles Hobbes's account of political subjects' relation to disobedience and resistance. To be sure, there are differences, and Hobbes's view is, in some ways, more straightforward; it certainly is put much more explicitly than Kant's. In a Hobbesian state, a subject has no right of resistance, and the sovereign is always within her rights to put a disobedient subject to death.[50] However—and here is the similarity of the two conceptions—the subject may nevertheless defend herself when the sovereign's minions come to kill her. This is because the right to self-defense is an inalienable law of nature, one that the subjects retain even in a commonwealth.[51] The sovereign has merely been given a wider use of *her* right of self-defense in the interests of other subjects. But when the sovereign intends to kill a subject, the subject's interests are no longer served, and she finds herself, for all intents and purposes, in the state of nature.[52]

Despite this implied possibility of resistance, Kant never makes it explicit. The fact that his rejection of the right of resistance is, apart from these few cryptic instances, unequivocal, ends up suggesting that he is willing to bite the bullet and even sacrifice the idea of autonomy to political stability. But, as Haensel points out, he simply *refrains* from developing a right of resistance, even though there is all this conceptual wiggling room in his doctrine. This seeming failure to carry through what was theoretically quite plausible raises the obvious question of why Kant chose to do this.

All kinds of explanations have been offered. Some have the more Straussian bent of seeing Kant as fearing state censorship and other forms of persecution.[53] These aren't at all implausible—Kant had, after all, gotten in trouble with Frederick William's court and had even been threatened with "unpleasant measures" (CF, VII: 6).[54] However, I briefly want to propose another explanation, one that is not necessarily in any conflict with the Straussian ones but that may be a little more illuminating for my purposes.

In the natural law tradition Kant is addressing, the right of resistance, when it had been affirmed, had been grounded on people's conception of the good and, in particular, on the principle of happiness (*Glückseligkeitsprinzip*). This was particularly true of Kant's most immediate predecessors in the tradition, Gottfried Achenwall and Christian Wolff, as well as of Kant's contemporary, the important *Aufklärung* figure Moses Mendelssohn.[55] As we know, Kantian ethics is a project that rejects the *Glückseligkeitsprinzip* as being able to ground intersubjectively justifiable morality, and my earlier discussion should bear out that the same is true for Kantian politics. Note, now, that much of what the debate in the late eighteenth century was about was *how* humanity was supposed to progress, or what form enlightenment was to take. Liberalism was not at all the only alternative, as Rousseau had shown in theory and the French Revolution would show in practice. In Germany, *Aufklärung* comprised all kinds of social and political programs from liberalism to nationalist patriotism to secret revolutionary organizations.[56] Most had in common their resistance to various kinds of oppression associated with religious and political absolutism. However, they differed greatly in their constructive programs, and in debates between, say, cosmopolitan liberals and nationalists, there was as much hostility as between Enlightenment and the counter-Enlightenment *Sturm und Drang*. If we put Kant's rejection of the right of resistance in this larger context, we can think of Kant promoting liberal pluralism against subjective principles: It is a mistake, we can take him to be saying, to think that if you oppose oppression, your position is necessarily correct. Thus, writing six years before the French Revolution, Kant suggested that "a revolution may well put an end to autocratic despotism and to rapacious or power-seeking oppression, but it will never produce a true reform in ways of thinking. Instead, new prejudices, like the ones they replaced, will serve as a leash to control the great unthinking mass" (WE, VIII: 36).

Of course, this explanation does not tell the whole story in that it begs the question as to why Kant did not justify a right of resistance in some other way, or at least justify a passive right to disobey authority. Altmann suggests that this is because Kant ultimately saw no need for it. That is, given the context in which Mendelssohn and his ilk were putting forth arguments for revolution, Kant thought they would only be counterproductive—and that he could not foresee history taking a turn to the worse and leading to the totalitarian systems we saw in the twentieth century.[57] He did explicitly reject English anti-revolutionaries' worries about history having taken a turn for the worse with the French Revolution as late as the 1790s: Only an enemy of humanity would claim that the new order in France was not progress (R 8077, XIX: 605)! But let's not be too apologetic and lay all our explanatory chips on what we now know was naïve optimism. There is something to be said for the tension that Kant fails to resolve, even though we may, in the end, want to retain some sort of right of resistance (since we now know that humanity's progress has been less than smooth since the eighteenth century).

Kant's view on obedience points to the theoretically important notion that even in liberalism, a social order that allows us to pursue our own conceptions of the good, that very pursuit may depend on some relatively strong commitment to a political authority. In a state of nature, not only is one constantly afraid because the institutions of security are missing [there can be no punishment in the state of nature, Kant says (R 7677, XIX: 486)], but there are even modes of life that simply do not exist. So it would be wrong to think of the legitimacy of obedience as negative, as a necessary evil. Liberalism is more appealing than merely the Hobbesian version of contract theory, and for a good reason: Our pale and Königsbergian liberalism gives, for the price of obedience, an entirely new mode of social life, namely, the realm of public reason. And unlike in the Rousseauian contract theory where the exercise of the general will is tantamount to *giving up* who you are, addressing others "as a scholar" is an expansion of who you are and can become but, most importantly, is still you. And it isn't incompatible with your other social roles.

"We Discussed Freedom and the Hats We Were Wearing"

We have seen the clincher for the Rousseau–Kant juxtaposition in the small but significant difference in the workings of *amour-propre* for the two theorists. Rousseau is right, Kant admits, about humanity being badly off. He is also right in that humanity ought to be going somewhere, somewhere where it, in some way, transcends its animality. In contrast to Rousseau and like many other liberals, Kant does not know *where* that somewhere is, and to pretend to know would be nothing but the articulation of a subjective *Glückzeligkeitsprinzip*. Unlike Rousseau, Kant does not think that we *really* can transcend our humanity. We will forever remain that ambiguous cross between angels and cattle. But there can and will be progress since the impossibility of one kind of perfection does not foreclose the possibility of other kinds, namely, the *procedural* perfection of perpetual, cosmopolitan peace.

The motor for this gradual transcendence is in us, and has been all along. All of us have the means of keeping *amour-propre* in check or, as the case may be, the means of healing inflamed *amour-propre*. The appropriate political structures are, then, ones that, first, prevent the inflamed *amour-propre* in those who suffer from it from having *social* effects and, second, promote the "self-healing" of inflamed *amour-propre*, both collectively and individually, by allowing people to seek ways for their improvement. This is a reformist project by definition: A revolution would amount to a forced introduction of some particular conception of where humanity should go. Yet, on thinking about the French Revolution, Kant still cannot help himself: Sometimes forcing a conception of the good on others may be better than putting up with another, *obviously* corrupt and oppressive conception. Again, this is not a case of senile Kant forgetting his own principles, but a historically intelligible instantiation of the principle that "one can be forced to leave the state of nature" (R 7648, XIX: 477), which, in turn, *is* consistent with the Universal Principle of Right.[58]

But while the French Revolution may have had morally praiseworthy features about it, Kant himself is *showing* us what kind of *political* action he prefers (since, by his definition, resistance and revolution are extrapolitical). His own writings on politics are not just writings *on* politics, whether political philosophy or public policy, but Kant showing us what he understands by political action: that very thing he is doing, writing and arguing and addressing the public—in short, making controversial claims about legitimate authority.[59] That the writings seem light does not mean that they are not serious; Kant was well aware of the different uses of language for different purposes: "This wise man [Christian Garve] rightly requires that every philosophic teaching be capable of being made *popular* (that is, of being made sufficiently clear to the senses to be communicated to everyone) if the teacher is not to be suspected of being muddled in his own concepts" (RL, V:

206). Kant was also trying to communicate, although not to "everyone" but to the "reading public" (WE, VIII: 3). This reading public was growing rapidly toward the turn of the century,[60] but it wasn't numbers that made it special; it was the sphere of human activity in which cosmopolitan citizenship would be realized. Because of this, it was important to play by the rules of the public use of reason: Kant took seriously those who challenged his doctrines "as scholars"—the respectful disagreements with Garve and Herder are examples of this—but refused challenges that he saw as subterfuge for personal political motives, as heteronomy smuggled into the democratic realm of autonomy.[61]

*   *   *

We now have two liberal accounts of politics that help us answer at least some of Schmitt's charges presented in Part I. Montesquieu and Kant have not taken on flights of metaphysical fancy, but gear their accounts as solutions to what they see as political realities. The accounts are normative, to be sure, Kant's robustly so, but that does nothing to condemn them. Furthermore, Montesquieu allows for the possibility that Kant spells out: A liberal citizen can have a robust sense of herself as a political agent—in addition to being many other things—without any conceptual contradictions or crippling schizophrenia. Rather, if anyone is in trouble, it is Rousseau, who would like to but cannot fathom how we, the victims of inflamed *amour-propre*, turn ourselves into the likes of that selfless Spartan mother. Liberal citizens needn't try to be anything that they really aren't, although, at the same time, liberal political institutions offer them a way to become something else. As I try to show in the following chapters, this feature of liberalism isn't just some nice theoretical possibility, but a powerful and politically quite useful idea.

Some of the anti-liberal charges remain unanswered. Most importantly, the accounts so far don't show whether the liberal principle of public reason really has any teeth beyond the nice picture of a reading public debating the merits of arguments. Remember that Kant's account is strongly normative. To be sure, there is historical evidence to show that his ideas of the egalitarian republic of scholars isn't crazy. Johann Christoph Gottsched's early Enlightenment "German society," for example, could be a textbook case for the Kantian model. In Gottsched's society, "the individual regarded himself as an equal among equals among whom force of argument alone was decisive, not the views of traditional authoritarianism."[62]

But even Gottsched's man of letters was quite happy to support absolutism "as citizen duty-bound to consider the reputation of his country."[63] And he was a man, at least in most cases, as many have pointed out.[64] Also, internal egalitarianism and commitment to reasoned argument were far from being the norm. Consider the way a nationalist poets' society, the Göttingen Hainbund, celebrated their idol Friedrich Gottfried Klopstock's birthday in 1773. Christoph Martin Wieland was a liberal cosmopolitan poet and thus the Göttingen Hainbund's rival:

We celebrated [Klopstock's] birthday in fine style. . . . A long table was laid and decorated with flowers. There was a comfortable chair at the head of the table, for Klopstock, adorned with roses and stocks, upon which lay Klopstock's complete works. Beneath the chair, Wieland's Idris lay in shreds. Then Cramer read some passages from the Song of Triumph, and Hahn some of Klopstock's odes to Germany. Then we drank coffee; the spills were made out of the works of Wieland. Boie, who didn't smoke, also had to light up and tread Idris into the dirt. Then we toasted Klopstock's health, the memory of Luther and Hermann, the health of the league, of Ebert, of Goethe, of Herder, etc. with Rhenish wine. Klopstock's ode to Rhenish wine was read, and a few others besides. Now the discussion grew livelier. We discussed freedom, the hats we were wearing, Germany, virtuous song and you can imagine what else. Then we ate and drank punch before finally setting effigies of Wieland and his Idris alight.[65]

Undeniably political, but with little resemblance to the Kantian ideals. Since these tendencies are still just as much, if not more, with us as the Kantian ideals, we need an account that can evaluate them.

While the institutional features of Kant's and Montesquieu's accounts are compatible with one another, I have only suggested that the same is true of the Kantian reason-based account of agency and Montesquieu's less sanguine conception. In what follows, I steer further away from exegesis and answer the remaining accusations against liberalism by turning to our contemporary world. The rest of the book shows how the doctrine plays itself out in the real world of politics. I occasionally return to exegesis—Kant gets a final word against Klopstock's passionate friends in Chapter 7—but the present tense is deliberate: The liberal conception of political agency I am defending here is not merely an ideal, but something already at work on the ground.

Part III

No Secret Agents

The differences in Montesquieu's and Kant's accounts point to real but interesting tensions that a *general* liberal account of political action ought to address. Of course, the two share much, too. Both reject, for similar reasons, the legitimacy of revolutions. This is only to be expected—although it isn't trivial that liberals have *principled* grounds for the rejection: Reformism isn't just weak-minded liberals' unexamined kneejerk. The tensions are nevertheless more interesting.

Consider: Montesquieu's account accommodates the fact of pluralism into political participation quite well with the *institutional* checks to the "passions" that motivate people. However, it does so at the expense of political agents' *autonomy*. They themselves needn't be trusted to check on their own passions. On the other hand, Kant's account does just that. It makes agents' autonomous consideration of reasons both the most valuable exercise of agency and the central mode of political engagement. But, like so much of Kant's philosophy, the apparatus still looks a bit impractical, despite the fact that it is more pragmatic than the textbook account has it. Although there are concrete places where "public reason" is exercised—coffee shops and reading societies, intellectual newspapers and learned journals—they are at best one of the spheres of political activity. Also, as anyone who has ever attended a faculty meeting or an academic conference knows, even in scholarly settings the supremacy of reason is iffy.[1] Scholars, readers, and intellectuals aren't really any different from other people (at least in these respects), and the cynicism about intellectual life Montesquieu made abundantly clear in the *Persian Letters* is consistent with many people's experiences. In the *Académie Française,* for example, the members "have no work to do except to chat endlessly: eulogy appears of its own accord, so it seems, in their eternal gossip, and as soon as they are initiated into its mysteries they are seized by a mania for panegyrics, which never leaves them."[2]

The general question is whether the Kantian model is a *practicable* solution to the autonomy deficit in Montesquieu's account. The question can be disaggregated as follows: How, if at all, does *actual* public reason, that is, political argument on the ground, relate to considerations of a society's political goals and ideals? Second, how does it inform actual political practices such as questions of strategy and alliance formation? Further, how, if at all, can it account for political engagement that doesn't prima facie make reason supreme? How, in other words, do emotions square with reasons? And if it does, how does it still amount to a meaningful standard by which to judge some political actions legitimate and some illegitimate? I take up these questions in each of the following chapters, respectively.

Public Reason, Political Argument, and Justification

First, however, I want to revisit briefly the relationship between this book and Habermas's theory of communicative action and his model of discourse ethics. I also want to sharpen my formulation of public reason so that it can do the work it will be asked to do in the following chapters.

As I briefly mentioned in the previous chapter, Habermas's thought has been on a tangent away from Kant. Simultaneously, it has forged a steady course from a contextual historical analysis toward greater "transcendental" robustness and universality. Whether that is a strength or a weakness with the theory is an open question on which reasonable scholars disagree; it nevertheless marks a crucial difference between the Kantian project this book pursues and Habermas's theory.

In his now classic *Habilitationschrift, The Structural Transformation of the Public Sphere,* Habermas offered both a theoretical analysis of the very Kantian concept of "publicity" and a historical account of its emergence in the empirical reality of eighteenth-century Europe. The interweaving of these two approaches laid the ground for a sophisticated *normative* critique of modern society and its institutions and ideologies. The critique, in fact, was undertaken in many ways: 1960s student radicals adopted the *Strukturwandel* as one of their key texts, much like they did with Herbert Marcuse's *One-Dimensional Man* (and others with *Quotations from Chairman Mao*). Habermas himself, in turn, began sharpening the theoretical foundations of the work. Where the *Strukturwandel* is at its normative best in applying the approximation of the Kantian sphere of public reason to *actual* social practices (consider, for example, the norms about shedding social hierarchies in coffee shops and reading societies or the supremacy of reasoned argument), the later works search for deep structural features in these and other communicative practices as new foundations for emancipatory politics.

Recall the solution: The very logic of communication presupposes a desire on the part of the communicator for an *understanding* among participants. This, in turn, presupposes a certain kind of equality: Whatever I think about you, whatever I want to achieve through the understanding I'm after, I must treat you as being capable of understanding me. In other words, communication pre-supposes a grant of agency by the communicator to the receiver, and that is a kind of equality. This presupposition, in Habermas's view, is quite robust since it is a conceptual one: It is a consequence of the metaphysics of communication. Habermas, of course, rejects the claim that it is a metaphysical account—he explicitly characterizes his theory as "postmetaphysical"—but if we understand metaphysics in the Quinean sense as the study of the ontological commitments of our various discursive practices, and not as nonempirical studies on what there is, the account is metaphysical: Habermas speaks of the "weak transcendental necessity" his arguments establish.[3]

But Habermas's account isn't metaphysical in the logical positivist's pejorative sense of nonsense. Nor is Habermas's project in any sense bad apriorism, another philosophical sin. The full articulation of the theory is very long in part because Habermas wants to ground it in the best relevant empirical theory about social action, communication, linguistics, and so on. He wants to keep it closely hooked to empirical reality. The account of how language works draws from Chomsky and other linguists, and the normative commitments of communication are developed out of J. L. Austin's speech act theory. And one of his central points is to understand the interplay of the *facticity* of binding institutions—say, laws as things that have coercive backing—and the *normativity* of those institutions—that we sincerely believe we *should* obey laws. (This is why the translated title of *Faktizität und Geltung*—"Between Facts and Norms"—is misleading: The account is not of something between those two, but of their curious hybridity.) All this is perfectly pragmatist and, as I pointed out in Chapter 2, convincingly sidesteps worries about the naturalist fallacy. As a theory of how legitimate constitutions can emerge, Habermas's recent work is compelling. But the problem is, as I have claimed throughout, that the thinness of the normative commitments presupposed by communicative practices isn't sufficient to get thick substantive norms off the ground. There remains, therefore, a sizable gap between the contextual account of how *a* legal practice might emerge and how the particular ones Habermas wants to advocate could be defended. In a way not intended, the title of the translation does get something right: The theory still falls between facts and norms.

Habermas doesn't, of course, imply that the fundamentally egalitarian structure of communication is particularly much in evidence in human and social interaction. And he has a theory about why it isn't: One of the central political problems of the nineteenth and twentieth centuries is that communication has been contaminated by *strategic* action, that is, by instrumental considerations aimed at some goals other than understanding. But the payoff of the theory of communicative action is that it offers a promise: It both grounds a critique of what is wrong with inegalitarian, domination-infested social relations (they violate the very logic of communication, that is, they commit contradictions) and it points to an emancipatory solution (the creation of "domination-free discourses").

The theory *is* powerful and exciting, and the formidable cottage industry it has spawned is a healthy sign of that. Not surprisingly, Habermas has been a great inspiration to scholars of democratic theory, especially to those working on deliberative democracy. Habermas himself is also attentive to the concrete policy implications of his theory. In addition to the "purely" theoretical works, he has always written about how the theory would inform concrete politics, from, say, the 1960s and 1970s student movements to environmental politics to the future direction of the European Union. So the theory of communicative action *is* normatively robust: It spells out, for example, why constitutional federalism is a better direction for the European Union than, say, the primacy of economic liberalization and integration.[4] But the gap remains, and the concrete arguments, as *persuasive* arguments, stand or fall on reasons independent of the pragmatic presuppositions of communication.

In contrast to Habermas's approach, this book won't come anywhere near policy recommendations as clear as Habermas's. The following chapters demonstrate that a reconciliation of Montesquieu's and Kant's conceptions of political agency generate a practicable but still normative understanding of what legitimate political action will look like. However, such an understanding is still far too broad to entail any direct policy recommendations. Liberalism is, as I suggested in Chapter 1, a cluster of political values, and it is a feature (not a bug) of my theory that it allows for internal disagreements among liberal actors.

The second relevant contrast is a worry about the wisdom of the search for a "domination-free discourse" that would approximate the egalitarian "ideal speech situations." The idea of institutionalizing such egalitarian dynamics through deliberative democracy, while attractive, misses crucial aspects of politics. Here, I add nothing to the concerns raised by various sympathetic critics of deliberative democracy: The point is simply that ideals of deliberation can be untenable, no more promising than the institutional practices already in place, and even practically pernicious (because they may systematically and problematically rule out some modes of engagement).[5] To simplify a little (but just a little): When the real problem of democracy is the systematic de facto disenfranchisement of some people, searching for the institutionalized equivalent of reasoned debate among equals wipes some of the central political quarrels under the carpet. In short, the issues discussed in theories of deliberative democracy don't cover the range of political action, even if we limit ourselves loosely to liberal-democratic circumstances.

At the same time, as a nod toward the Habermasian approach, one way of putting the aim of this final part of the book is to say it tries to chart some of the territory between justificatory, "ideal" political theory and some conventional empirical approaches to political action. Much of political philosophy is concerned with *justification*, that is, with the justification of the virtues of some political arrangement or another, while the conventional empiricist wants to *explain* political behavior. (Some empiricists are also or even only interested in prediction, but this book isn't trying to make a contribution in that department.) There is some room between these, and what I want to do here first is ask what the relationship between political action and political argument is.

To illustrate the project with an analogy, consider the distinction in philosophy of science between the *context of discovery* and the *context of justification*: namely, the factors that *lead* a scientist to think of a new theory may well be different from how one shows that the theory is *true*. Similarly, the considerations that *engage* a person in political action might be entirely different from why she thinks her action is *justified*. So if the empiricist studies the former, that is, the causal components of action—motives, interests—or what *explains* action, he doesn't say much about the *justificatory* reasons for action, which, I want to claim, are the stuff of which political arguments are made. This isn't the whole story, however. In these enlightened post-Kuhnian times we know that the distinction between the two contexts may itself be a little facile. We should wonder whether there really is a difference—or, if there is, what it is. You don't need to be a Kantian to agree that what engages a person in action is likely to be connected *in some way* with whether the person thinks her action is justified. There is no neat separation of the two contexts. At the same time, the distinction does help us see why attention only to individual motives and other psychological attributes might make us miss something about political action.

Legitimate liberal political action requires a justification. This does not mean that we always will see political action justified or even defended explicitly; it is simply a requirement that follows from the general concept of legitimacy, which, in turn, is what politics is about, as we saw in Chapter 2, as well as from how the *liberal* theory I am advocating conceives of legitimacy. This we saw in Part II. To understand how justification works, the next chapter focuses on cases in which it is made explicit, turned into public reason, that is. (In Chapter 7, I muddy the waters and consider whether and how arguments work outside textbook public justification contexts.)

Now, *what is* a political justification? I want to start with a cue from Rawls:

> [J]ustification is not regarded simply as valid argument from listed premises, even should these premises be true. Rather, justification is addressed to others who disagree with us, and therefore it must always proceed from some consensus, that is, from premises that we and others publicly recognize as true; or better, publicly recognize as acceptable to us for the purpose of establishing a working agreement on the fundamental questions of political justice.[6]

Some things are worth highlighting here. First, political justification always takes place *in a social context*; it is, as Rawls puts it, "addressed to others." To justify the claim that arithmetic is incomplete, it was sufficient for Kurt Gödel to show that the claim is *true*, but for us to say, for example, that "President Bush justified drilling oil in the Arctic wildlife refuge," requires that someone accepted his purported justification.

But, strictly speaking, we can't say even that. If justification is addressed to someone, it means that nothing is ever flat-out, completely justified, period; anything that is justified is justified *to* someone—and maybe not to anyone else. So it is possible that Bush may have justified the drilling to Congress, but not to Alaskans (or vice versa).

Rawls's general account of justification uses the so-called method of reflective equilibrium, originally developed for epistemology by Nelson Goodman in the 1950s. Crudely, reflective equilibrium is a state where our intuitions are in balance with more general principles. We get to reflective equilibrium by starting with our intuitions, from which we try to generate the general principles; if the principles are acceptable, we adjust our intuitions to match them; if not, we look for other principles, and so on.[7] My account draws from the same pragmatist sources, although there are differences relevant for the arguments at hand. For example, Rawls's passage is about the justification of principles of justice; I am interested in the justification of action. First, justifying action can actually take two forms: justifying the *end* that my action is to bring about or showing my action to be a good *means* toward the end. I may pursue revolutionary politics to bring about a socialist revolution, and it is a fair bet that I will be called on both to defend socialism *and* to show that my strategy will really help usher in socialism. (It is very likely that *different people* demand these different justifications.) I call the latter type of justification instrumental; my focus here is on the former.

To clutter the terminological universe still more, we might distinguish one more type of justification. You might disagree with me on socialism, but you might find the justification of my revolutionary actions sufficient to show they are legitimate *as* political acts. Or, to take a more pedestrian example, your voting for a candidate I reject doesn't make your act politically illegitimate. (The boundary isn't as sharp as this might imply, and I certainly may think it is *morally* illegitimate of you to vote for a repugnant candidate.[8]) Again, I bracket this category of justification out of my discussion here, not because it is not important but because the justification of the ends of political action is complicated enough. The legitimacy question crops up now and again in the rest of the book.

How does one justify the ends of one's action? The answer is simple: One articulates reasons for why some particular social state of affairs is something we should endorse and strive toward or reject and move away from, as the case may be. For pure-bred examples of these sorts of articulations, one can turn to arguments in traditional political philosophy. Much of it is, quite explicitly, concerned with the deduction of the legitimacy of the state, to use Robert Paul Wolff's slightly embarrassing phrase.[9] But much more counts as well, and I don't want the simplicity of my gloss to hide its unorthodoxy: In my view, the abolitionists' appeal to revelation in arguing against slavery was also an argument.

So I want to take "articulation of reasons" rather liberally. First, looking for theoretical sophistication or eloquence is going to make us blind to many perfectly good political arguments and can result in troubling elitism. This is exactly one of the problems with some proposals for deliberative democracy. In fact, Christopher Bertram has recently argued convincingly that this is not politically trivial: Too much theoretical sophistication and complexity may reasonably disqualify an argument in a genuinely democratic community.[10] Second, the articulation of reasons need not spell out complete arguments. As we will see in the following, if we think of justification as involving some kinds of arguments, all that often gets articulated is part of the argument; the rest is, as it were, assumed to be shared.

To forestall an objection from the cynical contingent, I want to keep things simple and assume that the arguments I am studying in the following are generally sincere. Of course, dissimulation, spinning, and outright lying are the stuff of which politics is often made, but assuming arguments to be sincere is useful. Talk may be cheap, at least in opinion surveys, as political scientists claim to have shown, but the very logic of political argument presupposes *some* causal efficacy. (*This* pragmatic presupposition seems trivially true.) My argument may just be a rationalization, but for me to *make* the argument shows that an argument is needed for *someone*. A successful argument, whether sincere or not, that satisfies *others* or moves them to act constitutes the real reason for action *to those* whom it moved. So while explanatory theorists often want to steer away from expressed views because of worries about insincerity, I embrace expressive actions simply because sincerity doesn't always matter. Of course, it does matter in some ways, as I briefly suggested in Chapter 2, but epistemic and methodological worries about it don't make thinking about expressions moot.

What about those successful arguments, then? When can we say that a political argument is justified? I want to suggest briefly two considerations and then return to the question at the end of next chapter by evaluating the NIMBY and environmental justice movements' arguments. First, as we saw, the truth of an argument is not necessarily the central criterion of its getting politically justified. Truth may be a criterion—if there is a common understanding or an explicit norm of it as a justificatory criterion. But both the common understanding and explicit norm are social features. In a way, then, the Hobbesian idea of "*Autoritas, non veritas, facit legem*" is quite right, even if the way he intended might be different.[11] As a general principle, I want to say that an argument is justified when those to whom it is addressed take it to be justified.

This will strike theoretically minded readers as dangerously insufficient. If basic rhetorical assent gets something justified, then what happens to the Kantian commitment that there be something fundamentally deliberative about arguments? Or, more poignantly, what prevents political communication from becoming nothing but rhetoric?

The following chapters spell out the answer in detail, but the central argument is the following. First, on the liberal conception, justification turns on reasons, and in principle every attempt at a justification takes place against at least a hypothetical *demand* for one. That's how the Kantian agent understands herself as a political claim-maker and, in general, that is what *legitimate* political action is like in the Kantian conception. But, of course, this is abstract, and as anyone who has tried to teach perfectly intelligent students the difference between "opinion" and "reason" knows, it doesn't really carve out any practically robust separation between reason-based reflective assent and merely rhetorical assent. Sometimes rhetorical assent only shows someone has been successfully duped, not that something has been justified.

To decide when we are dealing with duping instead of the justification, draw from pragmatic considerations: Communities do, as a matter of empirical fact, have practical standards for making a distinction between pure manipulative rhetoric and a justification based on reasons. Their application can be tricky and there are gray areas, but our discursive conventions suggest that we do use them. We do observe of others that "You can't really mean you agree to that; she's pulling your leg here," and we do often introspect our responses to see whether they are kneejerks to pleasing rhetoric or signs of conviction. We don't do that all the time, and we don't always do it successfully, but we do it. Furthermore, the criteria for these practices vary. For political situations that we know to be particularly tricky, we follow Montesquieu's advice: We build institutional solutions.

Ultimately, I dig in my heels. We are now operating with a liberal conception of political action, that is, with a conception that does have normative content. The normative content means that a *reason-based* model of justification can be required and that a total failure to engage other agents in some understanding of reasons can get one thrown out of the debate, as it were. But my point is that the reason-based conception doesn't, in every context, require that actual agents themselves deliberate and reflect on reasons; institutional solutions help us along the way. Our everyday political activities nevertheless are much more Kantian than people often would like to think, as I will show.

Consider briefly: Under what conditions will people regard some argument as justified? Let's begin with a trivial but illuminating example from G. A. Cohen:

> I might persuade my fellow middle class friend that, because my car is being repaired, and I consequently have to spend hours on the buses these days, I have a right to be grumpy. The same conclusion, on the same basis, sounds feeble when the audience is not my friend but a carless fellow bus passenger who is forced to endure these slow journeys every day.[12]

Among the middle class, the premise on which this argument rests, namely, the privilege of owning a car, is taken for granted and in need of no defense. However, those who do not enjoy the privilege are likely to take that *premise* itself to require a justification. There may well be one, but the point is that the initial argument cannot count as justified when it is offered outside the middle class.

For this reason, I want to suggest that political arguments, in order to be justified, need to be based on premises that are shared and, conversely, cannot trade on private premises. What is shared and what counts as "private" depend, of course, on what the scope of the argument is; it depends on what the relevant normative system in question is. What can be expected to be shared depends on whether the question is about new bylaws for the local scuba diving club or about state policy. I want to stress that the issue is about shared *premises,* not about shared or not shared social goods, privileges, or something else. We can imagine a society, say, an aristocratic one, where a carless person would be persuaded by a privileged person's claim about his right to be grumpy because he has to take the bus. At the same time, since *we* live in a society with general liberal and democratic ideals, arguments that trade on social privileges are likely to be based on unshared premises. (Although that's not necessarily the case. Consider the privileges celebrities have, for example; many think them legitimate.)

These brief remarks merely lay the ground for how my Kantian–Montesquieuian model will fare in practice. The following chapters spell out the details.

five
___

LANDFILLS AND JUSTICE
Political Arguments, Their Justification,
and Liberal Theory

In this chapter, I want to investigate the relationship between ground-level political arguments and the more abstract political theory of the previous chapters. I am interested in seeing how we might understand actual political arguments—public reason in practice—about specific issues as reflecting larger ideas about political values. I show that the Kantian job description of public reason is a meaningful: The dispute in question here is a dispute about the fundamental values and the political direction of a polity.

Let's be concrete. I want to look at what are ostensibly two kinds of environmental movements: so-called NIMBY movements, or people who say "not in my backyard" to perceived environmental risks, and environmental justice movements, which see certain kinds of environmental degradation as instances of broad social injustice, particularly racism. These movements have a lot in common, but they also differ in several respects. One of the differences is in how they defend their political projects. NIMBYs represent narrow self-interest politics—the *Homo economicus* as a regulative ideal—while environmental justice movements appeal to grand political principles such as equality, human rights, and democratic participation. These differences, I argue, can be seen to reflect theoretical disputes about conceptions of liberalism. The particular dispute I have in mind is between the view according to which liberalism ought to see politically salient relations between people as contractual and the view that defends a more communally oriented, "cosmopolitan" liberalism. I have suggested in earlier chapters that the reader forget the tiresome "liberalism-communitarianism controversy"; in this chapter, I argue that what we have here is a debate *within* liberalism. The Kantian model of agency can make sense of the dispute and of why the different ideals are defended.

Two Thumbnails

I want to begin with a very brief sketch of the two of movements as ideal types. The movements are interesting for this comparative purpose because of their many similarities. Both NIMBYs and environmental justice movements are local, or at least begin as local movements. While it is, in some ways, possible to think of the environmental justice *movement,* in singular, because of the importance of horizontal alliances, it is more accurate to realize that, just as in the case of neighborhood NIMBYs, we are talking about movement*s,* plural.

That both types are essentially local is no coincidence, but simply follows from the logic of the movements: They generally emerge as reactions to *localized* threats, known in the policy jargon as "locally unwanted land uses," or LULUs for short. These can be anything from plans to build waste landfills or incinerators or for other industries such as housing or road development. As we will see better later in this chapter, NIMBYs also target LULUs that have nothing to do with the environment: There are anti-multi-unit housing NIMBYs and movements against AIDS hospices, prisons, special schools, and so on. There is, however, significant overlap in the kinds of LULUs both NIMBYs and the environmental justice people fight.

There is also much overlap in the kinds of strategies the movements adopt. The strategies are, in short, very diverse. These are primarily straightforward citizen movements, embracing the range of strategies we have come to associate with them: petitions, call-your-representative campaigns, demonstrations and even nonviolent resistance, lawsuits, lobbying—the works for conventional citizen politics. Mobilization is generally through neighborhoods by some core activists, who often are women. (I will return to the significance of this point in Chapter 7.)

The central demographic difference between NIMBYs and environmental justice movements is that of race and class. NIMBYs are most often, although not solely, white and middle class; the environmental justice movements are primarily people of color and working class or poor. This difference isn't a coincidence, but has everything to do with what is different about the two kinds of movements, that is, what they fundamentally are fighting, why they are fighting it, and what those fights mean.

These *are* ideal types. NIMBY movements in particular encompass a wide range, much of which doesn't fit in the description here. The NIMBY label is itself a matter of controversy. According to many, the label is pejorative because it "implies that local activists are selfish, materialistic, and often naive and uncosmopolitan."[1] Some therefore prefer not to use the term at all.[2] It is true that NIMBY thinking can be seen as one of the purest examples of understanding politics as the pursuit of narrow self-interest; the *Homo economicus* is a standard bearer for NIMBYs. In the slogan "not in my backyard," the "my" is emphasized, and ". . . but someone else's backyard is OK" seems like an obvious implication. We need to remember, however, that political labels are not innocent, and it matters that the label was coined by the NIMBYs' primary opponents.[3] The label and its connotations still do a lot of political work for the opponents of local grassroots movements: Pathologizing NIMBYism as a "syndrome" casts the actors as suffering from something worse than just self-interest and suggests that the NIMBY phenomenon needs a cure, not a political solution.[4]

At the same time, despite controversy, there is some agreement on what the label denotes. Some NIMBYs have themselves adopted the label as appropriate for their movements. Obviously, the spin put on self-interest is different, but the idea is not necessarily contested. In the following, I want to argue that self-interest is the central defining feature of NIMBYism and one that sets it apart from other movements concerned with similar political issues, that is, those localized environmental hazards. The ideal type, then, isn't just a caricature created to conveniently pick out those features that make the argument here true.

That self-interest is a central feature of NIMBYism is not surprising; it simply means taking the NIMBY label seriously. This means that I am not going to take every local opposition movement so labeled to be a NIMBY. Some are indeed environmental justice movements maligned or simply misunderstood by their opposition; they present no particular puzzle for my analysis here. Slightly trickier are local opposition movements that rally around claims about unfair political processes. They look like NIMBYs except that their arguments resemble those of environmental justice movements. At the end of next section, I show why I think they are still NIMBYs.

"Not in My Backyard"

To see the centrality of self-interest, let's begin with relatively uncontroversial features and proceed to more controversial ones. First, NIMBY movements are political movements that emerge *in response* to a LULU siting policy. Most of the time, the locality is a relatively small one: a neighborhood—even a single street— or a small town. But the NIMBY logic can also be found on a larger scale: county-level NIMBYs are not rare, and there are even state, provincial, and national movements that appeal to the members of the political community against some supposed threat or potential threat. However, since small-scale local movements are the paradigm case of NIMBYism, I mainly discuss those in the following.

What constitute these LULUs is one of the first things on which NIMBY sympathizers and critics disagree. The sympathizers like to emphasize siting projects that bring with them serious harm or at least a threat of serious harm to people: for example, toxic waste incinerators and landfills,[5] nuclear waste storage facilities and nuclear power plants,[6] or highly polluting industries.[7] They also don't mind talking about opposition to projects that threaten ecosystems or at least some noninstrumental values such as natural beauty.[8] Opponents are eager to point out that these features don't constitute a relevant difference in NIMBY political practice from opposition based on mere prejudice or selfishness, such as opposition to AIDS hospices, mental institutions and outpatient clinics, homeless shelters, and even mere multifamily housing in traditional homeowner areas. As Michael Dear's attitude surveys show, a group home for AIDS patients ranks as "absolutely unwelcome" along with a garbage landfill.[9]

Langdon Winner, a NIMBY sympathizer, tries to downplay the significance of these less politically appealing NIMBYs: "such mean-spiritedness is the exception," he claims.[10] However, the fact that in community planners' professional publications NIMBY worries are just as often about opposition to multi-unit housing as about toxic waste suggests that the mean-spirited ones are relatively prevalent. Also, if we put NIMBYism in the historical context of "exclusionary land use" conflicts, it is quite obvious that environmental concerns are not the essence of the movements. Contemporary NIMBYs are heirs and heiresses to local movements against a variety of unwelcome neighbors of yesteryear: brothels, taverns, and gambling joints, but also hospitals (especially for contagious diseases), railroad tracks, and even schoolhouses.[11] So we need to keep in mind that for NIMBYs in general, a distinction between genuine threat and prejudice-induced opposition is not relevant. To be sure, we should be careful about condemnation by association. Just as the fact that Operation Rescue uses the same strategies as the 1960s civil rights movements doesn't mean we must lump the two movements together, we needn't assume that all NIMBY reasons are equally commendable. That said, I focus mainly on environmental NIMBYs in the following. This is not to sidestep the role of selfishness and prejudice: They can be present even in environmental NIMBYs. It is also not to suggest that we are dealing with environmentalists: Studies suggest that environmentalism and NIMBY activism are not strongly correlated even in cases of "environmental" NIMBYs, that is, NIMBY movements organized against an environmental LULU.[12]

Those who pathologize NIMBYism think that the conditions NIMBYs suffer from are social myopia and irrationality. These are aspects of the same phenomenon and are related to the vice of selfishness. Importantly, however, focusing on the nonnormative lends an air of objectivity to the critics' charges. Consider the accusations the protagonist in Stephen Wilcox's murder mystery, *The NIMBY Factor*, levels against the opponents of a local toxic landfill:

> "All this concern for the environment would be touching, if it wasn't so damn hypocritical," I said stonily. "Teddy, if you're that hot about reducing the waste stream, why aren't you out picketing your former employer [Kodak] to protest excessive packaging and throaway cameras? And you two—"I glared at the Hermskis"—if you're so worried about polluted groundwater, you should stop dumping chemical fertilizers all over your bean fields." I crossed my arms over my chest. "It's easy to turn this thing into an us-or-them feud: those wasteful city slickers versus us pure-hearted country folk. Well, Teddy, you spent thirty years making a damn good living in that city, keeping your mouth shut every time your company threw up another smokestack or leveled a few more houses to extend another parking lot for your gas-guzzler. And, Lily, I don't recall you and Ed bitching about all the milk and butter and cheese your dairy co-op sells to the eight hundred thousand county residents who don't happen to live in Kirkville, and I don't hear about your co-op arguing for a return to refillable glass milk bottles or biodegradable cardboard egg cartons. Oh, no—that might reduce profits, right?"
>
> I took a moment to catch my breath and straighten my halo, then applied the coup de grace. "So please save your sermonizing about poor Mother Earth and tell it like it is. This whole controversy comes down to one thing: the NIMBY factor—put your landfill wherever you want, so long as it's not in my backyard."[13]

I want to suggest that what remains powerful in this charge is its moral component, that NIMBYs are selfish even when the supposedly factual claims are arguable.

First, NIMBYs are supposed to be myopic because they want a certain quality of life and standard of living but are unwilling to look at the implications of those desires: More material goods and better jobs mean more energy consumption, more production, and more waste. But this charge is not as strong as its issuers would like it to be. First, the negative implications of the steadily increasing standard of living, especially in material terms, have not been obvious all that long. It is only in the last decades that the so-called technological optimism has become challenged on a large scale.[14] On smaller scales, the view that I will have to confront the negative consequences of my lifestyle choices, no matter how problematic morally, has not been obvious at all. There may be social myopia among the well-to-do of modern industrial societies, but it is certainly not at all unique to the NIMBY movements nor is it a particularly prominent element in the NIMBY logic.

The charge of irrationality is similar. NIMBYs are said to be irrational because they are said to hold contradictory beliefs: They want and they don't want a public good. They want wind energy, but when a "wind farm" power plant is proposed, they don't want it.[15] They call for increased recycling programs, but when a recycling center is proposed in the neighborhood, they oppose it.[16]

But like the charge of myopia, the charge of irrationality is weak. First, many people who support a policy for a public good in general are at least *less likely* to oppose an implementation of the policy "in their backyard."[17] But, second, there are more than statistical reasons to think that NIMBYs are not irrational. As Maarten Wolsink points out, a person's attitude toward some public policy often depends on the concreteness of the policy. I may "in principle" think that wind energy is a good thing, but if I find out that it would mean a noisy, environmental eyesore down the road, I may rethink my "in principle" position. There is no contradiction, and hence no irrationality, between the abstract "in principle" position and the attitude about the concrete project.[18] Attitudes aren't static, and they aren't merely affective. They can change, and cognitive elements, that is, knowing more, play an important role in their change.

Let's remind ourselves of where we are. The previous point does not show that NIMBYs are not selfish. It may be true that I come to oppose a public policy when finding out its concrete details, but it is still possible that one salient detail is that it is planned in my backyard and that I might be happy to support it elsewhere, in someone else's backyard. However, the point does call into question the viability of the claim that NIMBYs are irrational.

And there is a relatively straightforward way of interpreting NIMBYs as perfectly rational, even in cases where they genuinely seem to affirm the public good whose local implementation they oppose. They simply don't want to have to pay more than others for a public good. Despite the fact that LULUs are generally accompanied with some compensation—property tax breaks, increased revenue allocation in the target locality, jobs—NIMBYs perceive these as inadequate compensation for the burden.[19] From their perspective, they see a huge freerider problem where everyone but they themselves are freeriders. It is perfectly rational to oppose any such arrangement.

I want to emphasize that the freerider problem is a *perceived* one. Whether it is an objective one is open to question; I suggest later that it isn't. But the important thing is that the NIMBYs view the context as a bargaining situation where they are about to receive a bad deal.

Note that I don't want to stake too much on competing conceptions of rationality or on what is rational. The point here is that for the charges of irrationality, there are prima facie stronger claims of rationality. These are, of course, political questions in themselves: What is *socially* rational means making normative claims about social behavior. The NIMBY rationality claim hinges on the idea that it is legitimate to ignore one's class privilege in making political arguments, and as we saw in the introduction to this part, that's a normatively questionable proposition. For now, however, I simply accept the NIMBY defenders' claim about rationality as a legitimate and prima facie plausible position.

This picture of self-interested rationality at the center of NIMBYism certainly makes it intelligible, even when we might think the rational opposition depends on mistaken or ignored facts or pernicious selfishness (these being very different things). But we are interested in *justificatory* reasons here, not just in an intelligible explanation for political action. Surely NIMBYs themselves recognize that merely showing that their action makes sense is not enough. This is especially true as the demand for political justification comes under the guise of accusation of selfishness. When you are called selfish, showing that your action is rational is not a disarming response. What needs to be shown is why rational self-interest, even conceived of as "selfishness," is justified.

It is tempting to try to divide the kinds of justifications NIMBYs have for the unacceptability of LULUs into two: those that appeal to what we could call "basic" rights such as life, safety, and health and those that appeal to reasonable expectations. Examples of the latter have included claims to expected property values and expectations about the aesthetic or cultural character of a locality or "worsened general feeling" in it.[20] For example, in a suburban Illinois NIMBY movement, the activists appealed to the fact that the destruction of a nearby wetland would alter the aesthetic character of their village and thus also property values in it.[21] Similarly, the citizens of Giles County, Tennessee, justified their opposition to a toxic waste landfill partly by claiming it would change the image of the county.[22] Now, what makes the distinction tempting is that we might find ourselves (as people with a keen eye to sound justifications) in sympathy with NIMBYs insofar as they appeal to the health hazards of a toxic landfill, but not with the appeal to the preservation of the character of their locality. Some kind of distinction between basic, or primary, rights, on the one hand, and expectations, however reasonable, on the other, seems important. But insisting on it when discussing the NIMBY argument would be a mistake. These distinctions do not do much work in the NIMBY self-understanding, and it would be to beg the question to suggest they play a fundamental role in their arguments.

What actually does most of the work are "reasonable expectations." It is not that most NIMBY activists are stupid and can't make the distinction between important primary rights and the intangible goods that make their community valuable to them. "Reasonable expectations" simply include matters of life and death, that is, health and safety, but many other things as well. In particular, reasonable expectations are thought to include the right to enjoy the things one has paid for or otherwise "earned," whether they are a house in an unpolluted, quiet residential area by a lake or the character of one's neighborhood. The description by Gould et al. of the political campaign against the threat to local wetlands by homeowners in the Illinois suburb provides a good example of how people can think they *acquire a right* to intangible public goods. Wetland activist Lynn had moved to her suburb for "quality of life reasons," and part of her argument against developers was that *because of* the reasons she had moved there, it was reasonable to demand that the factors contributing to the quality of life remain there.[23]

Why is that reasonable? Why—or when—is this justification any good? Isn't change a fact of life? Aren't NIMBYs just conservatives who realize they can at least oppose human-made change, even if they can't prevent all of it? Not necessarily. There are two things NIMBYs can argue here. First, ours is a culture (and I mean Western liberal democracies in general) that believes people have a right to what they have justly acquired. So when we move into a certain kind of neighborhood because we like its "general feeling,"[24] nature, or culture, we are, in a way, acquiring those things as well, as public goods belonging to the locality, in addition to the house on the lot. Sure, there are many things that might change those elements, and some are beyond any individual's control: the forces of nature and the exigencies of macro-level social phenomena, for example. Those are, indeed, facts of life. But there are things that depend on people's conscious decisions. The latter, especially when they are costs or other changes for the worse, and when they are imposed upon us, are seen as unreasonable.

This doesn't yet make the justification good, and certainly careful observers would be quick to point out the several gaps in the logic and undefended assumptions in the argument. For example, framing the freerider problem around one public policy ignores the fact that, on the whole, the local costs of several public goods might be evenly distributed. Furthermore, the logic assumes some kind of local self-sufficiency, which, as we—and the NIMBYs themselves—know is at most a nostalgic myth: Villages and neighborhoods are not social monads or even close to being self-sufficient. But those assumptions, while perhaps false and certainly not universal, are nevertheless not unique to some particular locality. In fact, I suggest later on that they reflect one prominent conception of the political culture of liberalism.

Here, then, is a way to return to the slightly puzzling variety of NIMBYism I identified earlier. I noted that there is a kind of NIMBYism where the activists rally around claims about unfair political processes. Their opposition is primarily procedural since it focuses on the policy makers' refusal to consult local people in the LULU siting process, and thus seems like a different case from straightforward self-interested NIMBYism. But we can see that there isn't, after all, a great difference. First, in the "proceduralist" NIMBY movements, self-interest is still there: NIMBYs seldom oppose unequivocally good policies even if they are procedurally suspect; they oppose things they don't want. Second, taking offense at not being consulted in the planning of some policy taps into the same reservoir of political values as the idea that I have a right to what I have acquired. In fact, several studies show that these seemingly two kinds of NIMBYism are difficult to tell apart in reality: Vittes et al. show that "core cultural values" are among the primary factors in opposition to hazardous waste facilities; others note that people's perception of the fairness of a siting process correlates most strongly with their negative attitudes about the facility.[25] Professional planners are told that the best way to avoid NIMBY conflicts is an open and genuinely democratic procedure.[26]

Again, there are distinctions we might want to draw between better procedural arguments and worse ones. For example, there is a difference between criticizing the lack of local input and claiming that a local community can do anything it wants, including the violation of human rights. Relevant as that should be, it is not fundamentally relevant here where we are merely trying to understand the structure of the NIMBY justification. The point is simply whether there is some justification that can have appeal even outside the particular locality. We have seen that there is: NIMBYs' arguments are about self-determination and individuals' right to the life they have justly achieved.

Environmental Justice

There is, however, a way in which NIMBYism is myopic. NIMBYs don't pay much attention to systemic questions. They generally don't ask why their locality is targeted for the particular LULU. And as we saw earlier, what they think of the public good the LULU is supposed to provide needn't play a significant role in what they think of it in their backyard. They understand the threats of the LULUs in episodic, and not systemic, terms. Sure, strategic considerations may lead NIMBY activists to forge alliances with other localities or, most often, with nonlocal umbrella organizations, but the self-interested nature is still there: If and when the threat of the LULU is defeated, the movement disbands, even when the threat is simply moved elsewhere. Again, this self-interest needn't be narrow-minded parochialism in the worst sense of the word. In fact, successful former NIMBY activists are often willing to help other movements, *if asked.* It is simply that since the impetus of the movement is in the local threat *and* the threat is seen outside of a larger context, the local NIMBY movement cannot remain mobile without the threat—or without some serious reconfiguration of its argument.

Some, in contrast, have asked "why us?" or "why here?" Consider a dialogue between two African American women in Toni Cade Bambara's *The Salt Eaters:*

> "All this doomsday mushroom-cloud end-of-planet numbah is past my brain. Just give me the good ole-fashioned honky-nigger shit. I think all this ecology stuff is a diversion."
>
> "They're connected. Whose community do you think they ship radioactive waste through, or dig up waste burial grounds near? Who do you think they hire for the dangerous dirty work at those plants? What parts of the world do they test-blast in? And all them illegal uranium mines dug up on Navajo turf—the crops dying, the sheep dying, the horses, water, cancer, Ruby, cancer . . ."[27]

Asking these questions constitutes the first and perhaps primary difference between NIMBYs and the different varieties of the environmental justice movements. In many other respects, environmental justice movements resemble NIMBYs: Their genesis is local, and despite a greater importance put on alliances than among NIMBYs, their focus is still local, a response to a LULU just like with NIMBYs. In attacking the anti-democratic siting procedures they also resemble NIMBYs. But their inquiries into the systemic features behind the planning of unwanted projects in *their* backyards are meant to put the siting policies into a context of historical social injustice, primarily racism and colonialism. Correspondingly, their political arguments, as we will see, appeal *explicitly* to different principles of justice, albeit still within liberalism.

Why does it occur to some people to ask these questions about the systemic nature of LULU siting? Or, more pointedly, why is it primarily various people of color who have thought to ask the questions? What is the difference between them and, say the white middle-class communities who simply see a siting policy they don't like?

Michael Dawson's analysis of African American political behavior provides one possible explanation. "At least until the late 1960s," he points out, "individual African Americans' life chances were overdetermined by the ascriptive feature of race."[28] As long as this is a fact or reasonably perceived to be a fact, it makes perfect sense for an African American individual to ground her political action in the interests of African Americans as a group. Just imagine a Rawlsian original position where knowledge of one's race *is* permitted behind the veil of ignorance, along with the "general facts about social history" and the like. Dawson calls this mode of political reasoning "the black utility heuristic."[29] A component of the black utility heuristic is that it also guides how one *interprets* the political world.[30] Given the lack of full information (more or less a permanent condition in political life), it makes sense to assume that things like the planning of a toxic waste incinerator in a primarily African American community, for example, have to do with race. Facts might naturally prove the initial assumption false, but that has nothing to do with the rationality of the assumptions.

There are plenty of data to suggest that the assumptions can be taken seriously, and, in fact, the data are regularly incorporated into the political arguments. The environmental justice movements use statistical and other data-driven arguments quite skillfully. Consider examples presented in literature sympathetic to the movements: Sixty percent of African American and Latino communities and more than 50 percent of Asian/Pacific Islanders and Native Americans live in areas with one or more uncontrolled toxic waste sites.[31] Forty percent of the U.S. toxic landfill capacity is concentrated in three communities: Emelle, Alabama (78.9 percent African American), Scotlandville, Louisiana (93 percent African American), and Kettleman City, California (78.4 percent Latino).[32] A range of studies, beginning with the U.S. General Accounting Office's *Siting of Hazardous Waste Landfills* in 1983, have shown that communities of color are located near and bear the burdens of hazardous waste sites and other polluted areas in numbers disproportionate to white communities.[33] In his book aimed at supporting the environmental justice arguments, Jim Schwab describes Altgeld Gardens, a 10,000-resident, primarily African American public housing complex in the Calumet region, between Chicago and Gary, Indiana: There are forty-six toxic waste dumps and altogether sixty heavily contaminated sites within a few miles, and, in addition, illegal waste dumpers take advantage of the fact that police don't patrol the area.[34] The complex itself was build atop a dump of human and industrial waste in the 1940s. Residents suffer from disproportionate numbers from skin rashes and respiratory problems; 51 percent of births result in deformities.[35] Or consider examples involving Native Americans: According to Donald Grinde and Bruce Johansen, the Akwesasne Mohawk reservations in Canada and northern New York constitute the most polluted "native reserve" in Canada and one of the most severely poisoned sections of earth in the United States. They report that there are turtles in the area that qualify as toxic waste.[36] Many arguments point to the U.S. and Canadian governments having allowed Navajo reservations in Arizona, Lakota reservations in the Dakotas, and Dene and Métis reservations in Saskatchewan, to name just a few, to become, in the National Academy of Science's now notorious phrase, "national sacrifice areas" where the health and cultural costs of coal and uranium mining are deemed acceptable because of an overriding national interest.[37] And so on.

My point here is not to express skepticism about these data because they are deployed by partisans. Some of the data aren't straightforwardly partisan in the first place, and the fact that some of the data are doesn't, by itself, impugn them. It is happily beyond the scope of this book to evaluate the available data, explanations for, and inferences from them. The point, however, is what seems like a nonrigorous presentation of the data—the previous examples would seem a travesty in, say, the *American Journal of Political Science*—and the seemingly all-too-easy explanations do constitute an important part of the argumentative arsenal to flush out the intuitions generated by the black utility heuristic and similar devices. Furthermore, I want to claim that the level of sophistication is appropriate for the political arguments. (I'll return to this later.)

So, cases like the ones described represent what has come to be known as environmental racism and, to some extent, environmental colonialism. The latter term is invoked by some to highlight the particularity of the relationship between the U.S. and Canadian governments, on the one hand, and North American native peoples, on the other: Colonialism is the cruel flip side of the two federal governments' recognition of the various native peoples as sovereign.[38] Native lands and native peoples are harnessed into unequal relationships with the federal governments and their cronies, large corporations, for example, in which the big ones reap all the real benefits and wield all the meaningful power. The term is also used to highlight a link in the contemporary treatment of native peoples in North America and indigenous peoples elsewhere.[39] At the same time, the treatment of the native peoples can also be understood as a form of racism; consequently, I will mainly use "environmental racism" in the following to talk about both phenomena.

Let's assume, for the sake of argument at least, that the data documenting environmental racism are sound. The question that remains is why people of color seem to be disproportionately targeted with insidious siting practices. The question isn't so much of whether we "really" are dealing with racism and colonialism, but of what kind of racism. We can think of environmental racism as a form of institutional racism, that is, as a practice that operates on seemingly race-neutral criteria, but which nevertheless has an adverse impact on historically oppressed racial groups.[40] But saying *just* that is insufficient: We still need an explanation of *how* the race-neutral criteria can work in race-specific ways.

An early 1980s study about the difficulties of hazardous waste siting commissioned by the state of California has become a landmark example of how it all works. (Because of this, it has also become a popular target in the environmental justice movement's arguments.) In their report, the consulting firm Cerrell

Associates do not focus on race; they simply set out to look for communities "least likely to oppose a Waste-to-Energy project."[41] The logic is crystal clear: Jon Elster is not the first one to observe the fact that most political action forward may require some "steps backwards" and that, therefore, those who can't afford even one step backward are not likely to try to move forward.[42] In its final demographic profile, the Cerrell report skirts potential charges of explicit racism by listing attributes more specific than race and by including attributes that do not strongly track or single out people of color (e.g., political conservatism, Catholicism, old age). However, it still manages to highlight the appeal of communities of color to anyone looking for the most convenient way to site a waste incinerator or landfill, nuclear waste storage facility—or even a mine.[43] Housing discrimination tends to concentrate people of color together, often near or in industrial areas with low property values for housing.[44] Together with this, the history of racism has often ensured that these communities suffer from poverty, low levels of education, and high unemployment.[45] All of these are features that the Cerrell report lists as desirable demographics. It also notes that favorable attitudes about technology tend to make communities less resistant to LULU siting. One thing that many industries have found is that where people are initially neutral about such questions but in dire need of work, a promise of jobs can generate those favorable attitudes.[46] We saw this earlier in the case of the supposedly irrational NIMBYs: Some attitudes only become meaningful to hold when they are encountered as concrete proposals. (And again, those brandishing the facile "irrationality" label need to be careful since sometimes the calculus involves the rather simple options "food now" versus "potential risk down the line.")

NIMBYism has been implicated as a factor in generating environmentally racist approaches. The environmental justice scholar Robert Bullard observes that "a result of NIMBYism has been that environmentally destructive political pressure has intensified on communities that are relatively weak, that is, on communities of color in particular."[47] This for two reasons. First, were it not for the relatively successful resistance that better-off and generally white communities have been mounting against LULUs, there would be less need to look for the weakest link in the potential chain of resistance. It is not inconceivable that people would be willing to put up with the various "externalities" of the good life if their distribution was perceived as fair, for example. Second, since the NIMBY movements do not generally challenge the overall policies that underlie the siting projects, the projects remain legitimate. In other words, since there "has to be" a place for a toxic waste landfill, the search for the politically weakest community as a siting location is simply a sensible policy. Moreover, given the atmosphere of rational preference assertion the NIMBY movements give to these policy conflicts, those communities who do not say "no" can be claimed to have "freely" preferred to host the LULU in question.

The case of Native Americans illustrates a slightly different mechanism of environmental racism. Being targeted because of the relative political weakness of one's community is certainly true in their case as well, especially when it comes to finding host localities for nuclear waste storage sites. In fact, in some cases Native American reservations fit the Cerrell profile better than inner-city communities of color, as the Cerrell report finds rural communities more desirable than urban ones. But mining, primarily of uranium and, to some extent, coal, is different. Sure, whether some deposit is worth mining depends partly on where it is and what nearby communities think about it, and in this way the weak bargaining position of the Native Americans can be relevant. But more important is that it is no coincidence that most North American uranium deposits are on what are now native lands. The racist Indian relocation policy of the late nineteenth and early twentieth centuries was to find what then seemed like the worst land and force Native Americans into those areas, and what was discovered later was that often the lands were bad because of the radioactivity of the uranium.[48]

Another idiosyncracy in the case of Native Americans is the role treaties and their violation have played. Because of the recognition (however disingenuous) of the sovereignty of the native tribes and nations, the U.S. and Canadian governments have a history of governing their relationships to native peoples through various treaties. Some of these have been oppressive on their face, some beneficial in the letter and often counterproductive in the breach. The violation of these treaties, either sanctioned or committed by the central governments, has become a benchmark of the racism against native peoples: Native Americans have learned to understand the violation or deliberate nonenforcement of a particular treaty as belonging automatically to the history of their racist oppression. (Following Dawson's argument for the rationality of race-conscious politics, we can recognize an analogy here and call this perception a "treaty-violation heuristic": Given their history, it is rational for Native Americans to be pessimistic about treaties in general and to view the lax enforcement and the exploitation of their treaty rights as racism against them.) In this light, environmental racism against Native Americans takes on entirely new forms. Treaty violations haven't happened only in connection with resource extraction, toxics, and the like, but also in cases where Native Americans have exercised their treaty rights in activities that environmentalists tend to find suspect: logging,[49] grazing,[50] fishing,[51] and, most notoriously, in the Makah whaling case in Washington State in the late 1990s.

I've taken this lengthy detour into the mechanisms of environmental racism because it helps us understand how environmental justice movements must frame the political arguments they want to offer.[52] They begin with the questions I noted earlier—why us? why here?—and then answer them with the previous and similar observations. Their biggest challenge is to counter the sort of economistic rational preference account according to which poor communities freely respond to attractive offers. (Just consider the notorious memorandum by Lawrence Summers, then a World Bank economist, who argued that dumping First World industrial wastes into less-developed countries follows an "impeccable," "welfare enhancing" economic logic.[53]) This is tricky partly because the economist's model has politically attractive features: it grants rational agency to the communities, it takes them as "fellow bargainers." So they need to challenge the assumptions without selling the communities of color short as suffering from false consciousness. In short, they must show that, in the economistic view, the assumption of *free* rational agency is mistaken, but not rationality *simpliciter*. This is, of course, a notorious problem in both the theory and the practice of any political action (recognized famously by Rousseau and Marx), and ground-level evidence suggests the environmental justice movements must struggle with it in practice.[54]

All this points to why the *Homo economicus* isn't an appropriate model here. As an explanatory model, it sees the environmental justice movements as irrational—why *wouldn't* they accept "welfare enhancing" trade-offs?—and it gets confused about *what* they are doing. As a normative model, it points the environmental movements in the very direction they want to resist. Neither of these facts show that a comprehensive rational choice model would be *false*, but they do show how that very question is implicated in the political dispute. The Kantian model, which has us focus on the arguments, does better: It simply presupposes that people try to justify their political positions with *some* reasons, and that those reasons may but need not invoke the *Homo economicus* as the model citizen.

So the environmental justice movements' framing the issue in a historical and social context raises doubts about the usefulness and reliability of unvarnished preferences, the ones according to which people "want" a LULU in their community.[55] The environmental justice activists aim to show, particularly by highlighting the social context of poverty and racist oppression, that the targeted communities' choices are so limited that they make talk of freely expressed preferences meaningless and, at best, talk of rational preferences under duress more apt. They want to recast the attractive offers bundled with the LULUs as the kind of offer "one cannot refuse" or, as they have come to call it, as "environmental blackmail." The term isn't rhetorically innocent, of course, but its use is still couched—and in some ways, inseparable—from *reasons* for why it might be apt.

Furthermore, putting the particular issue they are dealing with in a larger historical or social context can help show what is problematic with the issue itself. So, for example, when the environmental justice movements point out that massive toxic waste landfills can only be sited by blackmailing poor and politically weak communities, they raise questions about whether the social practices that produce those wastes are sustainable in the long run. They have been partly successful in this: Both industries and the government now name the overall reduction of waste production, rather than the establishment of new facilities, as the primary goal of the U.S. waste policy. Contrast this to the NIMBY argument, which simply rejects a LULU on the self-interest grounds: They have a hard time saying anything about the badness of the LULU. Naturally, they might not want to, which is part of the point here.

Finally, since the social or historical context in which the single issue is seen is a context of injustice, political opposition to, say, a particular LULU can become a call for justice, not merely for environmental justice. In other words, the point is not only to issue a cease-and-desist order against practices that target communities of color. There is also a *general* call for the amelioration of the conditions that put people of color in a political corner, a call for the honoring of treaties and other contracts, a call for real a "place at the table."[56] How these issues are combined can be seen, for example, in the position paper Robert Bullard and Dana Alston of the progressive Panos Institute drafted for the People of Color Environmental Leadership Summit in 1991. The paper demands (1) procedural equity, the effective (and not merely nominal) right to participate in siting decisions and similar policy issues; (2) geographic equity, that is, attempts to redress the disproportionate impact on communities of color because of historical land use and housing patterns; and (3) social equity, which would, for example, mean targeted efforts to deal with the lead poisoning that inner-city children suffer in disproportionate numbers or the guarantee that services such as garbage collection or fire prevention are effectively available in communities of color.[57] What counts as an issue of environmental justice and what as social justice is inseparable here. That, too, is both rhetorical *and* a part of a legitimate argument.

Of course, some might argue that the demands of the environmental justice movements contain the seeds of their own ineffectiveness. Might it not be counterproductive to hook up a local opposition to a landfill with these wide-ranging and structurally deep social demands? After all, everyone knows that the demands can't be met very quickly or easily, even if there were more political goodwill than there is—partly because some of the problems are very structural and independent of any single set of political actors. In other words, the worry is that if this particular landfill problem is shown to be part of a large systemic social problem that is difficult to solve, shouldn't we just chalk up the landfill as another nonideal necessary evil? Possibly, and I consider the possibility of backfiring strategies in Chapter 8. But it needn't backfire. First, environmental justice arguments have, in general, been quite successful even in the individual political struggles. Second, the successes may be because of the very structure of the argument. By revealing these processes as instances of institutional racism, the movements have gained not only a moral upper hand but also an upper hand in terms of political arguments: The appeals to public good behind many of these siting policies become relatively hollow when they are shown to imply the violation of greater political values such as nondiscrimination or equality. Finally, even though the environmental movements well realize that not every demand can be met, their systemic arguments become one way to give substance to political ideals: "Equality" means not only political equality, but also equal access to a healthy environment, for example.

I will return to a more thorough evaluation of both the NIMBY and environmental justice arguments, that is, to the question as to whether we can really see them as having *justified* their respective positions. To prepare the ground for that evaluation, a return to the ivory tower is necessary.

Two Conceptions of Liberalism

Let's step back a little from the specific movement issues and show how they relate to a larger theoretical picture. The contrast between the arguments within NIMBYism and the environmental justice movements can be interpreted as a contrast between two substantive conceptions of liberalism. NIMBYism reflects an understanding of liberalism as essentially concerned with the individual, a system in which liberal values like toleration are seen as instrumental for *individuals'* pursuit of their good lives and where the notion of *contract* governs relations between people. Environmental justice, on the other hand, exhibits for us a more cosmopolitan liberalism, a kind in which liberal values in themselves are part of a public, even communal good and where the public good is hooked up to the degree of community between people.

Before elaborating on this claim, note that this is not the only way to understand the difference between NIMBYism and environmental justice. Ian Welsh, for example, sees the criticism of NIMBYism as stemming from the utilitarian commitments of a public political culture: NIMBYs refuse to act in the interest of the greater good.[58] Of course, given the enduring prevalence of the liberal view that self-interest is the best way to pursue common good, this interpretation is not a particularly convincing one.

But what about thinking of the NIMBY–environmental justice contrast as reflecting some constellations of the liberalism–communitarianism controversy? For example, we could view NIMBYs as the personification of self-interested liberalism and environmental justice movements, in turn, as communitarians. The problem is that while NIMBYs might fit the bill here, it is a little difficult to see how exactly environmental justice movements would be communitarian. Granted, a certain kind of identity politics is at work here: The black utility heuristic and treaty-violation heuristic and similar ways of understanding the issues do seem to appeal to something like "communal interests," where the communal is understood as "people of color in general" or something similar. Dawson's claim that African American politics is communitarian exactly because it is rational to hook up one's identity with the fate of the race at large is an example of this. One problem with this, however, is that it gets the order of explanation at least partially wrong: The "identity" alliances are forged in responses to shared *oppression*; they don't always predate anti-oppression as social ties based on culture, language, or general history.[59] And while I would be happy to view this kind of identity politics as a *type* of communitarianism, the label has come to have too many connotations that would be misleading here: Particularly important is the appeal of communitarians to some *fixed* set of *shared beliefs* (I will return to this point later).

Besides, we could also see the liberalism versus communitarianism dichotomy as explaining things *the other way round*, taking environmental justice movements as articulating universalist liberal values and seeing the NIMBYs as emphasizing the inviolability of shared local values, some cherished Jeffersonian idyll instantiated in a pristine subdivision. Either way we view the difference, some further arguments would be necessary. The situation is analogous—and in fact related—to the different possible approaches to Montesquieu's and Kant's theories I discussed in Part II. There *are* alternative interpretations. Some are better than others, as I urged in the case of both Montesquieu and Kant and am urging here. At the same time, the range of alternatives should keep us from imposing categories that are too neat. When I argue that the NIMBY–environmental justice tension illustrates too conceptions of liberalism and not, say, the liberalism–communitarianism controversy, we should not ignore the interpretive complexity. It matters that to some, NIMBYs, for example, look communitarian.

Part of the interpretive looseness is also a result of the fact that the political positions of the movements do not articulate comprehensive theoretical positions. The movements don't conceive of their positions as "liberal" or "communitarian" or "utilitarian." Their projects aren't theoretical, but practical. To the extent that they care about justification, it is primarily its persuasiveness, not its congruence with some comprehensive theory, in which they are interested.

That said, I do want to claim that the two movements' arguments can be put in a larger theoretical context. This is not separate from the idea that the movements want their arguments to be persuasive, but, rather, directly follows from it. We've seen how each argument appeals to ideals and political values that are shared or at least presumed to be shared more widely than just among the participants themselves. These different values, I am trying to argue, can be understood as representing two competing conceptions of liberalism, both of which can be found (at least) in the American political culture.

The picture of the relationship between the arguments of the actual movements and the theoretical issues is the following. There are three kinds of entities: the actual policy arguments activists make, general political values, and theoretical systematizations of those values. When I say that an argument "reflects" a conception of liberalism, I mean that the argument is related to a set of political values that, when systematized, can be called a particular conception of liberalism. The relationship between the specific arguments and political values can be conceived of in several ways. The first we might call strategic: *In order to* generate a successful argument, the activists appeal to those values that are likely to vindicate them. Thus, for example, NIMBYs appeal to a very robust conception of property rights. The second perspective is a conceptual one: Some set of political values is believed to *entail* the claims of the policy argument. The view I want to expound on here is that those "sets" of political values that help generate the specific arguments *can* be systematized into two specific conceptions of liberalism.

Some might, again, hear echoes of the Rawls–Habermas debate, and the perception is correct insofar as the quarrel between the two is about citizens' deliberative practices and theoretical principles.[60] But there are differences between my treatment and that debate. While my view is closer to Rawls's (and so implies that the Rawlsian position comes out ahead), I don't presuppose that institutional safeguards like free speech are stable parameters *outside* the political contests or that the contests are about some straightforward basic structure of society. *What* the basic structure of society is is among the questions for me. And, finally, I agree with Habermas that Rawls's distinction between people's "comprehensive conceptions of the good" and a "freestanding" political conception finds little support in practice. Again, part of the issue here is that people are trying to find *some* grounds of agreement to make their arguments persuasive; they aren't looking for a purely freestanding conception. And as G. A. Cohen's point about the contextual dependence of arguments showed, what is persuasive varies according to the audience.

In general, I want to stress that the theoretical systematizations need not play any active role in how the movements and the people in them conceive of their action. My claim is simply this: If a specific argument reflects a particular conception of liberalism, it means that an activist making the argument would, when asked, endorse a cluster of other values and principles central to that theoretical conception. Whether the activist would have anything to say about the theoretical systematization would not be relevant. The picture I have here is simply that precise *theoretical* formulations are not the core of political arguments.[61]

Now we come back to the matter of why we are not dealing with a version of theoretical communitarianism. Communitarianism is commonly conceived of as the appeal to *fixed* or at least unequivocally transparent shared political values, notions of justice or of the good, within a culture. But what the arguments of my two movements highlight is exactly that there isn't necessarily any fixed set of coherent or consistent values, but a range, even a multiplicity of sometimes vague or abstract and sometimes conflicting values. At issue isn't a "struggle for the soul of the American body politic," as Brian Barry calls political disputes conceived of in the communitarian fashion, because there is no "soul" or any other sort of monolithic center.[62] Louis Hartz's classic claim of a "Lockean liberalism" at the core of American political culture has been shown to be too full of gaps to be plausible; other similar attempts have fared more or less as badly.[63] There is not *a* set of core values; rather, one could say the core of the American body politic is to argue about what values there are and what there should be.[64]

This is an inevitable feature of modern political life, as my discussion in Chapter 2 suggested, and particularly so in liberal and democratic societies (but even elsewhere—just think of the disputes about what exactly the Koran says about women's place in Islamic theocracies). Even in a society that *roughly* exemplifies one political philosophy—liberalism in the case of the United States— no uncontroversial set of core values can be appealed to. This doesn't, of course, mean that anything goes. Some benchmark political principles set boundary conditions on what goes; they also constitute criteria for what can count as acceptable arguments, and the debates aren't ever limitless. Whether one wants to call this path dependency, it seems clear that the debates draw from a complex but ultimately finite set of values and ideas. Some political options will begin as nonstarters and others end up as seeming beyond the pale, as many political actors from the nineteenth-century socialists and anarchists to the defenders of fully state-provided health care have found. So the fact that the criteria might vary depending on the audience does not mean that there aren't any. There are worse and better ways of connecting the dots in what makes a coherent picture of a society's political values. What is particularly interesting about the two movements I am discussing is that each offers a plausible argument for how we ought to conceive of American liberalism.

The following tells us how to connect the dots, although we still shouldn't expect a theoretically fine-tuned and perfectly consistent picture to emerge. That could only be gained by abstracting so far from the actual positions that nothing would remain. This may be because perfectly consistent theoretical pictures require circumstances in which all political business is in order—the "well-ordered society" Rawls regards as his regulative ideal—and the kinds of political movements at issue are evidence that things aren't perfect. Two general pictures nevertheless do emerge.

First, NIMBYism represents a version of liberalism that puts a high premium on the idea of individualism and sees political institutions as essentially enforcers of *contractual* relations between people. These are related: The idea is that what is valuable is people's relatively uninhibited pursuit of whatever it is they think is worth pursuing. The idea that political arrangements are to make this possible makes the existence of political institutions secondary to the fundamental idea. Finally, since there is a diversity of opinions on what is worth pursuing, political institutions cannot themselves generate any substantive views of such matters, but must simply concern themselves with the enforcement of contractual relations between people. In other words, if Jill has legitimately acquired her bicycle, political institutions' only job is to make sure Jill gets to keep her bicycle, and political institutions should not be in the business of saying that since Jill has the only bicycle on the block it would be nice of her to share it at least a little. This is the liberal world of the *Homo economicus* and his close cousins. This is the kind of liberalism libertarians are most fond of—consider, for example, Nozick's *Anarchy, State, and Utopia*—but we shouldn't think libertarianism is its only instantiation. What we have is a liberalism of rights alone, as opposed to liberalism with a richer or differently conceived idea of rights and goods.

Contrast this liberalism of rights to a more egalitarian liberalism. The environmental justice movement instantiates the latter. Recall that the environmental justice activists, in Dorceta Taylor's words, "refused to say 'not in my backyard' without questioning or caring about whose backyard the problem ended up in."[65] This was because they perceived these policies as instances of institutional racism. First, since some particular locality was targeted because of its racial demographics, it would be likely that if the particular locality was successful in preventing the policy, some other similar locality would be targeted. Second, if the policy was racist, it would be racist in all instances in which similar demographics were the primary ground, not only in the case of one particular locality. Opposition to such siting was, then, opposition to racism.

What does one appeal to when one wants to oppose institutional racism? Since Reconstruction, at least, powerful egalitarian principles have been part of the legal and political traditions in America. Their application has been, of course, tenuous, but certainly they have been available as normative ideals. In general, there are important political values according to which the exigencies of birth should not count in one's ability to pursue happiness, and these can be and have been construed to yield egalitarianism about race and gender, among other things.

Of course, the kind of egalitarianism we are talking about is largely about equality of *opportunity*, the quintessentially liberal kind of egalitarianism. On this abstract construal, the *Homo economicus* and his NIMBY buddies are on board. But we needn't grant the NIMBYs their conception of the idea: Robustly conceived, equality of opportunity can generate effective and thick principles of redistribution and redress. This is not mere wishful thinking, as the (admittedly tenuous) existence of affirmative action policies shows.

So the egalitarianism that underwrites the anti-racism of the environmental justice movements is one way in which their political philosophy differs from the NIMBYs' thinner liberalism. But there is another contrast as well, namely, a more "communal" or "cosmopolitan" liberalism. It relates to the specific egalitarianism about opportunities by grounding the latter in a broader egalitarianism, that is, in a conception of a polity as a *community* of equals and, moreover, by conceiving of this community as *valuable*. There are, then, two essential differences between the egalitarian liberalism and liberalism of rights: (1) about how relations between people are to be conceived and (2) about what liberals can think of as bearing value. These are related; to show how, I consider the second difference first.

In the thin version of liberalism, objects of value are conceived in terms of their direct links to *individual interests*. In other words, what I think of as good or bad depends on how it fosters or threatens some interests that (I think) I have.[66] If there is no direct effect, I am neutral, or at least mainly disinterested. For example, when a proposed toxic waste dump in my neighborhood threatens me and my family or even the vista for which I chose this location, I think of the waste dump as nasty business and value greatly the state of affairs in which it never gets realized in my neighborhood. However, I am indifferent about it insofar as it is built somewhere where it has no effect on what matters to me. In contrast, however, a communally minded liberal, if she thinks of the waste dump as nasty business, will think that the world may be worse off even in cases where there is no direct effect to her personal interests.

Before elaborating on this, note that I am not talking about the contrast between purely individual and public goods in the way an economist understands them. The *Homo economicus* has no problem admitting the existence of public goods, that is, goods that cannot be enjoyed without others enjoying them as well.[67] In fact, it should be pretty obvious that local NIMBY movements are in most cases premised on the idea of a public good: Much as I might dislike my next-door neighbor, if I am going to continue to enjoy our clean neighborhood air, he will, too. (My neighbor might not care about it, but my NIMBY activism is largely about getting him to care.) The central issue here is that a public good is still in *my* interest; "public" just refers to how the good can be enjoyed.[68]

The contrast, then, is not in the mode of enjoyment of the good. Rather, the communally minded liberals think that in addition to goods related to individual interests, there are goods that are independent of any given individual's direct interests. Charles Taylor calls these *irreducibly social goods.*[69] Let's consider Taylor's example, friendship, as a holistic good. If I find the friendship between you and me valuable, what is it that I value? According to Taylor, I value no particular feature about you or me (although, of course, I may *also* value those things), but *the friendship,* a particular social relation. Moreover, I value it *because* friendship is a kind of social relation where we have a *common understanding* of ourselves as friends.[70] This common understanding of ourselves as friends is ontologically primitive *from the evaluative perspective,* even though the social unit itself depends on the beliefs and attitudes you and I have. So there is, in a way, a supervenience relation here: The value of the friendship supervenes on attributes at the individual level; however, in explaining the value, no reference to the individual attributes is going to suffice.[71]

Taylor's more political examples of these holistic goods include patriotism as well as a shared language in cases where the idea of sharing a language contributes to something like patriotism. Thus, for example, French is a social good in Quebec in a way English isn't, say, in the hugely multilingual Philippines, where it nevertheless is a common language.[72]

One common way of contrasting ways of valuing is to make a distinction between instrumental value and value "for its own sake." However, as Christine Korsgaard and, following her, Elizabeth Anderson have shown, this is a false contrast because there are *two* distinctions: Valuable "for its own sake" conflates *intrinsic value,* that is, being a *direct* object of valuing, and value as the *goal* of some endeavor. Instrumental value is a contrast to the latter, while *extrinsic value* is the proper contrast to the former.[73] When something is extrinsically valuable, it is valuable because of some connection it has to something intrinsically valuable. To illustrate, consider, first, Taylor's example of the French language. I may think of French as having instrinsic value because, for example, of its beauty. But I may also think of it as instrumentally valuable, as the means with which we can, say, bring about the independent Quebecois state. Anything that is instrumentally valuable is, a fortiori, extrinsically valuable: It has its value because I value something else, namely, Quebecois independence. But not everything that is extrinsically valuable must be instrumentally valuable: I might not speak a word of French, but I may nevertheless value it if, say, a loved one, a Quebecois nationalist, regards it as an important aspect of his identity. Of the four types of value, the only way the French language cannot be valued is as the goal of some endeavor, but that is simply because it already exists.

To muddy the waters still more, let's observe another type of distinction, that is, in the *grounds* of value, in *what* actually makes something valuable. We can distinguish between two kinds relevant for my purposes here: (1) goods whose value comes from the fact that they *make conceptually possible*, that is, are *constitutive of* individual or collective practices, and (2) goods whose value comes from their *contribution to* or *promotion of* individual or collective practices.

But what is the difference here? And how can Taylor—or anyone—possibly claim social goods of the second kind could be "irreducibly" social? By thinking about the first question, we also get an answer to the second. The difference lies in the way in which the two kinds of goods relate to other valuable things. In the case of (2), the relationship is literally instrumental. In other words, we are talking about some *causal* way in which a social good, say, the institution of taxation, contributes to valued practices, to individual and collective well-being, and so on. In the case of (1), on the other hand, the relationship is conceptual. It is, strictly speaking, wrong to talk about "contribution" or an "instrumental relation" in the first place; what we are really dealing with is a conceptually *necessary condition* between the social good and something else. Consider language, likely to have been one of the first social goods: Many human pursuits would be unthinkable without language. Or take the Kantian case I discussed in Chapter 4: In that view, the state, by enforcing the Principle of External Freedom, *makes possible* modes of human life that could not exist without it. Becoming a Kantian "scholar" represents a conceptual expansion of who a person is and can be. The same analysis can be offered, for example, to the state-guaranteed institution of property.

In this sense, then, it is perfectly conceivable for Taylor to talk about the first kind of goods being irreducibly social: No individual attitude, interest, belief, and so on about some particular social good of the second kind is possible without the existence of the social good. The existence of the institution of property cannot be explained by people's desires to be rich. Rather, the institution of property makes it possible for people to desire to be rich.

Now think of the kind of liberalism that views a rich variety of "experiments in living" as the best way to ensure individual and/or collective well-being. This is most famously the liberalism of Mill, but it is also the liberalism of Wilhelm von Humboldt. The difference between the two is that Mill is concerned with aggregate welfare, while von Humboldt, who is not a utilitarian, thinks that nonaggregated *individual* welfare is the most important.[74] I point to this difference to highlight the fact that one needn't be committed to any notion of collective happiness as the fundamental goal of political arrangements to think irreducibly social goods exist. The political project is, then, to establish political institutions that not only promote but also make possible a wide variety of lifestyles. The relationship here is both causal—"promote" can mean anything from noninterference to active encouragement and facilitation—and conceptual.

Some liberals like to think—perhaps because of Mill's choice of the word "experiments"—that diversity is good because it is a way of finding *the* best way of living. In other words, some think that liberalism is a way to run a high number of experiments at the same time and that only a few of those experiments will turn out to be successful. That is Schmitt's image of liberalism, as Chapter 1 illustrated, and certainly there are liberals who seem to hold such a view. But what the view (which I'm not claiming was Mill's) neglects are the effects of diversity itself. It is a reasonable empirical assumption that a diverse social context is more likely to sustain and foster diversity than a homogenous social context, no matter how free. In other words, if there are real examples of a variety of lifestyles, people have more choices and may even be more likely to take the possibility of their own "experiments in living" more seriously. The idea, then, is that diversity itself, and not just the institutions, can be seen as an extrinsic *but not only instrumental* social good from a liberal perspective.

But it is not clear that diversity is necessarily incompatible with the NIMBY style of liberalism I discussed earlier. "Sure," those liberals can say, "diversity is important to liberalism: It simply shows that pluralism is a fact, and effective diversity shows that political institutions manage to respect it. But forget this fancy talk of irreducibly social goods." What to say against that? Let's think about *what sort of* diversity we want to call an irreducibly social good. Someone can certainly say that a fragmented liberal culture is a diverse one, but it is not very plausible to think that it will foster a sense of experimenting with life very strongly. The diversity those whom I am talking about value is of a more "cosmopolitan" variety: That is, various different ways of life are seen to coexist on more equal terms so that any given person can *really* imagine herself at relatively great liberty to pursue the kind of life she wants.[75] I want to call this version of liberalism "cosmopolitan," although it needn't literally view some happy international commingling of individuals as its ideal; the "cosmopolitanism" viewed as the goal can simply be an equal coexistence of various ways of life. This deliberate openness sidesteps important ongoing debates on the relationship between local commitments and cosmopolitanism or on what cosmopolitanism means, but it does so by fixing the meaning to our ordinary uses.[76] Think of the contexts we call cosmopolitan in everyday parlance: the city of Monaco, for example, where people from various countries and cultures relate to one another as equals while respecting their cultural and individual differences. (It isn't, of course, a coincidence that Monaco is a *rich people's* city, but we can skirt that complication for now.) Or our ideals, if not the reality, of places like New York City and London, where the cultural diversity is exactly what gives them their special character and leads many people to like them. In other words, the ideal here is not bland, assimilated homogeneity or a society in which institutions cannot account for and respect differences, but diversity under conditions of equality.

Why equality? There are two related reasons: First, if diversity flows from the normative liberal ideal of *individuals'* right to engage in experiments in living, then those individuals had better have *effective* access to that diversity. It's not, I want to insist, a realization of a *liberal* conception of diversity if I get to be the "powerless social pariah" experiment and nothing else. The second reason is a little more complicated, and we need still another quick detour to get our hands on it.

Joseph Raz's account of what he calls "common goods," but what I continue to call social goods, helps us think about the relevant details. Consider Raz's discussion of the relationship between rights and interests.[77] On the one hand, rights are closely related to interests in the sense that we never really have rights to something in which we have no interest. On the other hand, however, there is a discrepancy between the valuations of rights and interests: In some cases, we value a right much more than the interest it protects. So, for example, I may think that it would be a bad thing if you stole a shirt of mine that I don't even like. Here the value of the right does not correspond to the degree of my interest.[78] Or, to use another example from Raz, I may have little interest in exercising my freedom of expression in any real way and yet have a significant interest in the freedom.[79] I feel that I don't have anything useful to say myself, but I nevertheless value a society in which people get to express their opinions freely. One of the consequences of this is that despite my lack of interest in the exercise of the right of expression, I am committed to *respecting* its exercise by others. In this view, then, the institution of property and the freedom of expression are social goods, as opposed to public goods: They promote and make possible the functioning of society, but they are partially independent of *any given* individual interests.

Think, now, of what it would mean to value genuine diversity as a social good. The idea isn't, and couldn't conceivably be, that citizens value all the different manifestations of diversity, but that they value that kind of diversity itself. Recall the discussion of friendship: In valuing this robust kind of diversity, they value the social relations that it establishes, based on the common understanding of citizens that it is valuable, regardless of their specific interests. But it does not establish this relevant complex of relationships among citizens unless they share an understanding about it. And if I am the powerless social pariah, I cannot conceive of it in the same way as those to whom it is effectively accessible.

This is the kind of political community liberals can be committed to; it does not have the potentially anti-liberal elements that make liberals leery of communitarianism. Where in communitarianism social and political norms are extracted from communally shared values, this is a community that *arises out of* a liberal conception of the political; it is the same social entity Kant saw in the "reading public," or community of scholars. The reader may have balked earlier when I described this account of liberalism as both communal and cosmopolitan since the two seem be almost oxymoronic, but we can see that the two fit together, at least here, coherently. In simple terms, the difference is this: In the NIMBYs' conception of liberalism, what matters fundamentally is *me*, and what governs my political relations to others is a contract. In the cosmopolitan account, in addition to me as the bearer of political value, social goods are also valuable. And what characterizes my political relations to others is my conception of all of us as equal members of a community.

The picture might finally begin to look familiar, although it is different from that other familiar picture of liberalism I attributed to NIMBYs earlier. There are familiar intuitions, some articulated in cornier ways than others: "I'm proud to be an American because in America you get to do and be what you want." It is important to realize—and I would argue that those who actually say these sorts of things often forget it—that the latter part of the statement is plausible only when all Americans can state it. And as the environmental justice movements, among many others, are arguing, we are nowhere near there yet. But the ideal is already with us, and the fact that it isn't so strange is a good thing, a sign that the narrow, self-interested conception of liberalism isn't the only thing kicking around in our repertoire of political values.

But what about those environmental justice activists? How is it, again, that what they are saying can be interpreted with this conception of liberal theory? First, the arguments made by the environmental justice movements are an attack against the plausibility of arguments for "separate but equal": They can point out that where there is no sense of a common good that effectively incorporates the idea of equal diversity, there is both a great temptation and little argumentative resource against taking advantage of the relative power differentials between separate groups, be they racial, ethnic, class-based, or geographic. If all liberalism was an account of contractual economic rationality, then, it seems, we would have to agree with Summers's argument that the logic of shipping toxic wastes to poor countries is "impeccable." In contrast, environmental justice movements argue, along the lines of the second style of liberalism, that politics that allows for "national sacrifice areas" is unjust. In showing that certain social practices are possible only when there are groups that can be deemed dispensable, they force society to reconsider whether some of its experiments in living are either sustainable or right.

This lengthy detour into liberal theory shouldn't imply that the political differences between NIMBYs and environmental justice movements are *primarily* differences over the "right" conception of liberalism. But in their disagreements over what the political problems with LULU siting are and over what kinds of political arguments—and, relatedly, what strategies—are legitimate and desirable, they disagree over some fundamental political values. I pointed out at the beginning of this section that viewing the disagreement through this framework of liberal theory is not the only way of theorizing about the two movements; but it is, I maintain, a profitable one, at least in the North American context (and perhaps elsewhere).

Justification?

There are, then, two defensible conceptions of liberalism reflected in the NIMBY and environmental justice movements' political arguments. Defensibility does not entail very much, however; that the arguments cohere with some general principles does not mean that they really amount to justifications of the respective positions.

I want to spend some time evaluating the arguments. Such an evaluation will, of course, be an incomplete business. We are dealing with political arguments, and the success of political arguments is tested in practice, as I argued in the introduction to this part of the book. Again, this point is not a cynical one, saying that minds are swayed and campaigns completed through illicit subterfuge of some kind. Even noncynical understanding of political arguments must consider persuasion as one of the final arbiters.

But how do we tell a difference between reasonable persuasion and, say, brainwashing? And does the requirement that those concerned be persuaded really mean that everyone relevant really *agrees*? And what does agreement mean? I take up the question of who that "everyone relevant" is in Chapter 7, but before that, several preliminary questions must be addressed.

Recall Weber's typology of legitimacy that I discussed briefly in Chapter 2. One way to express the difference between reasonable and unacceptable persuasion is to say that liberals would like people to be persuaded in a way that, if they would reflect on the question, their grant of legitimacy would be value-rational, not merely an emotional surrender. In other words, persuasion that enjoys something like the reflective endorsement from those persuaded *and* where the reflection invokes reasons open to all would mark the argument, and thus the proffered justification, reasonable. In short, this would be persuasion in accordance with a textbook Kantian version of the dictates of public reason. It would also be the model Rawls and others much like him endorse.[80] But, as I have tried to suggest, this is a bit too much of a textbook model, and the distinctions on which it hangs are only imperfectly tractable in practice. This does *not* mean that the conception of public reason should be abandoned. On that, the Kantians dig in their heels. It just means that the evaluation of public reason must be attuned to the contexts in which they are proffered.

So, to get our hands around something concrete, consider our NIMBYs and the environmental justice activists. That there is a defensible variety of liberalism to be found underlying NIMBYism doesn't mean that such a liberalism would, in the end, necessarily support every NIMBY movement. It is doubtful, for example, that the NIMBY claims of not needing to put up with any "externalities" of good living would be acceptable to all others. If unsolicited social burdens are a possibility in any locality, most people would reject the claim by some locality that they need not bear any such burden because of their entitlement to a burden-free neighborhood. Even if people were sympathetic to the kinds of liberal values NIMBYs rely on, they can simply point out that the NIMBYs are making a scope mistake in their argument: A neighborhood does not constitute a relevant kind of political community.

The NIMBYs who object to closed and nondemocratic political processes are likely to fare better. But this is precisely because their argument is much more general: Procedural violations are general wrongs, not just violations of these specific people's interests. So their argument is readily available to anyone. In other words, if they argue that what is problematic about a LULU siting is that they weren't consulted, then they do not have any theoretical resources to say that other people in some other locality may be neglected in the siting process.

Similarly, the kind of arguments the environmental justice movements are making, insofar as they appeal to something like the cosmopolitan liberalism I have described, are available to everyone. The scope of the argument is the same as the scope of the political society, and the only way to reject its general principle is to appeal to some "private," nonshared premises—in other words, to revert back to the NIMBY argument. Sure, it is possible and, in practice, probable that those who do not like the details of the environmental justice arguments—since they are, after all, redistributive—would challenge the arguments' details, not their major premise. They could, for example, try to argue that the inequities that environmental racism manifests are really an inevitable by product of other ideal political and social arrangements. How well those arguments would fare in the end is not clear, but I want to suggest they would have less bite than arguments based on the narrow NIMBY-style liberalism.

One important question when we consider the success of a justification *to* someone is whether justification really requires that *everyone* accept the professed justification. This is related to the notorious theoretical puzzle about the relationship between hypothetical and actual consent. The worry is that since my conception of justification follows the sociological Weberian idea of legitimacy, namely, that actual people find something binding, there is the risk that some stick-in-the-mud naysayer will hold up the proceedings by refusing his assent.

One way to solve the problem is through procedural and substantive requirements. It is relatively easy to build safeguards against that sort of sabotage in a conception of justification. We can say, for example, that the minimal rationality required for having standing in these matters amounts to responsiveness to others and their reasons, "intelligibly expressing our varied concerns to others."[81] Or we can build some other criteria of reasonableness into the process. Those who fail to meet these kinds of requirements are disqualified, and whatever they say in response to a professed justification can be ignored.[82] For example, if arguments based on private religious revelation are ruled inadmissible, as Hobbes already urged, then I can't counter your argument with the vision I had in a sweat lodge. However, as Jeremy Waldron observes, these criteria themselves are substantive and potentially controversial.[83] With a strong condition of reasonableness, one can agree to a requirement of full actual consent for something to count as justified, but that merely means that the reasonableness condition may itself stand in need of justification. This isn't a *theoretical* problem for the account I have presented here; in fact, my conception of the political (see Chapter 2) presupposes that very idea: Politics is controversy over what counts as legitimate authority, and we shouldn't be surprised to discover that the question of argument adjudication is one of those controversies.

This doesn't make it completely relative. The fact that polities have procedural rules shows that there can be agreements. Further, often such agreements are to create the institutional safeguards against our tendencies to make mistakes, just as the Montesquieuian model suggests. The fact that there are occasionally controversies over those agreements simply proves the point further. In short, *everything* is contestable some of the time, but not everything is contested at the same time.

All this said, it should be obvious that the schematic account can't be the full picture. It also should be equally obvious, if not more, that one of the things this view seems to ignore is the real-world contingencies that not only make the conception of equal political community a mere regulative ideal but also muddy the waters much more. Consider the familiar worry about so-called "false consciousness": Are we simply to accept the idea that some policy can't be justified, and thus be made legitimate, to some people even though it quite obviously would be good for them, if they don't want it? My revisionist discussion of justification here is motivated by the concern for the justifiability of arguments and policies *to* people, but it would seem politically counterproductive and ultimately quietist not to have to say something about agents' belief formation. Or consider the worry about incommensurability, discussed by anthropologists and philosophers alike: Can we even begin to think of the criteria for justification if we can't be sure whether the participants, as it were, speak the same language? Again, the Rawlsian answer is to float the political questions away from "comprehensive" conceptions; my point in this chapter and even more in the following ones is that such a conceptual move doesn't get us a handle on political practices.

Consider: I have done a little bit in this chapter to show how a liberal view can pay effective attention to issues of power, but matters of power seem to crop up anew with these questions, at the level of individual belief formation. This is, I want to claim, part of a larger issue, namely, that the agents' social location matters. This includes issues of power, but also of race, gender, class, age, and those other particularities liberals are often accused of forgetting theoretically.[84] It also includes what the agent thinks of herself and what she *feels*. I now turn to those questions, first by thinking about the issues of collective action and then by returning to the questions of standing and justification.

six

ON COLLECTIVE AGENCY

The previous chapter cheerfully presupposed that collectives—in the form of the two movements described—can do things like make arguments. Although the idea squares perfectly well with our ordinary intuitions, it is theoretically controversial. Many liberal theorists are uneasy about collective actors; many others, in turn, just forget the question of the relationship between individual political agents and groups. Anti-liberals, on the other hand, have made much of it. Evoking the Schmittian claims we saw in Chapter 2, one of Mao Zedong's key pieces of advice to political agents is for them to know who their friends and enemies are.[1] Since it does seem intuitively obvious that communities, especially those in which we are thrown together with all sorts of characters—our scholarly colleagues, to continue the Kantian metaphor—do generate groups based on affection and dislike, but also on shared interests, shared histories, and ascription of shared characteristics, something needs to be said about those groups.

In this chapter, I argue that liberal theory can have a robust account of collective political action and that, in fact, such an account is useful. I argue that the best such account is one that conceives of the collective actor as an *agent* similar in many ways to the individual agent this book has described: The collective agent can have its own reasons, goals, and projects, and these are both normatively and explanatorily irreducible to individual agents. I argue that this model both helps explain and successfully justifies such common political practices as alliance formation and compromise as well as symbolic collective action. It follows the liberal conception of a community I defended in the previous chapter, namely, the idea that the community is constructed and not organic; the chapter presents a liberal response to Mao, Schmitt, and other anti-liberals. But it also rejects any "hyperindividualist" liberal model, according to which legitimate collective action only emerges according to individuals' strategic considerations and, even then, is fraught with oppressive potential.

First: Political friends needn't be friends in the way we ordinarily think of friendship. Our private emotions of affection don't have to be deeply involved in political collectives and alliances, and we don't really need to like our friends or hate our enemies. Schmitt is adamant about using the concepts in "concrete and existential sense, not as metaphors or symbols," but that is exactly the point of disagreement here: The liberal conception needn't rely on deeply affective or other kinds of "organic" ties.[2] Aristotle thought that even political friendships among citizens required some feelings of fondness, but I would like, for now, to move a conception into a slightly more Kantian direction: All that is necessary is some degree of respect toward one's political friends, where the respect tracks the reasons one wants the "friendship" in the first place.[3] The next chapter focuses on the role of emotions in a liberal conception of agency; at this point, suffice it to say that, for a liberal, the ties *needn't* be affective, and they aren't affective in the first instance. The general idea about collective action for the liberal is the reasonable observation about strength in numbers. People realize that some political ends are best pursued in collectivities and that the larger the collectivities the greater their power and hence chances of success. However, I argue, the general idea isn't the whole story.

As David Hume observed long ago, people form alliances for other reasons as well. Loyalty to friends, to ancestry, to causes long forgotten may lead a person to forge or to maintain alliances. "Nothing is more usual than to see parties which have begun upon a real difference continue even after that difference is lost," Hume wrote. "When men are once enlisted on opposite sides, they contract an affection to the persons with whom they are united and an animosity against their antagonists, and these passions they often transmit to their posterity."[4] In other words, ties of affection may explain all sorts of political alliances where no search unearths any kinds of interests that are being served by the alliance. Similarly, Hume observed, commitment to a *principle*, rather than the pursuit of one's interests, may be the basis for alliances. Struggles for justice or against injustices of all shapes and sizes have historically fueled many a movement, even when those struggles have been directly contrary to the interests of the participants.[5]

That people have forged alliances for all sorts of reasons doesn't mean that they have been, first, *good* reasons or, second, *liberal* reasons. Hume, in fact, himself argues what the twentieth-century pluralists urged, namely, that interest constitutes the only "real," that is, rational, reason for alliance formation. Those political groupings based on affection toward the people with whom one's ancestors had at some point a "real" reason to unite are at best silly and, at worst, pernicious. It isn't just that the Montagues' and the Capulets' stupid animosity thwarts a beautiful courtship; similar irrational affective ties working their way through religion, national and ethnic identities, and the like still lead neighbors to murder neigbors en masse. Ethnic cleansing in the Balkans or massacres in Africa issue from neither good nor liberal reasons.

Where Have All the Collective Actors Gone?

The most obvious reason liberal theorists have paid scant attention to collective actors is that it isn't in their job description to do so. Standard Anglo-American political philosophy has concerned itself primarily with ideal, or "full-compliance" theory, as I pointed out at the beginning of this part. In full-compliance situations, the intuition goes, there is little need for actors, either individual or collective, to pursue political goals. The intuition is reasonable, and my point isn't to launch any tiresome complaints against ideal theory. As my analysis of Kant's theory in Chapter 4 suggests, ideal theory is not only a perfectly legitimate theoretical endeavor, but it can also inform imperfect-compliance contexts by articulating benchmarks against which the existing political shortcomings can be compared.

At the same time, it is *also* legitimate to ask about the pursuit of political goals, and once that question is off the ground, it becomes meaningful to think about some further reasons why liberals have been so quiet about collective actors. It turns out that in some cases, the silences aren't quite so warranted.

The most important reason is that liberals are uneasy with groups. Given the primacy of some variety of individualism in all liberal doctrines, it makes sense that they resist normative doctrines that put a premium on collective action. Rousseau's general will *is*, as I argued in Chapter 3, a profoundly anti-liberal concept, and models of action based on it sound problematic to anyone who thinks not only individual autonomy but also individual freedom important. The same goes for other classic models of collective action. Even liberals sympathetic to, say, Marxist critiques of capitalist exploitation find much to resist in what Marx recommends. They worry about what happens to individuals *in* the working-class movement conceived of in the Marxist way.

It isn't surprising, then, that insofar as liberals have thought of collective action, they have felt happy with the thinnest possible models. The most common model is very simple and steadfastly centered on the individual: The only grounds on which an individual will join in a collective action are strategic. There is strength in numbers, and if I want x but can't get it myself, I'll join in with others whose interests coincide with mine enough for me to get my hands on x. It is important to realize that interests may *coincide* even if they are different interests. You may be after lower taxes and work for a candidate while I join to bring about campaign finance reform. Also, while our immediate interests may be the same, we might have very different reasons for them. The alliances between the feminist and conservative anti-pornography movements are an example of how different the reasons can be. (I return to this point later.)

In the latter half of the twentieth century, this model became famous as the "pluralist" model of liberal democracy.[6] The pluralism in this model stems from the fact of pluralism principle I introduced in Chapter 1, but its deployment is for the analysis of politics, not for explicitly normative theorizing. One of the central units of analysis in politics is "interest groups," which are simply collections of people pursuing their interests with like-minded others (where the "like-mindedness" means only that the group members' goals coincide).

This pluralist model wasn't entirely new, but just a sophisticated version of a familiar idea from at least the nineteenth century. Although some earlier thinkers were torn between the value of interest group politics and its potentially pernicious effects—the Federalists' worry about "factions" is perhaps the most familiar example of this—the more economically minded liberals in the nineteenth century embraced it wholeheartedly. That set the stage for twentieth-century theorists to develop it either into the pluralist model or into some other variety of relatively thin and generally rational-choice theoretic model.

Liberals' normative misgivings about groups aren't the only reason the thin models have been popular. Even in the explanatory social sciences, there has been a general drift toward disaggregating collectives into a variety of "micro-foundations." The idea is that collective action is seen and therefore explained as aggregations of individual persons' actions. No normative commitment to liberalism has been a prerequisite for these moves. Some Marxists, in fact, have in recent decades opened valuable lines of inquiry into the microfoundations of Marxism and have even managed the controversial but intriguing interpretation of Marx himself as a rational choice theorist.[7] The sound rationale for all this has been the commonsense observation that collective actions do consist of individuals' actions, and that therefore making sense of the individuals goes a long way toward making sense of the collective action.

This doesn't mean that collective actors have disappeared from the social scientific radar screen. In fact, collective action literature has been a thriving area of scholarship in the social sciences particularly since Mancur Olson's tantalizing discovery of the collective action problem—that even when pursuing a set of interests with a like-minded bunch, it is in any given individual's interest to freeride.[8] Much ink has been spilled in the good cause of making sense of the obvious fact that collective actors do exist and successfully pursue a variety of projects. However, the microfoundations focus largely predominates that literature. And normative liberal theorists have been watching on the sidelines.

There are several reasons, however, for why normative theory can and even ought to be more proactive in these matters. One reason is that the micro-foundations focus, just like the pluralist model before it, runs the risk of dropping political agency out of the picture. Politics, in this model, takes place at the collective macro level, but events at that level are really aggregations of individual actions, not exercises of agency qua collective actions. At the same time, the disaggregative microfoundations story is often told in nonpolitical terms. In the classic example, individuals join a revolutionary movement for bread, not freedom.

Not Just for Strategy's Sake

The model of politics and political agency I have developed in this book generates its own reason for a richer account of collective action. No model that understands individuals' engagement in collective action in purely strategic and interest-based terms suffices for a theory of agency that turns on *reasons*. Whether people engage in politics out of interests—self- or otherwise—and whether their considerations are primarily strategic, their *justifications* can't just rest solely on either.

Further, when we think about the varieties of political engagement, it isn't even obvious how everything could usefully be reduced to interests and strategy. Recall the range of political engagements we have seen so far. For example, whatever motivates the environmental justice movements' participants, their arguments are separable from the interests of the persons making the arguments. There are reasonable practical worries about paternalist racism when middle-class whites make environmental justice arguments *on behalf of* poor people of color, but there is nothing incoherent in whites *also* making the arguments.[9]

Or consider the person who wants to walk her talk with Deja Shoes. It is an expression of her political valuation, and if and when that is the point of her action, then it is a secondary consideration whether the action succeeds as a strategy. Of course, we *can* meaningfully talk about "expressive strategies," but whatever they are, they aren't just strategies to bring about some states of affairs, as we saw in Chapter 2. The same goes for expressions of solidarity and condemnation. Recall from Chapter 2 the white environmentalists whose political campaign consisted in shows of solidarity to the Wisconsin Chippewa's right to spearfish. In that case, the environmentalist's interests differed from those of the Native Americans, but this wasn't a problem because their engagement wasn't about interests, but justice.[10]

Consider further the particular form these expressions of solidarity took. The strategy of the white environmentalists was to gather on the lakeshores on fishing nights to bear nonviolent witness to what happened, particularly to whatever the anti-Chippewa protesters might do.[11] "Bearing witness," a political strategy of nonviolent protest developed by Quakers and used dramatically also by Greenpeace, is certainly a strategy, but not one that makes sense without reference to reasons more robust than mere instrumental considerations.[12] So the point isn't that strategy is not a meaningful notion when analyzing the forms some political action takes or when articulating a prescriptive account. Greenpeace represents extremely masterful strategizing, and to suggest otherwise would be to diminish what is perhaps most creative about the organization, which otherwise is politically quite mainstream. But the point is that neither in an explanatory nor in a normative account is it sufficient to say that all relevant considerations by participants are strategic.

This becomes vivid when we return to collective political action. A political agent, I have argued, in principle always confronts a demand for the justification of her action. Whether she offers an interest-based or a purely strategic argument, or perhaps a combination of the two ("I'm joining the Republican Party because there is strength in numbers and because the Republicans are for lower taxes"), she is begging the question if we asked for a political justification. Her reasoning can be part of the justification, especially if we are appropriately disposed and share relevant premises (say, we are fellow Republicans), but it is still only a part. Further, there are cases of individuals' engagement in collective action where that set of considerations is entirely misguided. Individuals can join movements because it is the *right* thing to do, instead of the strategically efficient thing to do, because it is right to belong to some group or to be identified with some particular idea. That explains better the fact that people's engagement and participation in collective action or in movements in general aren't always efficient and that they often last beyond a particular goal orientation. Also, it explains why people sometimes insist on some particular collective that looks, from an instrumental and interest-based perspective, indistinguishable from another one.

My point isn't just to take "what is" as an automatic answer to "what ought to be." One could, of course, argue that regardless of the current ideas about collective engagement, it *should* just be instrumental and based on interests. That is, in fact, what Hobbes (at least in one interpretation) was doing: It wasn't that he thought people rational—they did do crazy things like die for their version of salvation, for example—but that they *ought* to have been. It is also the view that Hume defended: Although people thought they should group themselves in political parties on the basis of principles and affection, they *really*, in Hume's opinion, should just have forged interest-based alliances.[13]

So the point is a stronger one. The expressive conception of politics and the reason-based conception of agency liberals build atop it afford no reasons for restricting the conception of collective political action to instrumental-strategic considerations. The reason for this is simple, and stems from the role justification plays: If there are justified (or justifiable) arguments for noninstrumentally strategic political engagement, then a conception of agency that rules out that kind of engagement is too narrow. If noninstrumental collective action makes sense, then it makes sense, period. In other words, I reject the Humean idea. (Given the historically contingent reasons Hume—and possibly Hobbes—argued for the interest-based views, it is an open question whether they would argue similarly in today's context.)

The question now is what particular conception of collective action *best* squares with the reason-based model of political engagement.

Persons and Movements

I want to evaluate a typology that describes a variety of relationships between individual and collective political action. The criteria for the preferable model are that it (1) incorporates the conception of individual agency I have defended here; (2) coheres with the liberal idea (defended in this book) that justification is central to political action; (3) is empirically adequate, as specified in Chapter 1; and (4) is *political*. In other words, the model can't just show that liberals can live with collectives but, further, that they can live with political collectives.

Note that the typology doesn't describe models for explanatory but for normative purposes. Explanatory models look for *explanans*, grounds that explain phenomena. Usually, these are causes (although there are some, not particularly successful, noncausal explanatory theories around). The normative models are after reasons: The goal is to understand *what kind of reasons* inform (and ideally justify) some type of action. There is a connection between the explanatory and normative purposes, to be sure: The pluralist model I discussed earlier, for example, can serve both. But, at the same time, the adoption of one model for one kind of purpose doesn't determine the model for the other purpose. All that is required of the normative model I am interested in is condition (3), that it be empirically adequate.

Call the first model epiphenomenal. According to this view, collective action should be informed solely by micro-level, or individual, considerations. The fact that micro-level considerations might converge in a way that results in collective action is, in this model, neither here nor there. This model is *not* the same as the instrumental-strategic model I rejected earlier. A person doesn't choose one action because she thinks it might coincide with that of others or because she thinks there is strength in numbers. Second, her action doesn't have to be based on a consideration of her individual *interests*, which the common strategic-instrumental views insist on. It can be based on the principles the person subscribes to, and they needn't have anything to do with her interests. For example, the person who wears Deja Shoes as a political statement of her environmental principles, regardless of the consequences or social meanings of her action, is engaging in political action we can call epiphenomenal at the collective level if, by some coincidence, many people do it at the same time.

Although there are cases where it is intelligible and even defensible to be engaged on purely individual considerations, the epiphenomenal model can hardly be defended as *the* model for political engagement. And, by definition, it is not a satisfactory conception for thinking about collective action since it, in effect, denies it. There is nothing wrong in saying, "I am doing this because it is the right thing to do and for no other reason whatsoever," but it makes little sense to insist on it as the principle on which all political action ought to proceed.

The strategic-instrumental model is another possibility, and although I rejected it earlier, it is worth making a few observations about it. First, although the strategic-instrumental model usually comes combined with the idea that individual interests have priority, it doesn't have to. As the case of Greenpeace suggests, an individual can be committed to values independent of her interests and then engage in collective action out of strategic-instrumental considerations. The model only requires that all collective reasons be understood in instrumental terms, as means to *some* micro-level considerations. Again, the point is not to deny the value of strategic-instrumental considerations in political action, but merely to deny that this is the *only* appropriate model. A political agent ignores strategic considerations at her peril. She needn't, however, limit herself to those.

Note that the strategic-instrumental model corresponds most closely to a rational-choice microfoundations model on the explanatory front. To tell a microfoundations story about a collective action is to give a complete explanation for it. Moreover, since the considerations are purely strategic, all one need assume about agents at the micro level is that they are capable of choosing effective means to the ends they happen to have. This proximity is no coincidence but, as I suggested, neither model entails the other, even in a loose sense of the word. The rational-choice model might be empirically false, but we might nevertheless urge people to engage in collective action only for strategic reasons. Or I might be satisfied that the rational-choice model adequately explains collective action and yet lament this fact, hoping for a social context in which it doesn't. Or, finally, I might think that the rational-choice model powerfully explains at least some collective action but think that insofar as *justification* is concerned, something more than strategic considerations is needed. (The latter is, of course, the view I have been presupposing in this and the previous chapter.)

Move now to models that do accept the possibility of genuine collective agents. At the extreme here is what we might call normative holism. In that view, *only* macro-level considerations, that is, reasons relevant for the collective, are acceptable. It is important to realize that normative holism needn't go hand in hand at all with methodological or explanatory holism. In fact, since the normative holist model still accepts the validity of *reasons* (although it just limits them to the macro level), one could argue that it is entirely inconsistent with classic holist models such as Durkheim's, where reasons of any kind or at any level are motivationally inert. Normative holism, on the other hand, is not inconsistent with the general idea of methodological individualism in explanations.

Rousseau's general will is a textbook case of normative holism. Given Rousseau's illiberalism, we have a reason to wonder whether normative holism can be a useful model of collective action for liberals. It certainly facilitates a robust idea of a collective *agent*, that is, the idea that the collective has its own reasons, projects, goals, and the like, but at a cost that a liberal may find difficult to accept.

It is important to understand that normative holism is not an incoherent idea. Both Rousseau's general will and Schmitt's political theory show that it makes theoretical sense. It is perfectly intelligible as an empirical idea as well. Recall the variety of collective goods I discussed in Chapter 5. There is nothing crazy in thinking that, at least in some contexts, the only relevant *and* legitimate considerations for some action invoke the good of the collective. We do this for the friendship, for the country, for the party, and any other consideration would be inappropriate. But how is that *really* possible, given that on the explanatory front we nevertheless want to tell a microfoundations story about the collective action?

One answer is to point to the existence of social *roles*. As a member of the Communist Party, as a *citoyenne* of Sparta, as an executive of Microsoft, I adopt the goals and values of the collective agent and let them generate the reasons for my action.[14] This isn't psychologically implausible: People are capable of internalizing norms that say they oughtn't let their individual considerations inform their reasoning as parts of the collective agency. As a private citizen, the former New York governor Mario Cuomo opposed abortion; as a governor he upheld women's legal right to it. Further, anyone skeptical of the psychological plausibility of this kind of role internalization can be reassured by noting that these roles don't only depend on people's psychological abilities; they also get help from enforced sanctions. Here, we have another way in which the Montesquieuian institutional solutions get worked into the theory. Whether I personally care about the goals of my employer, I will lose my job if I don't play my part appropriately. In that case, the microfoundations story obviously would end up invoking individual interests, but at one remove: *Just* to talk about my interests would be insufficient. (We might observe, as an aside about explanation, that this means that a *reductionist* microfoundations explanation, that is, the one that invokes only micro-level considerations, can be incomplete in many cases.)

So normative holism simply means that the role I have by virtue and as a member of the collective is not immediately connected to my "purely individual" considerations. The specific lack of connection is in the *reasons* offered at the individual and collective levels.

This actually suggests that normative holism in general needn't be illiberal. There are many collective endeavors where the reasons at the individual and collective levels are very different. Unless one is prepared to say that having a job is profoundly illiberal, it seems intuitively obvious that in many spheres of social activity, normative holism is a perfectly common and benign phenomenon, and nothing a liberal can't accept. There are, of course, limits, and many of our ordinary intuitions track those limits. Many of us think, for example, that whistle-blowing—acting against the demands of some specific role out of an individual conviction—ought to be permitted. But I don't become a whistle-blower when I realize that my individual reasons differ from the reasons of the collective agent I serve; I become a whistle-blower in cases where there is some *particularly egregious* discrepancy.

Things get a little trickier when we start talking about political action, however. The reasons are theoretical and political. First, if an agent's individual reasons for her adopting a role as part of the collective don't count, as normative holism says they don't, then there are no grounds on which we can take the individual to be exercising the same political agency as the collective agent. Of course, what she does *as* part of the collective agency is political, but if we don't care about her individual reasons, then she is not political as an individual.

Why is this a problem? Simply because of the value liberals put on individual autonomy. At least if we take the variety of liberal theory I have advocated here seriously—that individuals must be able to conceive of themselves as autonomous political agents—then an account that ignores their *political* considerations is simply unacceptable as a general model.

Again, this doesn't mean that all cases of collective political agency where the individuals aren't political agents are illegitimate. There is nothing fundamentally illiberal about someone choosing to work for a political party, say, simply because she needs money, and not because she shares the party's commitments. To deny that possibility would, in fact, be illiberal. But that relationship shouldn't be the rule for thinking about the connection between individual and collective agency in politics.

At this point, I want to remind the reader that my discussion of "roles" that "individuals" adopt shouldn't be understood to imply some kind of presocial identity. I rejected that idea in Chapter 3, and there is no reason to think it is being smuggled back in. Roles aren't masks we can strip to find the "pure individual"; I follow Simmel's view according to which an individual is a particular unique nexus of social roles and other affiliations.[15] All my distinction between the individual and the role points to is that a role carries with itself *specific* norms and considerations, whereas the individual's norms and considerations stem from the unique nexus of roles and affiliations a person happens to follow. To be an individual is to be, say, a father and a husband and a recreational rock-climber and a chess club president and a journalist and to take all those roles into account when thinking about what to do. To play the part in the particular role of a journalist is to bracket, at least to a great extent, those other considerations. When I act in a particular role, the considerations are still mine in that I have adopted them; the question at issue is what *other* considerations have led me to adopt that role. The argument against normative holism is that it ignores such considerations *before* a person adopts a role.

Note that Kant's slightly unusual understanding of "private" and "public" described in Chapter 4 helps this account. Kant's distinction allows us to track roles in the manner I am doing there. That is also why mapping the individual/role distinction onto the private/public dichotomy would be a bad idea.

The ideal liberal picture is one I call an *interactionist* one. It resembles normative holism in the sense that it allows for collective agency but, at the same time, regards the individual's pre-role reasons as important. Finally—the reason for the name of the conception—it incorporates the idea that an individual's adoption of a particular role in a collective agency has an effect on who she is, but, at the same time, the individual's considerations have an effect on the collective.

The interactionist model has different variants. The most straightforward, almost trivial one (one that informed my critique of normative holism) is that I join in a collective action because my individual political goals and reasons for action coincide with the goals and reasons the collective has. (And they needn't just be strategic, which is why the strategic-instrumental model won't suffice.) I may join the Communist Party USA even when I know a socialist revolution is not in the cards because I want to make a statement about politics and take the CPUSA to be doing just that. This differs from normative holism: Since individual reasons matter, they serve as a check on what can count as legitimate reasons at the collective level. The collective agent's reasons and goals are partly independent of individuals' reasons—they are not *reducible* to individuals' reasons (I'll say more about this shortly)—but they nevertheless *also* depend on them. To say that individual reasons matter, as the interactionist model does, is to suggest that I have a say about the role I adopt, not only in terms of whether I adopt it, but also what it looks like.

The collective agent's goals and reasons aren't reducible to individual agents' goals and reasons either in explanatory or normative terms. As I have suggested, considerations at the collective level may play an explanatory role for the individual, both for her motives and for her reasons. The collective goals and reasons may help the individual articulate her own reasons. There is nothing mysterious about this; the point is none other than the one made in Chapters 4 and 5: Some collective level arrangements make possible new modes of being. I may consider myself a communist even if the Communist Party is, say, banned, but I won't be able to be a Communist, and there is a difference. This isn't a fancy metaphysical claim: The new modes of being I am talking about have concrete social consequences. At the same time, the new modes constitute a change in *who* the person is.

Third, although the interactionist model looks for overall coherence between reasons and goals at the individual and collective levels, it doesn't require an identity between considerations at the two levels. This, too, should be virtually trivial: The pursuit of justice by the environmental justice movement may also constitute my personal pursuit, but *how* it informs me and what considerations for action it entails for me are likely to be very different from those at the collective level. Collectives can be agents, but they are different kind of agents from individual ones. Agency simply isn't only a feature of individuals, and to call collectives agents is not to talk about some metaphorical persons. *Pace* Hobbes, a collective agent is not an "Artificiall man." The difference isn't merely strategic, that collective agents pursue ends with different means than individuals. The differences can involve straightforwardly normative considerations about, say, what is *appropriate* for an agent to do. I may, for example, be a member of a feminist political movement, have a legitimate role in it, and share the movement's goals and reasons, but it may nevertheless be inappropriate for me, as a man, to engage in some particular actions, and not just because it might be bad PR. It may *also* be bad PR, but it may undermine the principles of the movement in much deeper ways. (This doesn't, of course, mean that men can't act on feminist causes, only that there may be some instances where they shouldn't.) Consider the reasoning by an organizer's husband in Mothers of East Los Angeles (MELA), an environmental justice movement: "I have no role; I'm part of a coalition. My wife is involved with MELA. They have put up a successful fight. All I can do is back my wife up. I can't be a Mother of east L.A., since I'm a man. They should have control. They have started this fight. Personally, I believe that no one priest or no one man should be in charge."[16] Of course, given my conceptualization, this man does have a role; he is "part of a coalition" where his "backing his wife up" is a normatively appropriate role.

"Appropriate" shouldn't be taken to imply that the man is somehow put in his place by some external norms, but that, given his *own* understanding, the appropriate role for him is a supportive one. Call this self-understanding "personal microfoundations": It is a person's making sense to herself of her involvement with the collective agent. And all that the liberal interactionist model requires is that my personal microfoundations cohere politically with the collective goals.

New Social Movements

While the need for an account of collective agency and the interactionist model I have offered may be new to normative liberal theory, they have close relatives in social scientific literature. The so-called New Social Movement (NSM) theory has defended a similar position for some decades now. I want to spend some time highlighting some of the similarities and, more importantly, the differences between my model and the NSM theory.

The NSM theory has been regarded as a response to the so-called "resource mobilization" paradigm in collective action literature. The resource mobilization view, which emerged originally in the 1960s and which was developed in now classic works by Charles Tilly and others, explained collective action in terms roughly similar to what I have called the strategic-instrumental model: Particular forms of collective action were understood as rational, strategic deployment of available resources by instrumentally rational agents. Among other things, the advocates of the NSM model saw the resource-mobilization paradigm as too narrow; the central idea was (roughly) that people join particular movements not only because available resources make it an efficient means to a given end but also out of a range of thicker reasons.[17]

The idea of the NSM theory as a response to the resource-mobilization paradigm is, at best, historical shorthand. The two approaches to social and collective action are partly historically parallel, the former having enjoyed prominence particularly in Europe and the latter in North America. Also, the two approaches have different goals. The resource-mobilization theory is more conventionally explanatory, while many NSM theorists inherit critical theory's normative preoccupations. However, as I am not concerned with details of intellectual history here, the shorthand suffices.

It is ambiguous what the attribute "new" in the New Social Movement theory denotes. The NSM party line, insofar as one can talk of anything like a party line with a diverse set of theories, is that the movements themselves are new. The other view is that it is merely the theory that is new. The idea for the former is that, toward the end of the twentieth century, a new kind of civil society emerged at least in Western democracies, and that this civil society, in turn, both created the need for and facilitated new kinds of movements. Where the "old" social movements were, according to the NSM theory, concerned primarily with strategies to achieve concrete and well-defined goals—higher wages, better laws, cleaner air—the new social movements emerged in "postmaterial" conditions and were interested in "identity creation" and "lifestyle politics."[18] The new movements mobilized to take advantage of and create spaces in which people could engage in self-fashioning of various kinds. For example, in this view, "new" feminist movements were just as much about new kinds of identity formation as about getting rid of sex and gender discrimination; movements by people of color as much about new forms of racial and ethnic identity as about racial justice, narrowly construed; environmental movements as much about ecological lifestyles as about pollutant-free air.

While the transformations in Western industrial societies may indeed have increased the "social spaces" for movement activity that isn't immediately strategic or after material goals, one doubts whether the divide is so stark that the NSMs really represent something radically new. It is virtually trivial that social movement activity in general, not only among postmaterial Western middle classes, has "identity effects," that is, effects on the participants' sense of who they are, who they want to be, and so on. Furthermore, often this is far from a byproduct; it can be closely connected to the concrete goals of the movements. Working-class consciousness and working-class identity are merely the most obvious examples of this. And even where the effects of movement activity may be a byproduct in the sense that it hasn't been articulated as a goal, it can be politically significant and even constitutive of the further political direction of the movement. For example, as Michael McCann has shown in his study of American women's pay equity movement—surely an old-fashioned "strategic" "resource-mobilization" goal if anything is—the emancipatory effects of the organizing activity were significant even when the movement failed to reach its concrete goals.[19]

My point is, then, that what, if anything, is "new" here is the theorizing, not the movements themselves. *That* aspect of the NSM theory coheres with my interactionist model of individual and collective political action. Where my account differs is on the question of how one can call many of the postmaterialist social movements political. It isn't because they are concerned about "identity"— say, about the importance of *being queer*, as opposed to the importance of achieving the *right* to marry for gays and lesbians—that they might not be political. Being queer, fashioning new gender identities (or getting rid of them) by making "gender trouble," and achieving "ecological identity"[20] are ways of being political, and they can be well-articulated and defensible political *goals*. But that's exactly what the interactionist model insists on: Political articulation—political *reasons*—must be available, and it must be plausible. Pure identity orientation or, perhaps more strongly, pure lifestyle orientation can fail to be political, regardless of how much of a social movement activity it embraces if it can't be articulated in political terms. This is the lesson from Chapter 2.

Put this in terms of a distinction we owe to Jon Elster.[21] Political activity can be conceived of on a "market" model or on a "forum" model. On the market view, politics is about achieving some particular ends on more or less strategic grounds. (In Elster's recent thought, the tendency seems be toward the "less.") On the forum model, on the other hand, political action resembles an idealized version of the Greek polis where the very goal is to engage in a deliberation of The Good itself, rather than the pursuit or even deliberation of any *antecedent* goals.[22] While my account resembles the forum model in some ways, it does of necessity, as the account in Chapter 4 should convey, presuppose *some* antecedent goal. A social movement activity that is purely self-referential—just about identity or a pursuit of a lifestyle for its own sake—isn't political. Its reasons needn't only be concrete goals, but they need to be political. To put this in less abstract terms: Generation X youth's rave parties may be a "new social movement" that is political if it can plausibly be articulated in political terms. That requires, among other things, that it embraces a lifestyle that is a claim about some legitimate authority.

Alliances and Compromises

The virtue of the interactionist model lies not in its difference from or resemblance to some other theoretical position but in the fact that it helps make sense of actual, ordinary movement practices. I want to consider moves commonly made and also commonly rejected by political movements. (I talk about "moves" to avoid having to use the term "strategy" simply because of its particular substantive connotations in this context.) These moves are the formation of alliances between political movements as well as other kinds of willingness to compromise. One question is how to make normative sense of (and not merely explain) alliance formation between, say, ideologically oppositional movements that happen to share some immediate goal. A few examples: the alliances between anti-pornography feminists and religious conservatives to enact prohibitions against pornography; the alliances between environmentalists and industrial labor unions against supernational trade organizations such as the World Trade Organization (WTO); the alliances between progressive and nationalist movements against the European Union in countries contemplating joining the union.

I raise these questions because they are ones where the strategic-instrumental model seems to shine most brightly. When we ask why feminists would ally with religious conservatives against pornography—or, more poignantly, when the participants in a feminist anti-pornography movement ask themselves why they ought to forge such an alliance—the strategic-instrumental model offers a ready answer: because it makes strategic sense. It's simply an extension of the principle that there is strength in numbers. The same goes for other compromises.

Again, my point is not to reject the eminent sensibility of these strategic considerations. I want to reject the strategic-instrumental *model.* That is to say that focusing only on these considerations actually doesn't make normative sense of what political movements do.

The reason is simple. Deliberation on what the strategic goals ought to be and on whether and what boundary conditions limit their pursuit has to be extrastrategic. There must be *reasons* for why in this particular case this alliance with the unsavory partner is acceptable and why it might not be in another case or with another potential ally.

Consider three collective players in the 1999 demonstrations against the WTO in its ministerial conference in Seattle. The WTO meeting was opposed, among others, by a variety of environmental organizations; by organized labor, including conventional large industrial unions such as the United Steel Workers of America (USWA) and the International Brotherhood of Teamsters; and by an enigmatic but well-organized collection of people who called themselves anarchists.[23] Each had a fundamental opposition to the WTO in general. For the environmentalists, the liberalization of global trade purely on the basis of economic principles left important environmental considerations unaccounted for and thus in jeopardy. The labor organizations worried about the rights of organized labor on similar grounds. The anarchists professed opposition to the very idea of global economic liberalization because of its general costs to the environment and to people.[24] At the same time, there were great differences. Labor and environmentalists, in particular, haven't seen eye-to-eye on many issues in history, especially when it comes to large industries. Yet, during the week of demonstrations and other protests, labor activists and environmentalists were marching, sometimes literally, hand in hand, while the anarchists alienated many people, including several sympathizers.

To suggest that one can make sense of this just by thinking about strategy is too simple. First, while the labor–environmentalist alliance was, in many ways, a show of collective unity, it remained uneasy in some cases at the individual level. While one could chalk up some uneasiness to generational and class differences—a young green-haired environmentalist dressed as a sea turtle might not square with the stylistic sensibilities of a stereotypical middle-aged truck driver—some individuals expressed more explicit principled concerns about the reasons their allies had.[25] Second, while the anarchists' alienation from many other protest groups looked like a *result* of their willingness to engage in large-scale vandalism and chaos generation—a strategy disagreement—the anarchists' *reason for* this strategy involved their belief that an alliance with the other movements would be a compromise of their fundamental principles because it would be an alliance with "the accomplices of the system."[26] And, of course, the overwhelming rejection of the anarchists' strategies by the other groups was a combination of views according to which they were counterproductive *and* wrong. So the strategic-instrumental model would beg the explanatory question and would leave the participants' self-understandings—the normative stuff—quite obscure.

Now what is the connection to the interactionist model? The interactionist model helps make sense of the combination of strategy and reasons by locating the two types of considerations at the different levels of agency in different ways. Think of the matter from an agent-centered perspective. An individual steelworker, say, finds himself considering how he should relate to the WTO meeting taking place in his hometown, Seattle. His union, USWA, has taken an official stance against the WTO, most recently because of the extension of a WTO membership in China. USWA's official rhetoric combines concern for the economic effects of the move on American workers and outrage at the Chinese treatment of labor.[27] The rhetoric may or may not reflect this individual worker's views, but he endorses it in principle. USWA also plans demonstrations, some jointly with environmental and Third World human rights organizations. Although he is leery of environmentalists—both because he finds them middle-class hypocrites and because he knows some goals some environmentalists have may be in conflict with those of industrial production—he can accept the strategic alliance at the collective level. And, finally, because of that, he understands that qua a union member he can put aside those individual reasons when he marches with green-haired sea turtles. The "compromise" is not a compromise of his reasons, but his playing his strategic part as suggested by the reasons at the collective level.

Furthermore, the virtue of this model is that it also allows for *errors* that aren't merely strategic. An alliance or some other kind of compromise can turn out to have been a mistake not only on strategic grounds. For example, the principled disagreements between two movements may be so large that no alliance succeeds, despite clear shared goals. During their early and mid-1990s push for membership in the European Union, many countries' "No to EU" movements tended to consist of two rather disparate groups. On the one side, were progressives who worried about the overwhelming weight of economic grounds for unification, especially in the pre-Maastricht situation, which they saw as threatening environmental regulations, the welfare state, workers' rights, and similar issues. On the other side, were conservative and even xenophobic movements that resisted the invasion of a supernational body and the likely increase in "dirty foreigners," crime, and the general erosion of national power. While there were points of contact, in many cases these movements kept their distance, often on principled grounds. When they didn't, many activists regarded the temporary alliances as great mistakes.[28] Or, to take another example, many feminists, even among anti-pornography feminists themselves, think that the alliance between feminists and religious conservatives to get anti-porn laws enacted are great mistakes, regardless of the outcomes. This is because the two have profoundly different reasons: The feminist anti-pornography argument turns on conceptions of wrongdoing to women, the conservative one on notions of obscenity. Of course, again, there may be points of contact in these reasons, but they are nevertheless largely different.

This view that errors can be accounted for nonstrategically can naturally be challenged: One can argue that there isn't anything to be said beyond the strategic considerations, and that anyone who laments their unholy alliance or a humiliating compromise is being irrational. But note that when this takes place in an actual situation, between the principled nostalgic and a strategic pragmatist, the latter's argument amounts to *reasons*. And it is an open question whether the reasons are convincing. An alliance with someone—say, a Nazi—may be *wrong,* and not just because it's a bad strategy. The liberal Kantian account that is the engine of the interactionist model helps make sense of all this.

None of this is to suggest that there always are some principles that are sacred. Sometimes there are, but as I suggest in the concluding chapter, my view is that those cases are *appropriately* rarer than we would like. All I want to insist on here is (1) that the question of *whether* and *what* compromises collective agents make is extrastrategic and (2) that the interactionist model offers fruitful ways of understanding of how the reasoning on those considerations might go.

Conclusion

The argument of this chapter is that the idea of collective political agency makes perfect sense. And although there are important differences between collective and individual agents, there is also overlap that allows us to analyze some aspects of collectives' exercise of agency in the same terms as we analyze that of individuals. Talk of reasons that are irreducible to something more "basic" is the most important commonality for my purposes.

At the same time, as this chapter also argued, this thesis about the validity of collective agency also complicates things. It opens a new area of analysis, namely, the relationship between the individual agents and collectives. The best normative way to understand the relationship for the liberal model I am advocating is the interactionist model I have described. It is a model that allows for the importance of political reasons both at the individual and collective levels and makes sense of their relationship.

Again, however, the account has been schematic, and it does not address the concrete questions of power and other situational contingencies that I identified as complications to the idea of justification at the end of the previous chapter. In other words, where my account of justification in Chapter 5 didn't account for the difference power inequalities make, my position in this chapter hasn't accounted for *how* individual differences affect individuals' relationship to political collectives. The earlier example about the difference roles make in movements shows only that they can be accounted for, but not how.

So there are both good and liberal reasons for alliance formation on non-interest-based grounds. (And we shouldn't romanticize interest-based alliances in contrast to the other ones since interests obviously have also gotten implicated in all manner of nastiness.) There is nothing illiberal about alliance formation on the grounds of a political principle or value, and, as Chapter 5 should show, there are good reasons to be committed to a host of values that are at least partly independent of an individual's interests. Northern abolitionists, the white environmentalists in support of the Wisconsin Native Americans' right to fish, or the Angry White Guys for Affirmative Action aren't about the pursuit of self-interest, but all have perfectly defensible liberal reasons for their movements.

But it isn't just the shared end—be it principled, such as justice, or interest-based—that tells the whole story of these and similar alliances as alliances, nor is it just the idea that there is strength in numbers. Membership in an alliance can be an important marker of an exercise of agency. It is a way of identifying oneself, just as the wearing of Deja Shoes, as we saw in Chapter 2 is a way of identifying oneself with a political cause or a principle. In some cases, then, *being* something, say, a member of a coalition or a party or a movement, is an exercise of agency, regardless of what one *does*.

All this means that we need to begin asking questions about how we should conceive of individual agents. Specifically, I want to look for criteria for deciding who counts as an individual agent and under what circumstances. That is the goal of the next chapter.

seven

WHO IS AN AGENT?

My account of the political entails, as we have seen, that all political action requires justification. In principle, that is. In practice, if we want it to square with any intuitions we have about politics, the requirement gets served with a list of conditionals: An agent should be able to justify an action or a position in a suitable setting, and that suitable setting might be different from the context of the action. I needn't justify myself to a rabid throng of anti-abortion protesters when I'm defending a Planned Parenthood clinic, but if I can't, in some less volatile situation, offer any good reasons for my action, my action is unintelligible. And I don't have to tell the election officials why I want to vote for Barney Frank, but if I don't have any reasons for my choice, my voting makes a mockery of electoral politics. When and how a justification ought to be offered depends on all sorts of considerations. Some of them are strategic, but there are also substantively normative ones. Also, as Montesquieu's theory reminds us, our human foibles often make it necessary to ensure the proper justificatory contexts by institutional solutions. The secrecy of the ballot, for example, exists to ensure that citizens can in fact make their choices for good reasons and to prevent illegitimate factors from entering the process.

Recall the story so far. I have defended the Kantian conception of public reason as a model for the exercise of liberal politics: A liberal political agent is one who addresses others within the requirements of public reason. But that account still seems awfully abstract, and as the previous chapters began to show, politics can't be quite as simple as that learned intercourse among scholars. We have seen that the question of justification is complicated by a host of contingent facts about the social context, and the Kantian model, even with a little help from Montesquieu, is put to real task to deal with such contingencies. To show that the model nevertheless can function in political practice, I now want to dig deeper and consider the question of *who counts* as a political agent. The theoretically straightforward answer—everyone within the relevant justificatory community—only begs the question, as I show in this chapter. It leaves open the question of how we draw the boundaries of a justificatory community. First, I explore the "outer" boundary of a justificatory community. I consider a radical but prima facie plausible proposal to extend the boundaries of the justificatory community beyond humanity, reject it, and argue for a qualified anthropocentrism. Second, I take up the question of what kinds of engagement might still exclude some humans from membership in a justificatory community. The trickiest issue for any Kantian model is emotional engagement, and my discussion focuses on whether and how affective agency can be politically legitimate.

Boundaries of Justificatory Community: The Question of Scope

If political justification always takes place in a social context—things get justified *to* someone—there ought to be some criteria for the relevant social context. It is not immediately obvious who gets to count among the relevant "someone," and the question is far from trivial. As G. A. Cohen's example from the introduction to this part suggests, I may be able to justify my policy proposal to all those who agree with me quite easily, but it is unlikely that *everyone* to whom I *should* justify it agrees with me. At the same time, it seems both reasonable and intuitively obvious that not everyone gets to count. I might find the social policies of, say, Ethiopia quite unfair, but it does not mean that the Ethiopian government owes a justification to *me*. Philippa Foot suggests in a usefully analogous discussion of approval and disapproval that for someone to disapprove of another's project, the former must have *standing* of a relevant kind.[1] Standing can come from a particular bond between those concerned—they might be parents and children, for example—or from some shared ends.[2] These are regulated by social norms: by norms of convention, morality, law, and so on. Importantly, however, to put it in terms familiar from the previous chapters, the boundaries of the relevant political community or membership in it are not obvious; what seems at least intuitively right is that agents' subjective ideas about that do not settle the matter.

One potentially attractive and at least conceptually straightforward solution for this boundary problem is to say that justification is owed to all within the scope of the relevant norms, "to all who have to live under" the regime in question.[3] NIMBYs owe a justification not just to those who agree with them but to others under the scope of the same norms, and in these cases those norms are the norms that guide public policies. Of course, given the overlapping sets of norms in the real world, part of the puzzle in concrete cases will be to find ways of making sense of the fact that the different sets of norms have different scopes. The overlapping scopes of federal and state rules make for a relatively neat example of this phenomenon which can get very muddy. But the conceptual idea at least gets us going.

The problem, however, is that even if the question of overlapping scopes gets postponed until later, to the pragmatic stage, the idea calls for some serious sharpening. First, it is not obvious what it means to be "under the scope of (the relevant) norms." The very same boundary and membership problems pop up again. In fact, they not only pop up but look even more intractable than before because, as we will see, it isn't clear that the scope of norms is limited to other agents or even humans.

The Question of Standing: An Argument for Anthropocentrism

Consider the theoretical idea that justification is owed to all who live under the relevant regime. Who is this "who"? It isn't just your textbook agents, rational and reasonable able-bodied adult humans: There are children and severely disabled people, for example; moreover, there are animals, future generations, perhaps even inanimate nature. All will, to take the idea literally, have to *live* under the regime. At the same time, if we wish to maintain that justification is a type of communication, it seems that justification cannot be offered to the members in those groups. We can hardly even talk of members of groups in some cases.

The theoretical intuition is that *a being*, perhaps even a thing, may have a political *standing* regardless of his, her, or its agency. Historically, claims about agency and standing have often gone together, but they needn't (and haven't always). To be sure, Aldo Leopold exhorted us to "think like a mountain" to learn to consider the interests of nonhuman nature, but in most cases the arguments about the political standing of nonhuman beings do not appeal to the agency of these beings. The general question is how the nonagents who will live under the norms are to be accounted for.

The case of future generations escapes some of the problems. There is a sense in which we can talk about justification being offered to future generations: That is, they can reject and revise the norms and their justifications we leave as a legacy to them. They can revise our laws, even constitutions. At the same time, it is obvious that what our generation does will have an effect on the future generations, such a profound effect in fact that what those future people will be like—or whether they are going to be there in the first place—depends in part on the choices preceding generations make. Who they are and what their options will be depend so much on preceding generations that it is still useful, although of course very difficult, to think of them more as nonagents to whom justification cannot be offered directly but whose interests may nevertheless count somehow.

The problem is a tricky one, especially for liberalism. One possible conception of liberalism is to see it as being based on a kind of social epistemology: That there is no single truth about the best mode of life and, therefore, the perspective of all provides the most reliable account. This, further, results in the liberal-democratic norm that all must have a say in the organization of social arrangements. But this very epistemology hits liberalism particularly hard when it encounters beings that can't have a *say*. A theory that is skeptical about anyone claiming to speak for someone else has no immediate response in cases where we don't know how to discover the interests of those who can't express their interests. The environmentalist charge that liberalism is just another form of chauvinist communitarianism—anthropocentric "speciesism" in favor of humans—is not without some bite.

One strategy people sympathetic to this worry have tried is to render the de facto nonagents *hypothetical* agents. The deep ecologist's exhortation to "think like a mountain" isn't all that different from the attempts to accommodate future generations and nonhuman animals into political argumentation (and not just into arguments). Adjustments to the contents of Rawls's justificatory mechanism, the original position, are an illustrative example, both in terms of the promise it offers and the problems it nevertheless fails to overcome.

To deal with the problem of so-called intergenerational justice, the general idea is to make not only the social location but also the *historical* location of the parties in the original position fall behind the veil of ignorance (although Rawls himself rejects this construction[4]). If I don't know where I am in the history of a polity, the "maximin" heuristic that is supposed to have me opt for the two principles of justice will also, on the further stages of the deliberative process, try to make "those who come after" as well off as possible. But as Brian Barry compellingly argues, the idea is fraught with difficulties. First, since preceding generations' actions make a difference as to who—or whether anyone—comes after, the original position begins to look rather messy: an original position in which all generations who might have existed will include parties who don't know whether they actually existed and what sorts of choices made them nonexistent.[5] Second, there is the problem that if one thinks of justice in terms of mutual advantage of all parties concerned—"convenient articles of peace," in Hobbes's words[6]—the idea doesn't even get off the ground: There is no obvious mutual advantage across generations since backward-looking benefits are difficult to conceive of.[7] The damage future generations can do to our reputations is, while possibly important to some, nevertheless orders of magnitude different from the power we hold over future generations. One way for me to assure that my grandchildren won't think ill of me is not to have children.

Similarly badly, Barry argues, would fare attempts to extend the original position to include animals, although for slightly different reasons. The normative leverage we get from imagining we didn't know what species we belonged to is nothing in addition to what we humans already know about the interests of nonhuman animals and other species: "Once we concede that bears suffer from bear-baiting we have the basis for condemning the practice. To say that if I were a bear I would suffer is to say *no more* than that bears suffer, but it weakens the force of that assertion about bears by obtruding puzzles about cross-species identity."[8] Extending to animals the kind of rational agency we so far have limited to humans grinds hypothetical deliberation to a halt until we know what it is like to be a bear. The same goes, I suggest, for other similar attempts.

I am saying, then, that there is something different in the historical denial of political standing to women and people of other races and lower classes, on the one hand, and the denial of political standing to much nonhuman nature on the other. At the same time, I don't want to deny that nonhuman nature ought to be within the scope of political (and moral) concerns; further, it is possible that, say, some higher primates might even have *some* kind of political standing eventually. My point is merely that imaginary agency is not the way to go about it.

Given the difficulties with the hypothetical approaches—and given the fact that so far they have been relatively marginal in on-the-ground disputes—it is not surprising that especially those more actively engaged in the actual disputes have sought more straightforward routes to protect and to serve nonhuman nature. I want to explore a more pragmatically prominent strategy, one that we could call the argument from interest. There are several kinds of arguments; I focus on what I regard as a representative sample. I am not, in this context, interested in the philosophical merits of these arguments and I won't try to settle any disputes here. My primary aim is to think about what they say about the possible boundaries of justificatory communities. To put it simply, I am interested in considering *how* disputes involving nonhuman nature would be settled.

A now classic version of the argument from interest is Christopher Stone's "Should Trees Have Standing."[9] The argument is significant both for its ambition—Stone develops an argument for concrete legal *rights* for natural objects, both animals and plants, out of their having an interest-based standing—and for its influence: Supreme Court justices William Douglas, William Brennan, and Harry Blackmun, for example, have found Stone's argument at least partly compelling.[10] My rendition here does not do justice to the nuances of Stone's argument, but will suffice for our purposes:

(1) For something to hold a legal right,
    (a) there is a public authoritative body prepared to give it some amount of review; and
    (b) it has recognized dignity and worth *in itself*, that is
        (i) legal action can be instituted *at its behest*;
        (ii) the court must be attentive to *injuries to the thing*; and
        (iii) relief must run to *its* benefit.[11]
(2) (1)(a) is just an operational criterion which depends on the satisfaction of the factual criteria in (1)(b); so, if all the criteria of (1)(b) are satisfied, then (1)(a) ought to obtain.
(3) It is an established legal principle that (1)(b)(i) doesn't require that the thing *itself* institute legal action or even be competent or able to do so.[12] In my terms, agency is not required for something to count as a rights-holder.
(4) Both ordinary intuitions and scientific evidence support the idea that we can make sense of injuries and of what is beneficial to non-human living things: we can and do know many things which make animals and plants suffer and which promote their lives.
(5) So non-human living things, in addition to humans, satisfy the requirements of (1)(b).
Therefore, (1)(a) ought to obtain for non-human living things.

For our interests here, the most intriguing aspect is Stone's solution to the problem of agency. "One ought, I think," he says, "to handle the legal problems of natural objects as one does the problems of legal incompetents—human beings who have become vegetable."

> If a human being shows signs of becoming senile and has affairs that he is de jure incompetent to manage, those concerned with his well being make such a showing to the court, and someone is designated by the court with the authority to manage the incompetent's affairs. The guardian ... then represents the incompetent in his affairs.... On a parity of reasoning, we should have a system in which, when a friend of a natural object perceives it to be endangered, he can apply to a court for the creation of a guardianship.[13]

The notion of de jure guardians for the interests of mute rights-bearers is not only legally plausible, perhaps even compelling, but also consistent with the political commonplace that much of politics is *representative*. And if that is the case, why couldn't some of it represent the interests of nonhuman beings? To broaden this idea, then, beyond the specifically legal context to politics in general and to the topic of this chapter, we could say that political justification about nonagents is owed to their guardians. Just as parents get to argue about matters pertaining to their underage children, the guardians of nonhuman beings get to argue about matters pertaining to those whom they represent. All that is needed is the idea of injury and benefit. And it is not an abuse of ordinary intuitions to talk of these as amounting to the thing's interests.

At the same time, there *is* a point at which talking of interests in anything more than highly abstract terms might become difficult. Whether the problem is conceived of in epistemic terms (we have no way of knowing what the interests of some very different lifeforms are) or conceptual (consider, say, lifeforms where the boundaries of an individual being are blurry, or very low levels of lifeforms), it sets constraints on how the idea of interests gets used. A close relative of the argument from interest aims to avoid this problem. Rather than developing an argument for the "worth" or "dignity" of a thing *from* its having interests, as Stone does, this view *begins* with the assumption of a thing's intrinsic worth and infers a political or legal standing from that.

Deep ecology, which philosophers and aestheticians will recognize as resembling G. E. Moore's and his Bloomsbury friends' intuitionism, is the most common form of this kind of valuation.[14] This is because those who hold these views tend to be critics of anthropocentrism and want to reject theories of value that say something has value if we, or somebody, value it. Rather, they postulate the value to be an objective property of the value bearer, something it has regardless of the existence of valuers. Some disagree on whether the value is intrinsic, that is, something the bearer has independently of *anything* else, or extrinsic, by virtue, say, of its being a part of an ecosystem that is seen as intrinsically valuable, but both converge on the objectivity of value.

Whatever one thinks of the metaphysics that underwrites this sort of intuitionism, it leads to practical difficulties. Those difficulties are familiar from the realm of aesthetics, which isn't surprising at all, given the aesthetic inspiration of the Bloomsbury-style intuitionism. The most obvious question is, Who gets to count as an authority about the value? Who perceives, conceives, or intuits the value of nonhuman natural objects? Or, to put it slightly differently, what would it be like to know the value? People certainly have all sorts of *attitudes* toward nonhuman natural objects, but to pick out of the great variety of those attitudes the "right" ones without some a priori conception is impossible. Given that there are disagreements about the values, the intuitionist approach seems paralyzing. (The nonliberal way out of the paralysis is simply to *decide* you are right; I discuss that later on.)

It might seem obvious that the intuitionist arguments run into these problems, but even the more straightforward argument from interest encounters them as well. Consider: If the argument for an object's political standing is based on interests, that is, on intelligible and at least in principle epistemically accessible notions of injury and benefit to the object in question, we get a conception that extends beyond objects that can be easily individuated—for example, to species of animals or plants. It makes perfect sense to talk about the interests of an ecosystem or a "bioregion." And often the interests of the members of some specific species within an ecosystem may be exactly opposite from those of the system. It would be a crude anthropomorphism to apply our *intraspecies* principle of individuating rights-bearers to nonhuman natural objects, especially if, ex hypothesi, we are talking about nonagents.

My point is not to use this to defend some thoroughgoing skepticism or relativism; I don't think such a conclusion would be warranted. One can quickly notice that Stone's approach to expanding the notion of rights to nonhuman nature has a quick response to this worry: The rights he expounds just entitle the object to its day in court. The account can allow both ecosystems *and* individual species to be rights-bearers; it is for the legal—or political—processes to render a verdict on whose or what rights make the weightiest claims.

Of course, the quick response is perhaps a little too quick, and it actually points to a weakness in Stone's account of what it means to be a rights-bearer. For surely one's day in court is just one aspect of the things one is entitled to when one is a rights-bearer. It is an aspect of the larger idea of the rights-bearer as a constraint or even as a source of duties on others.[15] Stone doesn't say anything about what this larger, not merely procedural conception of rights would be for the nonhuman objects, and that leaves their legal rights still relatively hollow. That, however, is not central to my interest here, and despite its weakness, Stone's procedural notion is important.

This is because it points to the fact that there simply isn't a way out of political questions. Whether one would thicken Stone's picture of a rights-bearer with a utilitarian conception of rights, with some kind of Kantianism, or with something else, the point is that there is no antecedent and process-independent truth about them to be discovered. Rather, solutions to these questions emerge out of argumentative processes among agents and, as such, are always contingent.[16] Now doesn't this create a nasty sort of tension? I began the discussion by thinking about how nonagents might be accounted for in political justification, and here we have, it seems, once again brought them entirely to the mercy of agents, who, as we have seen, include only humans. The critiques were founded on a rejection of anthropocentrism, and here we are in the grips of seemingly inescapable anthropocentrism.

Notice, however, that there are at least two different ways to understand anthropocentrism. First, we can think of anthropocentrism as an attribute of *interests*: I'm anthropocentric if all I think that matters are human interests and don't give a hoot about nonhuman nature beyond its role in satisfying human interests. It is well known that this needn't imply, say, uncaring attitudes about the nonhuman nature—just think of preservationist hunters—but it has limitations.[17] But we can also be anthropocentric about *justification* without committing ourselves at all to the more thoroughgoing anthropocentrism. It is, in a way, a form of ecopolitical humility to admit that the way I value nonhuman nature can only be justified to my fellow humans, but that doesn't mean that I and others cannot think of nonhuman nature as having value that is independent of our *interests*. We needn't lament this sort of anthropocentrism, and Stone's distinction between the kind of guardianship for natural objects he defends and the representation of nature on the *qui tam* model, that is, representation that *combines* my interests and nature's interests, shows that it is intelligible as an operational political idea.[18]

This needn't, of course, mean that the political standing of nonhuman nature must either be assumed right from the start or even be concluded at the end of the justificatory process. There are, after all, conceptions of justice that simply cannot accommodate such considerations, and if those conceptions happen to prevail, too bad for the environment.[19] Given the anthropocentrism of justification, this is an obvious "risk," as it were. But it is, I want to insist, a risk with which we must live. What is important is to realize that the risk isn't at all limited to the consideration of these new candidates for political standing, trees and seals and such. Even in the (in my view implausible) case that *moral* realism is true, it doesn't at all follow that the current holders of political standing *naturally*, in some metaphysical sense of "natural," ought to hold it. There is a difference between, say, the expansion of political rights to women and to nonhuman nature—because it is very difficult to deny that women are agents—but it is a difference in the *weight* and *kind* of the reasons that can be given for the expansion.

The reasons are political, not metaphysical: They have to do with what a human being can be and do as an empirical being, in response to actions from others. History knows of cases where metaphysical and a priori considerations have guided policy decisions, but often, although not always, those a priori considerations have turned out to be false. A pertinent example for us is the extension of legal responsibility to animals in early modern Europe: After a while the system simply became untenable because of the empirical contradictions it involved in practice.[20] Despite the much greater belief in the existence of otherworldly forces, people came to realize that hanging dogs for "stealing" served no purpose. It is those practical considerations and empirical knowledge, not metaphysics, that would show that the denial of political standing to, say, women or slaves is unsupportable. For example, as James Oakes has shown in his study of American slavery, because of the slave-owning culture's needs to regulate slave behavior, slaves had to be granted a kind of moral agency even though it was technically denied.[21]

This doesn't mean that the issues are arbitrary or the decisions up for grabs. Let's assume, for simplicity, there is an in-principle agreement on interests. This obviously doesn't mean that matters are settled, but there are ways of beginning to settle them. First, to render the interests of nonhuman nature intelligible, there are various sorts of experts with better epistemic access to those interests than nonexperts. Most of us can interpret, at least to some extent, the behavior of domestic animals enough to tell whether they are suffering, and most of us can recognize some signs of, say, plant suffering, but there is a large area where biological experts are needed as interpreters. They aren't, of course, the final authorities; in fact, some of the disputes begin at the level of interpretation when experts disagree. There are also those disputes about how to tally different sorts of interests: for example, whether the interests of mountain goats that threaten the interests of the park in which they stay should count more than those of the ecosystem as a whole, and if not, how exactly to draw the boundaries of ecosystems and bioregions.[22] Even when the biological facts themselves aren't in question, they don't determine the political solutions.

Do Emotions Disqualify Agency?

The historical denial of political or even full human agency to women or nonwhite people points to the fact that the politically salient question is less about the *outer* boundary of the justificatory community than about the reasons people have used to limit some humans' participation. As my earlier argument suggests, these questions are themselves political ones, and the fact that they are largely factual provides no automatic solution since the political disputes can be about the normative relevance of facts. However, I do take it as firmly established—as a matter of empirical political practice—that gender and race and similar "contingent facts of birth" do not justify any denial of political agency. Simply, I take it as a political given that adult human beings prima facie count as political agents.

Even then, important theoretical and practical questions remain. A crucial one is whether some particular *mode* of human exercise of agency should be privileged and whether some other mode should be seen as grounds for exclusion. Consider: There is a common tendency to discount or even ignore political action that seems to issue from strong emotions or just appears "emotional." For example, many local grassroots movements, especially those led largely by women, have had to struggle simply to get standing as agents in political processes. They have been dismissed as "hysterical housewives,"[23] too emotional and thus too myopic to engage in what political action requires, namely, reason and reasonableness. As a consequence, in many public policy issues, for example, the more mainstream participants have felt justified in not responding to these "mad women's" demands for justification. The idea is that democratic processes are based on the idea of reasoned deliberation and that those who don't participate in it on those terms voluntarily shut themselves out of the game.[24]

A related and sometimes indistinguishable way of dismissing other actors' agency is to make claims not just about the grounds of engagement—"They're *being* emotional, not reasonable!"—but to shut out others by claiming they are simply *incapable* of what it takes to engage in politics. Where in the previous case, "*mad* women" are ignored, in one instantiation of this phenomenon all women are ignored *because* they are, "by nature," mad, or emotional, or whatever. The impressive variety of ways in which this phenomenon has manifested itself has included, in addition to such descriptions of women, claims about the subhuman nonagency in people of other races, ethnicities, and classes. As we know, classical conservatism was premised on the sometimes genuinely felt worry about the "lower orders'" inability to engage in anything that was needed for governing.[25] But we should note that while this logic has often been used for what we now deem illegitimate purposes, the logic itself is understandable. For example, the same logic rules out children from a range of exercises of agency. The assumption is that children lack the maturity to be able to choose from among political candidates, to marry, to drink alcohol, and so on. These sorts of presuppositions about who could possibly count as a political agent shape, in important ways, the question of to whom one takes oneself as owing a justification.

Anyone wishing to dismiss emotionally charged agency might run to Kant for an argument. Kantians, after all, are generally taken to have a straightforward position: Insofar as political claims issue from emotions, and not reason, they are illegitimate. This is because emotions "contaminate" the effect of morally worthy and valuable reasons. If you helped the proverbial old lady across the street because you coveted the shiny merit badge and not because it was the right thing to do, you weren't acting morally. Emotional promptings, we may recall, need to be suppressed out of reason's way. That's why Kant is different from that proto-emotivist Hume, the view goes. '

Two options seem available. We can either accept the textbook Kantian picture, bite the bullet, and dismiss emotionally charged political action and claims, or we can reject the textbook Kantian conception, if we think such a dismissal misses something essential about politics. I opt for the latter, arguing simply that the *textbook* Kantian account is mistaken, but that the historicist Kant from Chapter 4 can handle emotions nicely. This isn't just to make Kantianism compatible with all things wonderful, but because a Kantian defense of emotional political agency in fact affords us valuable criteria for evaluating legitimate and illegitimate emotional action. After all, we might think that while citizens concerned about a toxic waste dump in their neighborhood have good reasons to be angry, citizens upset about "dirty foreigners who'll steal our jobs" don't. The Kantian account explains why.

The textbook interpretation of Kant's treatment of emotions is certainly reasonable. In rough outline, the argument is straightforward: First, only *autonomous* exercise of agency can make the agent's action morally worthy. This is intuitively intelligible: *I* have to be the author of an action for which I am claiming moral approval for me. Second, it follows, a fortiori, that heteronomous action disqualifies one from moral praiseworthiness. What makes actions heteronomous are causal forces arising out of sensibility, that is, of our natures as physical beings. They make practical reason depend on "an underlying feeling where reason could never be morally legislative" (G, IV: 461).[26]

In the second *Critique*, Kant couches this view in rhetoric that seems to leave little doubt about the inappropriateness of emotions in moral action.

> It is a very beautiful thing to do good to men because of love and a sympathetic good will, or to do justice because of a love of order. But this is not the genuine moral maxim of our conduct, the maxim which is suitable to our position as *human beings*, when we presume, like volunteers, to flout with proud conceit the thought of duty and, as independent of command, merely to will of our own good pleasure to do something to which we think we need no command. (CPrR, V: 82)[27]

A few pages further, Kant's tone turns reverential, and the exclamation marks come out:

> Duty! Thou sublime and mighty name that dost embrace nothing charming or insinuating but requirest submission and yet seekest not to move the will by threatening aught that would arouse natural aversion or terror, but only holdest forth a law which of itself finds entrance into the mind and yet gains reluctant reverence (though not always obedience), a law before which all inclinations are dumb even though they secretly work against it.... (CPrR, V: 86)

We might think the enthusiastic tone a little ironic here; I suggest later why it isn't. The point seems clear: Feelings grounded in sensibility or inclinations are not an appropriate ground for morally valuable action. Kantianism does seem as emotionally arid as its critics charge.

Things get complicated quickly, however. First, this very chapter on the "Incentives of Pure Practical Reason," on the relationship between reasons and motives, is far from unequivocal on the role of emotions, and not just because Kant loses his cool when it comes to worshipping at the altar of duty. Recall also Kant's enthusiasm about the French Revolution in Chapter 4: Despite their potential misgivings about the revolution, even disinterested spectators would find in their hearts "wishful participation that borders closely on enthusiasm" (CF, VII: 85). We can infer that Kant shares such enthusiasm himself, although "affect as such deserves censure," as he says on the next page. However, "affective participation in the good" (*Theilnehmung am Guten mit Affekt*)[28] is not only excusable but is sometimes appropriate and, importantly, compatible with reason, not with the self-interest that rises out of our sensibility: "genuine enthusiasm always moves only toward what is ideal and, indeed, to what is purely moral, such as the concept of right, and it *cannot* be grafted onto self-interest" (CF, VII: 86, emphasis mine).

So we have a theoretical tension in our hands. Feelings based on our sensibility cannot ground autonomous action but may, in fact, "deserve censure." At the same time, emotions, even enthusiasm, can be morally appropriate. It isn't ironic that Kant seems so excited about duty: it is *proper* to feel reverential enthusiasm toward it. Similarly, insofar as the French Revolution reflects, despite its bloody flaws, the moral tendency of humans toward freedom (via a republican mode of governance), it is appropriate to feel sympathetic.

I want to rule out one possible answer right away. Kant is not merely saying that emotions are acceptable when they are *caused* or otherwise occasioned *by* autonomous and right action. Sure, it is, in some cases, fine to feel happy, proud, elated, and so on *upon* your having done something right (although it would be wrong to do that something *in order to* feel that way). But the view is stronger: Some emotions can be part of an acceptable motivational apparatus, albeit not in the form, "I'm doing *x* because it makes me feel *y*."

Some terminological clarifications are in order. Kant uses several different terms when he talks about emotions, and although the full meaning of his terms would require a substantive philosophical accounting, some rough outlines can be sketched. "Rough" is operative here also because (1) Kant himself isn't always consistent in his use of the terms and (2) his translators also aren't consistent.

The general term for emotion in Kant's work is *Affekt*, although, in some cases, he also uses the less ambiguously causal term *Rührung*. Like the term for "feeling," *Gefühl*, *Rührung* connotes states of affairs in a physical world of cause and effect. However, there isn't much mileage to be gained by charting the differences between *Affekt* and *Rührung*; the tricky question is to understand what *Affekte* are, and that is far from obvious. A full accounting of how *Affekt* should be understood would amount to a well-nigh complete interpretation of Kant's theory of cognition and psychology, and although I have something to say about that later, it is important to keep the incompleteness in mind. For now, it is enough for us to think of emotional as roughly synonymous with "affective."

Emotions, as affects, differ from *passions*. Passions—*Leidenshaften*—are emotions that an agent has adopted as her maxims. Kant describes this difference briefly in the third *Critique*: "Affects are impetuous and unpremeditated, passions persistent and deliberate. Thus resentment in the form of anger is an affect, in the form of hatred (vindictiveness) it is a passion. Passion can never be called sublime, no matter what the circumstances; for while in an affect the mind's freedom is *impeded*, in passion it is abolished." (CJ, V: 272n). In the *Metaphysics of Morals* (hereafter MM), Kant supplements this by saying that affective action merely lacks virtue whereas passionate action is an active bad, a vice (MM, VI: 407–408). There is, in other words, a definite evaluative hierarchy between affects and passions, one that stems from a difference in how they disturb reason as a motivational ground. Similar evaluative hierarchy applies to enthusiasm (*Enthusiasm, Enthusiasmus*) and fanaticism (*Schwärmerei, Fanaticismus*). Kant's terminology over these varies a little over time, but the ideas remain the same throughout. In the pre-Critical *Beobachtungen über das Gefühl der Schönen und Erhabenen* (Observations on the Feeling of the Beautiful and the Sublime), *Fanaticismus* is offered as a synonym to *Schwärmerei*, and refers a feeling of "immediate and extraordinary communion with a higher nature" (B, II: 250, 251n). This is distinguished from enthusiasm, which is a state where the mind is "heated above the appropriate degree" by some principle (B, II: 250, 251n). In the third *Critique*, fanaticism is described as "the delusion of wanting to *see* beyond all bounds of sensibility" (CJ, V: 275). Fanaticism is like a *mania*, whereas enthusiasm is merely like madness, Kant says: "Of these [fanaticism] is least of all compatible with the sublime, because it is ridiculous in a somber way. In enthusiasm, an affect, the imagination is unbridled, but in fanaticism, a deep-seated and brooding passion, it is ruleless" (CJ, V: 275). In the even later *Anthropology*, the analysis remains the same. A person who habitually fails to square her emotional imaginings with the laws of experience is an enthusiast, Kant says (A, VII: 202); enthusiasm is a kind of emotional daydream, and as such a madness. However, in a mania, the very capacity for judgment is disturbed because the reason fails to provide the concepts with which we arrange our ideas (A, VII: 215).[29] Fanaticism is thus a far more serious condition.

This evaluative hierarchy is, not surprisingly, visible in Kant's use of the different terms. Enthusiasm, as we just saw, is an emotion a person may legitimately have in some cases, even if it is a kind of madness. In contrast, in Kant's rhetoric, fanaticism is always a term of abuse. For example, in the B preface to the first *Critique*, it gets included in the laundry list of all things detrimental: "Criticism alone can sever the root of *materialism, fatalism, atheism, free-thinking, fanaticism*, and *superstition*, which can be injurious universally" (CPR, B, xxxiv, Kant's emphasis). In his 1783 review of Johann Heinrich Schulz's *Attempt at an Introduction to a Doctrine of Morals for All Human Beings Regardless of Different Religions*, Kant held that Schulz's quasi-Spinozistic argument for a universal morality entailed a determinism that did away with human agency. And from this, Kant thought, "must arise the grossest fanaticism, which does away with any influence of sound reason" (RS, VIII: 13).[30]

Although the terminology has its part in Kant's philosophical apparatus, it is worth observing, as James Schmidt, among others, has reminded us, that Kant and

Kantians were hardly the only Enlightenment thinkers who took a dim view of whatever they thought was fanaticism, and used the term as one of abuse.[31] The fanatics to be attacked represented the superstition, religious and otherwise, which held the Enlightenment back and for which, as we saw in chapter 4 the Enlightenment was to serve as a corrective. But, as we also saw at the end of chapter 4, there were fanatics among the cheerleaders for the Enlightenment: The Göttingen Hainbund's party, where a rival poet was burned in effigy, was a perfect reminder. It is not unreasonable to see such behavior as detracting from, instead of contributing to, the ideals Enlightenment thinkers sympathetic to the more Kantian ways regarded as ideal. And it's not unreasonable to think it a kind of fanaticism, fanaticism with political consequences to boot.

Of course, it is ironic to call this an example of what a Kantian might have regarded as fanaticism when Kant himself expresses that cautious enthusiasm for the French Revolution. First, surely there is a difference between debauched effigy burning and guillotining thousands. Second, as is clear from Kant's text, his enthusiasm wasn't about the behavior exhibited by the "gifted people" of France, but about the maxims that informed the revolutionary process. The question then remains, How do emotions feature *legitimately* in maxims? since they clearly sometimes do.

My argument turns on the general idea I outlined in Chapter 4. We need to make a distinction in Kant's theoretical discussion of emotions between *conceptual* and *psychological* claims. The question isn't settled by thinking about whether emotions have a *causal* impact on our minds, since they always do, but rather by sorting out what conceptual role they have in our maxim creation. Inasmuch as Kant's general conceptual apparatus remains unaffected, emotions may legitimately enter into it and in fact play an acceptable motivational role. When they can't, they are illegitimate.

Making this distinction isn't novel. It tracks, in fact, a longstanding controversy over whether, or to what extent, Kant subscribes to and discusses the so-called "faculty psychology." According to one view, Kant's theory of cognition in general is of little interest because the psychology on which it is based—that our mind has distinct and clearly demarcated "faculties"—is outdated. According to the opposite view, the cognitive end of Kant's theoretical philosophy, particularly as expounded in the first and third *Critiques*, isn't about the structure and functions of the human mind but about the conceptual relations with which we gain knowledge and make judgments about the world.

Let's think about Kant's discussion in the third *Critique* about whether the feeling of pleasure precedes the judgment of an object as beautiful or follows it (CJ, V: 216). The question is tricky by itself and is confounded by the fact that Kant seems to be giving two opposite answers in different parts of the *Critique* and in an unpublished version of an introduction to the book. Commentators who insist on reading Kant as writing about psychological processes in the human mind tend to have a hard time getting rid of the air of paradox, whereas a nonpsychological reading dispels it. Consider the solution Hannah Ginsborg offers in her important contribution to the debate: "*Qua* judgment about the pleasure, the judgment of taste has as its determining ground the universal communicability of the pleasure. *Qua* judgment demanding agreement with itself, the judgment has as its determining ground the feeling of pleasure."[32] The relationship between the judgment and the feeling of pleasure is a purely conceptual one, not a causal one. The aesthetic judgment is a predication of a state of mind as one that is of self-perpetuating character because that's just what pleasure is conceptually, in the Kantian view. None of this is, of course, independent of causal relations—the aesthetic judgment is, after all, about a state of mind occasioned by the world impinging on the agent's sensibility—but the relevant considerations aren't about the causal relations.

When we extend our discussion to practical reason, the same distinction applies. Again, it's an inevitable given that we are physical beings subject to the world of cause and effect. But, at the same time, if we are to have morality or any kind of agency at all, we must conceptualize ourselves in alternative terms, as rational wills capable of making choices on the basis of noncausal reasons. This is all familiar. One standard question it generates is the question of how an agent is to square the alternative viewpoints with her phenomenology, that is, how she is to think of herself both as a physical being subject to causes and as a rational will.

My discussion in Chapter 4 was an answer to that question. The self-love test, whereby the agent checks whether a (potentially causal) inclination toward something could be *understood* as a rational maxim toward an end, is that mechanism. Recall also that the self-love comes fraught with a risk: If unchecked by reason, it can become self-conceit. This hierarchy of evaluation between the two kinds of self-love—proper self-love and self-conceit—tracks the two other evaluative hierarchies we saw earlier. Self-love is like enthusiasm—problematic but controllable—while self-conceit resembles manic fanaticism. The relevant distinction is again the way in which the affective component relates to maxim formation. As long as it remains in place and doesn't try to fight or overthrow the majestic reason, it can be legitimate. Not only legitimate: Emotions can, as we have seen, serve *as* the determining grounds in practical reason. All emotion as such (*"Aller Affekt als ein solcher"*) deserves censure, as Kant says (CF, VII: 86; see earlier), but (to offer my gloss on what he means by that "as such") *not* necessarily when it can be incorporated into maxims via reasons. Further, emotions, especially strong ones, are risky because letting them into the conceptual apparatus means letting them act on us, and there aren't guarantees that we manage to keep them in control.

The discussion so far has been quite abstract, and it's time to clamber back down from the heights to think more concretely about political questions. Recall that the problem is an actual argumentative move in political practice where, for example, women's agency is dismissed because they are taken to be "too" emotional. What helps disqualify emotional engagement from politics is, in Naomi Scheman's words, "the myth about the emotions, women's emotions in particular, that tells us that they are irrational or nonrational storms."[33] The idea is that many emotions are psychophysiological givens and *purely* causal. (We should note that Kant, the old misogynist, thought this way particularly about women, at least in the pre-Critical *Beobachtungen*.) To the extent that they are taken to be open to the agent's reflection, it is merely as a spectator that she can look at them. Of course, the view is hopelessly naïve. First, even if we suspend judgment on the Kantian analysis of emotions, it is quite uncontroversial that emotions in general have important cognitive components. In many cases, although not in all, what emotions we have depend on our beliefs. I may feel *Schadenfreude* because Jim was called into the principal's office for what I believe to be a scolding, but if in fact it is to award him a prize, my emotion would be, if I knew better, unfounded.

So even if emotions were just psychophysiological causes, they would not be independent of other highly cognitive elements to which we have easier introspective access. I want to emphasize this because it is independent of any particularly Kantian interpretation of emotions (mine or someone else's). The point is not that emotions are easily manipulable beliefs—beliefs themselves aren't *easily* manipulable. Rather, I want to suggest that we can talk about the justifiability of emotion and that one kind of justifiability hangs on the justifiability of the belief. If, say, anger is my emotional response to someone doing better than me, then my feeling angry at that someone is "justified" as long as the person has indeed done better than me.

One could still say that they are irrational or nonrational storms that sweep us with them once the right kind of cognition is in place, and as such still *inter*subjectively invalid. If I am the type that gets horribly angry at others who do better, my anger toward Jill may be "justified" when Jill runs the mile faster than I—justified, that is, in the sense that the relevant type of belief that triggers my anger is justified. But that is just a kind of pathology I happen to have. Certainly there is another way in which my anger isn't justified at all. Envy is a vice, and it is not clear what sort of story would need to be told for us to take feelings of envy as *justified* in the sense we generally use the term.

However, emotions aren't just hooked up to cognition in this way. In fact, as Scheman suggests, our very interpretation of our emotions is deeply *social*.[34] *What* the emotion I happen to have is depends on social practices and background norms. For example, people would readily point out to me that what I take to be anger at Jill is better characterized as envy. Anger might even be appropriate if, say, Jill had done something to *wrong* me, say, beaten me on the mile because she used steroids, but without something like that I have no good *reason* to be angry at Jill. It is not that anger would necessarily be an illegitimate emotion: I may, for example, have good reasons to be angry *at myself* if I spent the night before the race drinking Scotch instead of stretching. But even then, the legitimacy of the anger depends on certain kinds of background norms of what is appropriate for someone to feel angry about. If I did my best, and Jill just happens to be better, I have no good reason to be angry at myself.

Furthermore, the interpretation depends on social relations. As Philippa Foot argues, expressions of approval and disapproval require that whoever expresses them has standing to do so.[35] If a person on the street tells me he disapproves of my clothing, I can tell him to mind his own business. If my spouse tells me she disapproves of the clothes I'm planning to wear to her parents' house, her disapproval really is disapproval. The rude person's attitude is just an expression of dislike or some such thing. My spouse has standing with regard to my clothes by virtue of the kind of relationship we have: Our marriage is, as it were, a joint project in whose success she has a say.

It is important to observe that her disapproval gets to count because of this, not just because of some difference between my attitudes toward her and the rude person on the street. She doesn't have standing to approve and disapprove of some of my doings and beings just because her opinion matters to me; rather, her opinion *ought to* matter to me because of our relationship.[36] There is a difference in her disapproving of my clothing and her telling me she doesn't like something I wear even if the causal impact is the same because her taste matters to me.

So we've gotten reasons, as grounds for emotions, as well as social norms back into the picture. With them comes justifiability, in the way we need it for political justification and, subsequently, for the kind of agency we want. If someone engages in political action because she is angry, the demand for justification may nevertheless be met if the anger is justified with reference to relevant grounds. For example, if a citizen enlists in the military because she feels patriotic anger toward the enemies of her country, her engagement is justifiable as political action, but not if she sees enlisting as a way of settling a personal vendetta.

However, there are still worries. First, the question of motivational economy: If there are good reasons behind someone's emotional engagement in political action, why take the circuitous route via emotions and not simply on the basis of those reasons? This is an important question for anyone subscribing more strictly to the duty-exclamation-mark interpretation of Kant. Further, it has to do with what we might call political sincerity: If you *really* believe that the reasons behind your anger justify your engagement, then the anger seems unnecessary, something extra that the good Kantian that you are wouldn't really need. And if you *don't* see the reasons behind the anger as sufficient, then your anger is not really based on them, and you are just giving a rationalization for your illegitimately emotional engagement.

The worry is misplaced; it misunderstands the role of the anger. The emotion is not the motivational fuel for some political action, but the appropriate *political judgment* of some state of affairs, and as such *part* of political action. We can say that it is evidence of your understanding of what it means to be a political agent that you know that the expression of certain kinds of emotions is appropriate in various circumstances, and that you know what they can be. Of course, what expressions you find appropriate depends on the particular values you hold—pro-choicers won't feel elated at the news of the bombing of an abortion clinic—but the general idea is that emotions and their expression are strongly connected to your agency. Controversial issues aside, we might recall Montesquieu's picture of citizenship, in which passions play a central role: *Some* kinds of patriotic emotion may be legitimate, while others might not.[37]

There is nothing mysterious about this, and I want to suggest that, in fact, the idea of justifiable emotions is acknowledged by the very practices that seek to discount them. It loosens the connection between reasons and emotions when those emotions are framed as the merely psychophysiological causes and not as emotions connected to any reasons. The more physiological, the better: *Voilà* PMS-crazed hysterical housewives. Hysterical anger or fear are pathologies, and thus can be ignored, the logic goes.

How, then, does this account help us drive a wedge between legitimate and illegitimate emotionally charged politics? What is the difference, if any, between angry anti-immigrant rhetoric and Lois Gibbs's Love Canal toxics campaign, for example? First, I don't want the response to ride on the effect my conveniently chosen examples might have on our intuitions. My point certainly isn't to drive the wedge in such a way that right-wing populism always comes out as illegitimate and concern for cute does or doe-eyed children as legitimate.

The Kantian answer follows neatly from this discussion: If one's emotional engagement is justifiable, that is, *compatible with legitimate reasons,* which themselves depend on agents' attentiveness both to the world of facts and to the world of other agents, then the emotional engagement is legitimate. This conception rules out, for example, disrespect of the humanity of persons. It doesn't rule out anger, but it does rule out hatred. This isn't particularly tricky theoretically but is a Kantian given. Further, the conception rules out emotions based on straightforwardly false beliefs. Of course, life is largely about uncertainties, and, arguably, much of politics arises out of the uncertainty about outcomes. These uncertainties make it difficult to judge some beliefs as true or false and also make legitimate *some* emotions. For example, emotional fears about the future—say, about the influx of immigrants—can be legitimate. However, there are constraints on *what* gets legitimated, even under conditions of uncertainty. How this happens deserves far more discussion than I have room for, but, as a quick legerdemain, one could argue that a fear motivated by uncertainty about the effects of a policy justifies raising concerns about it and seeking more knowledge. It doesn't justify drawing empirical conclusions that aren't justified. A change in the immigration policy doesn't, as a matter of simple logic, *entail* "foreigners coming to take our jobs."

This makes my conveniently chosen examples not solely a case of cheap partisanship. Arguably, the modus operandi of populism is to play on the affective, instead of seeking to collate the affective with reasons. All political engagement that merely plays on the affective does, the Kantian liberal would say, deserve censure. This isn't a metaphysical point, but a claim immediately deployable in political practice.

What is important about the account here is that it helps us sidestep a question about the phenomenology of emotions. It is certainly true that emotions "feel" the same, regardless of their genesis. But that doesn't mean that an agent can't tell the difference between an unjustifiable emotion and one that is justifiable. As I've argued, justifiable emotions emerge as *judgments* of a particular kind, based on a set of observations and some epistemic and normative principles of judgment. Unjustifiable ones don't. Of course, it may still be the case, as a matter of an individual agent's phenomenology, that the background of his emotions isn't immediately transparent to him. Two emotions, regardless of their genesis, may simply "feel" the same. The Kantian view here would be that in such a case, an appropriately acting agent would want to scrutinize these emotions or, at least, be responsive to scrutiny by others; to be, in other words, responsive to reasons. And, again, Montesquieu's corrective would be to urge institutional safeguards against illegitimate action for contexts where we know we aren't likely to be even minimally reflective.

Conclusion

We now have a sense of how agents' standing gets determined and therefore a sense of to whom we owe a justification for our political engagement. Of course, a central point of this chapter has been that those determinations aren't *et nunc et in die aeternitatis*, but contingent on the particular situations in which they take place. This isn't a concession—or, worse, a move—to relativism since the idea itself is nonrelativistic. It just depends on the context of how it gets carried out.

Now, finally, we are ready to be specific about what a liberal political agent may *do*. We can frame the point of departure skeptically: I want to raise worries about the whole theory by wondering whether it makes sense to talk of *justification* as something central to politics in the first place.

eight

AGENCY AND LIBERAL LEGITIMACY

In the previous chapter, I defended the idea that politics is essentially anthropocentric. Not everyone accepts that view; much environmentalism is premised on the rejection of anthropocentrism. I begin this chapter by considering such a rejection because such an exploration gives us a liberal criterion to distinguish between illegitimate and legitimate political action. Rejecting the essential anthropocentrism about justification can motivate political action that is illegitimate from a liberal perspective. Such political actions aren't the only examples of illiberal political action—we can always think of fascists and Leninists or the anti-WTO anarchists—but the cases are theoretically instructive.

Note first that many of those who *claim* to be rejecting any kind of anthropocentrism actually do seem to accept the anthropocentrism about justification. Deep ecologists write pamphlets in which they *urge* their fellow literate beings—who, they readily acknowledge, are all humans—to think like a mountain. And the militant radical environmentalists of Earth First! who refuse "any compromise in defense of Mother Earth" are willing to commit to reams of (presumably recycled) paper to defend and publicize their positions, not to mention participating in political organizing with people who disagree with them. Obviously some of this is to mobilize people, not to justify the position. However, the aggressively defensive tone of, say, Christopher Manes's *Green Rage* or the debates in the pages of *Earth First!* cannot but convey a desire to have others see and perhaps accept these radicals' point of view.[1] Even Edward Abbey, whose monkey-wrenching eco-terrorists of *The Monkey Wrench Gang* and other novels eschewed the need for justification, himself engaged in debates endlessly.[2]

Of course, a literature search will not find those who refuse to write, and to point to texts in order to show that their writers imagine communication important doesn't mean there aren't people who don't bother. Those to whom justification or even visibility to humans is irrelevant are not particularly prominent, but they nevertheless exist. There are activists who have modeled themselves after Abbey's ecoterrorists and who take themselves to be accountable only to Mother Nature, or the ecosystem, or Gaia. While Paul Watson, the controversial founder of the radical Sea Shepherd Society, isn't a paradigm of an invisible eco-terrorist—he goes on talk shows, gives popular lectures, and offers a sophisticated Web site—his anti-anthropocentrism gives us a good example of what eschewing the need for justification would look like.[3]

Watson is generally not interested in offering justifications for his strategies or his views about the moral landscape for humans and nonhuman animals. The *explanations* he offers for his politics cite visions he has had in shamanic rituals, decidedly not publicly accessible or generally accepted sources of epistemic authority. Yet he takes his position to be the correct view about environmental politics in general—correct in a relatively rigid sense of moral and nonmoral realism—and he goes to great lengths to promote them against competing views.

Now why is it uncontroversial to us that what he is doing is political, even if we don't think he should be taken seriously as a participant in the discussion of ecological questions? I take it that at least part of it is exactly his demand to be taken seriously when he offers no "reasonable" justification for it. In other words, he is making a controversial claim to legitimate authority. The logic is something like this: Watson is an ecological utilitarian for whom the biological well-being of the earth, measured by biodiversity and other factors that contribute to the long-term survival of life on the planet, matters most. To the extent that there is any intelligible notion of individual moral accountability, one is accountable to the "earth." Now how does someone who subscribes to this view orient himself toward other humans? In the way Watson does.[4] So one reason why he is taken seriously by some is the consistency between his principles and his actions, the conventional understanding of what it means to "walk your talk." The claim he is making, then, to speak of matters ecological is as a moral authority.

This kind of action is undoubtedly political. Watson is virtually a live exemplar from Max Weber's conception of a political actor.[5] And Watson is, despite his belief that he needn't justify the position, expressing an unequivocal claim to authority about human relationships with the marine world. But it is illegitimate, I want to argue, in the sense that it refuses accountability to the justificatory community.

It is important to appreciate the sense of illegitimacy I want to attribute to the Watson-style politics, and the way in which it is *not* illegitimate. It is illegitimate in the sense that it refuses engagement with the justificatory community. Importantly, however, this doesn't make Watson's or similar *actions* automatically illegitimate. The liberal "rule" of legitimacy goes like this: When you do *x*, you must also do *y*; when you engage in arguably political action, you owe a justification for that engagement. What Watson has violated is to follow *x* up with *y*, but this doesn't necessarily say anything about the legitimacy of *x* itself. We can call that narrower conception of legitimacy the *strategy legitimacy*, an issue to which I return later.

At least in this case, strategy legitimacy and justificatory legitimacy are loosely related in that indifference to any human justificatory community also informs Watson's indifference to the rules that emerge from that justificatory community. In general, however, there is no necessary or other sort of strong connection between the kinds of legitimacy. The question is what we can make of Watson's strategy—and similar styles of activism in general—with regard to its legitimacy, especially in a liberal polity. On the first glance, it seems straightforwardly illegitimate. Liberal principles are engraved in the rule of law; radicalism such as Watson's breaks laws, ergo it is illegitimate.

But that is too quick. First, it is a well-established principle of liberal politics that breaking existing laws may be an important and legitimate political strategy. Although there may be controversies over individual instances, the principle of civil disobedience is defensible from a liberal perspective. In Chapter 4, I sketched what a Kantian defense might look like; others have offered many different versions.[6] Legality and the legitimacy of political action do not go together. Neither does conformity with some looser but nevertheless real set of rules or norms. It simply follows from the conception of the political as I have expounded on it here that many political actions are political because they challenge the authority of some set of norms. And in the Montesquieuian conception, laws are merely institutional safeguards against contingent human folly, but they aren't sacred first principles. If politics means controversies about what norms should apply in a given situation, then it thoroughly misses the point to say that political action is legitimate only when it abides by norms.

What Does "Radical" Mean?

Let's take a little detour to conceptual analysis. In ordinary speech, "radical," as a label attached to an agent, seems to describe either the means or the ends she embraces, or both. Those who use the term perceive that there is some relatively obvious mainstream of either means or ends, and the ones embraced by the radical are clearly off that mainstream. Of course, what that mainstream is—or whether there really is a reasonably demarcated one—can itself be a matter of controversy, and thus the label "radical" can be deployed for rhetorical purposes. Some use it pejoratively and others proudly wave it as their flag. But the conceptual picture is nevertheless clear.

It is not, however, the full picture. First, more needs to be said about radicalism with regard to one's political ends. What I regard as my ultimate end may look radical in the sense that it is very different from the contemporary political reality, but it is possible that I envision political transformation as incremental steps toward that goal. So, for example, I might agree with Marx on the communist utopia as the ultimate end of political action, but might find the Marxist steps toward that goal too drastic and, instead, sympathize with social democrats who wanted to get "there" through incremental steps, beginning from where we are and proceeding by making the ideas slowly more popular or powerful. It seems that there would be something not quite right in calling that kind of position radical, with reference to *either* the ends or the means.

Granted, a great discrepancy between what one perceives as one's ultimate goal and one's intermediate goals can be politically problematic. It can be puzzling, as is the discrepancy between what Rousseau wants and how he doesn't want to get there: If the political goals you spell out seem radical but you yourself reject any kind of revolutionary means, you leave your sympathizers at a loss and your detractors with handy charges of utopianism.[7] It can also make people suspicious about your commitment to the incremental steps. Western social democrats have notoriously faced this suspicion: "Sure they say they are committed to parliamentarism," the doubting bourgeois have said for more than 100 years, "but if we vote them in, they'll get rid of it as soon as they are in power."[8] And, of course, there are many cases where these suspicions have proven true, although it is not social democrats who are the worst culprits. The theoretically important point is, however, that although one's ultimate ends may look radical, one's intermediate ends might be perfectly "moderate" and reformist.

We could quibble on whether liberalism can conceivably be radical about ultimate ends since in most conceptions it is agnostic on ultimate ends. Certainly there is a way in which liberalism denies the whole idea of an ultimate end. But, at the same time, its procedural ideals make it perfectly conceivable to think of what a society in which those ideals were fully realized might look like—think of Rawls's well-ordered society, or even the ideal world according to the *Perpetual Peace*—and if it is the case that that vision is very different from where we are now, it doesn't seem to me a momentous issue to wonder whether liberalism can have ultimate ends.[9] Its ideals are close enough that one can reasonably talk of ultimate ends.

More interesting is the point that the converse about the conceptual looseness between ends and means holds as well. There is nothing conceptually contradictory about embracing piecemeal liberal reformism and being a strategic radical. At the same time, given our relatively uncontroversial intuition that ends circumscribe means and that liberalism, in particular, is big on procedural conceptions of legitimacy, it can't be the case that anything goes as far as means are concerned.

We can get a handle on the matter if we think of the reasons behind some political strategies that we might call radical. For although Watson and his type snub their noses at those who demand justification, it doesn't mean that they themselves don't have reasons for the strategies they adopt. As we will see, some so-called radicals are perfectly willing to accept the demand for justification. In thinking about their and others' reasons for their strategies, we will see, first, that there *are* legitimate liberal strategies that are radical without presupposing any sort of radicalism about ends, and, second, what the criteria of liberal legitimacy are.

Punctuating Arguments with Fists: The Relationship between Strategy and Justification

Some examples of radicalism: The first took place at a seminar of a Danish natural history society at the University of Copenhagen in 1969. A participant and one of the founding members of the Danish environmental organization NOAH, Carl Herforth, relates the following:

> We locked them all in. We were about twenty people. After we had locked the doors, we cut off the ventilation and started to poison them. It was pretty violent. We got up on the stage and talked about air pollution. We burned garbage and tobacco in large quantities. We poured waste water from a nearby factory in an aquarium with goldfish who slowly died. On the side walls we

showed films about cancer and pollution and we had a loudspeaker with a traffic alarm blasting. We sprayed water in the audience from Emdrup lake. And we had taken along a wild duck which we covered in oil. "Come and save it," we screamed. "You talk about pollution. Why don't you do anything about it?" Finally we cut off its head to end its suffering, and we walked down along the first row of chairs so that all who were sitting there got blood on their clothes. After an hour we opened the doors and said that we wanted to start an environmental movement and that the founding meeting was being held in the next room.[10]

The second example comes from the same corner of Europe. In 1985, the Greens of Finland were debating the direction of the movement.[11] The Greens had gained their first parliamentary seats the year before, and one of the topics was whether the movement, then organizationally a "registered association," ought to become an official political party. This was an aspect of a larger discussion, which was, in many ways, similar to the debates among the German Greens between the *Fundis,* who opposed the conventional politicization of the movement and wanted to focus on narrowly environmental issues, and the *Realos,* who wanted to participate in traditional politics and expand the focus of the movement to include social issues. During a televised discussion in which the Finnish equivalents of the *Fundis* and *Realos* argued about the imminence of the ecological catastrophe and of the priorities of the movement, an invited speaker, Pentti Linkola, a radical deep ecologist and in some ways the grand old man of the Finnish preservation movement, knocked out a participant. He did this, he explained, to push the envelope of the discussion about what sorts of means would be required in the "war of life-preserving against life-destroying individuals."[12]

Were these two actions legitimate? In Finland, most people thought Linkola's move wasn't. Even ignoring the illegality of the assault—since we have decided that an action's conformity with statutes doesn't afford us relevant distinctions— it seemed to violate the norms of acceptable political discourse. At the risk of spelling out the painfully obvious, I want to consider why.

A relatively common view holds that there is no simple, context-independent principle about legitimate means. To judge whether an agent's employment of one strategy or another is legitimate requires paying attention to the context in which she acts. In a familiar application of this view, some forms of violent resistance are seen as acceptable in cases where, say, a tyrannical regime has outlawed or otherwise made impossible other forms of political action. This is a liberal-democratic view: The premise here is that somebody who *ought to* have a right to engage in political action is barred from it. The general idea is that *if* those who ought to have a right to act politically are prevented from doing so, then they may try to enforce their right and determine what means are legitimate. In the Kantian terms of Chapter 4, they find themselves in a state of nature and therefore are themselves the sole authorities of norms about legitimate action.

It seems to follow from this that Linkola's act was illegitimate. He was the invited speaker at the Greens' meeting, so he can't have considered himself to be under a regime that excluded him from taking on means other than violence. (He was also one of the most prolific and widely read polemicists of the Finnish environmental movement, having begun his influential writing career in the 1960s.) The act of violence was, after all, just an aspect of his presentation, which was otherwise perfectly within the limits of legitimacy. Punching someone's lights out was not the only thing he could have done or in fact did.

But what of the idea of pushing the envelope? And what if he thought that safely legitimate means, at least from his point of view, were ineffectual? These are related questions, but worth considering separately.

Let's begin with the second. When we talk of an agent's ability to engage and participate in political action, we are talking about *effective* action and parti-cipation. The history of criticism of purely formal but practically empty political rights, whether we articulate the view with Anatole France or Marx, has been con-vincing enough at least at the level of principle. At the same time, it is mad-deningly difficult to achieve anything like a consensus on what counts as an effective, and not purely formal, right of participation. Many Westerners viewed the former Soviet citizens' right to choose from among different communists as an instance of political participation with skepticism, and when the postrevolutionary elections in Iran involved differently colored ballots for different candidates, many people saw the practice as a cruel mockery of the citizens' right to participate on equal terms. At the same time, some of these same people think that although gerrymandering some American voting districts makes it consistently impossible for some citizens' preferences to register, the right of participation is *not* violated. Similarly, some people don't think that the lack of limits in campaign spending, which keeps poor people from seeking office, is a denial of effective participation. My point isn't that this is such a denial, but simply that where the line goes in reality is another contested political question and one for which no abstract principle provides an answer.

One could argue that Linkola felt a speech, a debate, or an argument were just so many empty words in a context fundamentally designed to undermine his position, and that therefore the more radical resort to physical violence was one of the few effective options for him. Perhaps, one could suggest, the Greens' invitation was just a polite formality accorded to the grand old man of the environmental movement, and unless he really did something drastic, he wouldn't really be listened to. It seems that being attentive to this kind of dynamic in political discourse is important, but it is unlikely that the argument would succeed in this context. Linkola's speech by itself did make a difference, in several ways. The chroniclers of the Finnish Greens note that the audience was shocked and disappointed by Linkola's "survivalist" program. The few who agreed with him left the "official" Greens and formed a new political party. This, more than most abstract discussions about the principles of party formation, then led the Greens to become a party, lest Linkola's survivalists would capture the votes of the increasingly green-sympathizing Finnish electorate.

The one thing Linkola's speech didn't do—and here people actually cite his violence as a significant factor—was persuade people. But success, understood as an agent's achieving her intended ends, can hardly be the standard by which we judge whether the agent can effectively participate in politics. Some theorists go as far as to view an agent's responsibility for the unintended consequences of her action as one of the central components of political, as opposed to moral, agency.[13] In that view, irony, the fact that one's aims are easily frustrated and almost never realized as such, is what makes political life what it is. Liberals think that the demands for effective participation have been met when an agent gets taken seriously, a principle which, as we have seen, is controversial, but not in the sense that it could be taken to require the unadulterated realization of one's hopes. Even if we ignore the logical difficulty involved in thinking that success is what matters—we could tell whether someone effectively participated only though an ex post evaluation—the fact that Finnish Greens didn't rush under Linkola's flag is hardly central in deciding about the legitimacy of his act.

Let's consider the argument about pushing the envelope. It is hard to disentangle it from the effective participation argument in this case, but the logic is very different. The name of the strategy indicates its clearly causal nature: The idea is to shift or broaden political discourse ("discourse" understood here in a straightforwardly non-Foucauldian sense) to take seriously or at least to be open to a broader set of alternatives than it does at the time. So, to use a familiar example, the American left has relatively unsuccessfully tried to push the envelope of political discussion to consider social policy alternatives that are perfectly commonplace elsewhere—often as close as Canada—but have traditionally been seen as beyond the pale in the United States. As the American lefties have so often discovered, pushing the envelope can be very difficult. One of the risks is that since one is advocating something that is viewed with suspicion, perhaps even as illegitimate, pushing the envelope can, instead of rendering the issue acceptable, delegitimate the messenger.

Consider Antonio Gramsci's concept of "hegemony" as a way of making sense of pushing-the-envelope strategies. Recall that Gramsci developed his notion of hegemony to complicate the orthodox Marxist view that political institutions were parts of a merely epiphenomenal superstructure that rose on the causally efficacious material reality of production and ownership relations. In the orthodox picture, gaining control over and changing those relations were sufficient to achieve the socialist revolution. Thus, for the orthodox Marxist political activist, it was simply the economy that needed taking over.

Gramsci, on the other hand, argued that the superstructural institutions—not merely the state, but institutions of culture, education, religion, that is, the "civil society"—are not epiphenomenal, but independent of the economic base. Because of this, a successful political transformation required "two revolutions."[14] The second revolution, supposedly the more difficult one, is the revolution in which one hegemony is replaced with another. These days, many see Gramsci's critique of orthodox Marxism as less important than the general potential of the concept of hegemony, especially in contrast to the notion of power. There are two central ideas about the conceptual independence of power and hegemony: First, someone can have power—a position Gramsci calls "domination"—without having hegemony, or "leadership," an occasional synonym in his writing. The former communist regimes of Eastern Europe are an excellent example of this condition: Under those circumstances, only one revolution was necessary to bring about a political transformation because the hegemony the regimes had had was gone. Few considered the regimes and the system they represented legitimate.[15] Second, an analysis of the relations of power in a society doesn't necessarily reveal the most interesting political relation, because hegemony may contain several organs or institutions that may each be equally powerful in ways that might even seem to be in conflict. Having read his Montesquieu, Gramsci points out that liberal hegemony is centrally the idea of division of powers. So it doesn't really make sense to claim that the institutions taken together still amount to the state apparatus: Part of the hegemony is the idea that all legitimate politics—whether actions by the state or in putative opposition to it—takes place through these divergent and potentially conflicting institutions.[16]

That is the point that critics of liberalism want to push—not, I want to claim, entirely without merit. Even in cases where there is no obvious political unfreedom as a result of the exercise of power against some agents, hegemonic structures can render political playing fields extremely uneven in ways that an analysis of power relations misses. For some agents, the problem is not the lack of effective access to a political forum, nor even the failure of audience uptake, but, rather, that the audience's *judgment* is a consistent and automatic dismissal because the position is regarded as being beyond the pale. In other words, in some situations the liberal requirements for participation have been robustly met, but there is still somehow a failure for the agent to secure the genuine uptake of her message. To put the critical point in terms I introduced in Chapter 2: Liberal institutions make it the case that some formally efficacious participation fails to turn some agents into political claim-makers.

This doesn't look altogether different from the view according to which *efficacy* is a mark of effective participation, a view we reasonably dismissed. Not everything ought to be efficacious: There are bad arguments and bad positions. Why should they not be dismissed? The difference, in the Gramscian analysis, is not only that the dismissal is systematic, that is, that there is a recognizable pattern to them (for there is, of course, a recognizable pattern to the dismissal of bad arguments as well, namely, that the bad ones get dismissed), but that there are no good reasons for the dismissal *and* there are alternative explanations for it. These alternative explanations can, for example, highlight the interests the "unacceptable" political positions threaten, but in ways more sophisticated than the orthodox Marxist account of ideology does. Roughly, hegemony is not false consciousness, but something that can be reflectively endorsed, importantly even by agents whose interests it doesn't serve. It can enjoy legitimacy.

So how does hegemony help here? One of the things it does is point to the contingency of a given legitimate order and to the fact that there may be political positions that get systematically dismissed even though they are defended in procedurally appropriate ways and are perhaps even "good," however one wants to conceive of goodness. In other words, even a system that claims to take arguments on their merits may fail, on a systematic basis, to really see the merit of some arguments. In those contexts, resorting to pushing-the-envelope strategies is one way to try to shake the hegemony.

Pushing-the-envelope strategies are a subclass of political strategies aiming to send a message under conditions in which straightforward avenues of traditional political arguments are counterproductive. Another prominent subclass is the vigil of silent witnesses. It is different from pushing-the-envelope strategies in that it is premised on partly self-imposed restrictions of agency, generally nonviolence. An important Quaker tradition, the idea is that while one doesn't "actively" interfere with, say, an injustice, one can communicate one's condemnation of it by bearing witness to its taking place. Sometimes the presence of witnesses naturally does have a strong direct impact on the events—people tend to be less willing to engage in obviously bad actions with witnesses present—but even when this happens, the mechanism tends to be the same: The point of the witnesses is to stand as placeholders for the *reasons* for the actions' putative badness. However, since matters aren't always so black and white, the witnesses end up standing as one among many other positions. For example, Greenpeace's media-savvy witness bearing to nuclear tests in the early days of the organization served as an argument in the 1970s nuclear debates.[17] Recall the connection between reasons and the expression of emotions: The moral outrage implied by the silent witness is a powerful way of making a very specific message.

This way of categorizing strategies says little about how they are actually carried out. The Greenpeace version of silent witness is not very silent, and in fact it earned the organization a reputation as extremely radical in the 1970s. Similarly, strategies to push the envelope needn't themselves be radical. What counts as counterhegemonic depends on the context, and given the ambiguity of the meanings of actions as well as uncertainty about outcomes, there is no obvious criterion for what specific kinds of acts are counterhegemonic. Importantly, however, this needn't mean that anything goes: There can be criteria of legitimacy, even for nonconventional political strategies such as attempts to push the envelope.

So what can we say about Linkola's attempt? His point was to criticize the norms in which the Greens had framed their collective agency and to illustrate how they, in his view, *must* proceed to achieve their aims (or the aims he thought they ought to have been pursuing). The principles of democratic debate, respect for a multiplicity of perspectives and viewpoints, and the desire to achieve a consensus were in his view hopelessly ineffectual, too slow, and, most importantly, fundamentally wrongheaded. In enshrining the principle of respect for others the Greens missed, in his view, the point that global survival required a radical return to a mode of social life in which the weaker simply had to lose. His goal, then, was to push the envelope about procedural political norms among the Greens and in society in general to include, among other things, the idea that physical strength mattered politically. In other words, in his view, left hooks and roundhouses should have become a part of the Greens'—and eventually everyone's—argumentative repertoire. Of course, if this had happened, the earlier norms about equal respect and so on would have been undermined. But that, according to the radical view, would have been just right.

One way in which the Gramscian analysis has come under criticism is its seeming adherence to a kind of Marxist realism about social and political relations: Roughly, the idea is that some hegemonies are objectively better than others. Postmodern critics, by tweaking the concept of hegemony to look more like Foucault's notion of discourse, are increasingly arguing that all hegemonies are, at least in the end, oppressive and that counterhegemonic struggles remain emancipatory only insofar as they remain counterhegemonic. There is far too busy a cottage industry around that topic for me to try to set up shop here, but I want to acknowledge *another* sort of difficulty with the supposed Marxist realism.

Regardless of what the objective hegemonies might be, if you explain the concept to ordinary citizens, say, in the United States, and ask them what they take the prevailing hegemony to be, you'll get a variety of puzzlingly interesting answers. Consider the claims of those engaged in what the right (in ironic bad faith) has begun to call the *Kulturkampf*: According to the right, there is a hegemony of a multicultural "political correctness" in American culture; according to the left (though these labels are increasingly uninformative), the hegemony in, say, education, is still very Eurocentric, racist, and patriarchal. Or consider attitudes about the preservation of wilderness. Environmentalists argue that the existing hegemony favors environmentally destructive practices, while the "wise-use" movement argues that there is a green conspiracy afoot and it has turned America into anti-business and pro-environment to an extent that nothing can get done any longer.[18] These perceptions of hegemony shouldn't be taken as givens, of course. There are better and worse reasons for holding them, plenty of bad faith and false consciousness to go around, but it is important to realize that they aren't *just* bad faith or false consciousness and that in many cases brute facts massively underdetermine the reasons for holding the views.

Is there, then, a way to evaluate the legitimacy of attempts to push the envelope, especially if those attempts are about procedural norms themselves? Would it have made a difference if Linkola's violence had persuaded more Greens? And if so, do numbers matter? To condemn Linkola outright, his sympathizers have argued, merely reflects the prejudices and timidity of most of the Finnish Greens, which Linkola tried to shake out of them. Only a few have the courage to countenance the harshness of the truth about the world, Nietzsche suggested— and the survivalists' putative truth is much like Nietzsche's—and our condemnation of those who spell it out just shows we belong to the herds.[19] More generally, where we draw the line can simply be said to reflect the norms under which we operate, and if those are the ones that are being challenged, whence does any judgment come? If this is true, then attempts at pushing the envelope are simply beyond questions of legitimacy.

A very Machiavellian point, this, at least if we understand Machiavellianism to refer to the most straightforward reading of the *Prince* as advocating an "ends justify the means" doctrine. These so-called Machiavellians and other self-styled "realists" have always defended their views as best accounts of how politics "really" happens. To put it very roughly, the idea is that the strategic-instrumental model I discussed in Chapter 6 is taken as the correct and complete conception of legitimacy: There are no relevant considerations of legitimacy beyond those of strategy, expediency, or prudence. Here, one could argue that since there don't seem to be any meta-norms by which to assess the legitimacy of pushing-the-envelope strategies, the only reasonable way to think about those strategies is strategic: If they worked—whatever that means—they were legitimate, and if they didn't, they weren't.

But things are more complicated. We still shouldn't rush to grant the strategic-instrumentalist claim. Again, the point of Chapter 6 works here as well: The strategic considerations are themselves ineluctably entangled with relatively robust nonstrategic claims about legitimacy. They are entangled with reasons.

Think about how strategic considerations work. It is a common strategy among those fighting for environmentally friendly legislation, say, for the protection of endangered species, to deliberately propose what even they consider excessively broad criteria because the demand sets the outer boundary of negotiation so far that most compromises will be acceptable. U.S. Senator Robert P. Griffin dubbed this idea "brinkmanship" in 1970.[20] This is, of course, simply the principle familiar to anyone who has ever had to bargain for anything: Ask for more than you hope to get, offer less than you are willing to pay. But there are boundaries: Claims that are perceived as too outrageous will backfire because they won't be taken seriously. I can't expect to make $100,000 on my first job even if I request a $1 million salary with a straight face, and if you offer $2 for my titanium frame bicycle, I won't waste my time with you. The same goes, I want to claim, for procedural pushing-the-envelope strategies. Even if the strategy is purely Machiavellian, it must be attentive to the existing boundaries of legitimacy *in order to* be effective. After all, even a "thief orients his action to the validity of criminal law in that he acts surreptitiously."[21]

None of this means that strategic considerations and broader considerations of legitimacy can't be in conflict. Surely they very often are. But the fact of such conflicts doesn't show that there is a bug in my theory; it's a feature of the theory that it acknowledges them. I have been trying to develop a liberal account of political agency, which means that the account is normative, that is, that it specifies what sorts of norms circumscribe the exercise of political agency in a liberal regime. If there were no conflict with the Machiavellian picture, the account would be quite toothless—and uninteresting to boot, because the Machiavellian picture isn't, despite the claims by its advocates, any less normative than this one.

Conclusion

So what I have tried to say complicates at least the most simplistic picture of liberal politics, according to which something is legitimate if it has been publicly defended with arguments whose premises are uncontroversial and accessible to all, and if all have, on due reflection, found those reasons acceptable. We have an account of political agency where the idea of justification is central without making it seem as if all politics is is a reasoned debate. This has been a way, I argue, to render liberal theory sensitive to the real-world variety of political practices while retaining some normative bite with the principles. The theory is capable of producing criteria for the evaluation of the legitimacy of the different practices. But at some point, it seems one can raise the question of whether it really makes sense to talk of justification or even of something like justificatory practices. We have seen, first in Chapter 2 and again in this one, two ways in which "purely" causal political action needs to be connected to justification: Either it is *unintelligible* as political action, as I argued in Chapter 2, or it is *illegitimate*, as I have argued here.

It is, then, both *who* and *what* that determine the legitimacy of an exercise of political agency from a liberal perspective. Liberalism requires from an agent a commitment to the in-principle justifiability of the reasons for her engagement. An agent without such a commitment may be doing something political, but it won't be legitimate from a liberal perspective. At the same time, there is a considerable variety in how that in-principle commitment gets manifested in practice, and it is here where it matters who the agent is. It makes a difference for the legitimacy of expressions of emotions about abortion whether they come from women or men. At issue is not the sincerity of those emotions, but who can reasonably expect their opinion to count. Similarly, it makes a difference for the interpretation of the legitimacy of some particular strategy as to who engages in it, what sorts of relations of power and hegemony are in place, and so on. Sometimes, therefore, this commitment gets translated into the legitimacy of *institutions* that safeguard political practices in contexts where individuals themselves won't or can't be very reflective. The Kantian model for the exercise of agency that we saw in Chapter 4—that of scholars engaged in reasoned deliberation of arguments on their merits—is not at all irrelevant to this picture, but, rather, informs it as the kind of benchmark against which existing conditions are evaluated. We interpret political actions in the world as if all agents who are committed to this reasoned deliberation among scholars were engaged in it.

A contractarian theory such as liberalism needn't mean that the idea of contract governs political relations and interactions. As Elster, among many others, has argued, the "forum," and not the market, informs (even if not to the extent some argue) the best model for politics.[22] And as I have tried to show, liberal political agents can view their relations with other agents, both individual and institutional, not in narrow market terms, but in terms of shared membership in a community that must, despite profound disagreements, get along. None of that turns them into Schmitt's cowardly intellectuals: Their reasoned engagement in politics isn't all talk.

CONCLUSION

The essence of being human is that one does not seek perfection, that one is sometimes willing to commit sins for the sake of loyalty, that one does not push asceticism to the point where it makes friendly intercourse impossible, and that one is prepared in the end to be defeated and broken up by life, which is the inevitable price of fastening one's love upon other human individuals.

What Happens to Responsibility?

In philosophical ethics, one of the central issues in any discussion of agency is *responsibility*, the question of whether, and how, praise and blame are to be apportioned. I have, it seems, said very little about this question in the preceding chapters, which may strike one as odd in a book devoted to the discussion of agency. I might answer that this isn't a book on ethics, but on politics, and while the concept of agency makes sense there, it is sufficiently different from a moral philosopher's concept, and thus the idea of responsibility is beyond the purview. However, that answer would still beg the question. At least according to Max Weber, whose "Politics as a Vocation" is a classic discussion of political agency, "a sense of responsibility" is one of the three qualities a good politician will have.[2] While I have approached political agency in ways very different from Weber's, I have not said anything to repudiate his account.

To clarify, then: The question of responsibility is a reasonable question about political agency even in the way I have discussed it in this book, but, at the same time, it is not a central question. I didn't undertake the foregoing discussion to enumerate the criteria by which responsibility could be assigned to political agents. The purpose of the book has been to understand what we could call the "normative psychology" of political action and the related role of the institution of public reason.

Moreover, since I have argued for situational contingency in what count as reasons and how they are understood, this implies that responsibility, as a robust notion with definite content, is *partly* outside the purview of the book. Given the normative connotations of the concept of responsibility, I prefer to follow T. M. Scanlon and Marion Smiley, who adopt, for slightly different reasons and for different purposes, the concept of *accountability.* That concept figures here meaningfully, but relatively trivially. I borrow the concept from Scanlon and Smiley as a means to an inquiry into an agent's *reasons* for her actions and beliefs, without rendering any normative judgment on her.[3] In other words, to call an agent accountable for some action is to say that we can legitimately demand from her her reasons for the action. In that sense, of course, accountability figures trivially in the very idea of justification I have described: My political agents are accountable for their political engagement in the sense that they owe a justification for it. The concept of accountability is not only prior to the questions of substantive responsibility, but also broader. Only after we have ascertained that you are accountable for something can we even *begin* to raise the question of responsibility.

Of course, although accountability is conceptually trivial for my account, it isn't practically trivial. To say that agents owe justification for their political engagement to other agents is a substantive normative position that liberals needed to defend. That was the project I undertook in Part II and elaborated upon in Part III. Beyond this kind of accountability, however, this book has remained agnostic on responsibility, not because the question isn't important, but because it cannot be given a *general* answer.

One way to characterize the liberal account of political action I have advocated here is, in fact, to say that it steadfastly refuses certain kinds of general answers, answers that are both general but also have robust substantive content. In the following concluding section, I want to suggest that offering such answers would be profoundly illiberal.

Neither Mao nor Jesus

In his 1937 pamphlet "Combat Liberalism," Mao Zedong wrote: "But liberalism rejects ideological struggle and stands for unprincipled peace, thus giving rise to a decadent, philistine attitude and bringing about political degeneration in certain units and individuals in the Party and the revolutionary organizations."[4] This articulates nicely the position we've seen expressed by Carl Schmitt as liberalism's "cowardly intellectualism." It is the position I have wanted to reject in this book, and the previous chapters on why liberals can be committed to a *principled* peace, political reformism, and other supposedly cowardly modes of political engagement should have done that. At the same time, the previous chapters have also tried to show that my theoretical response to Schmitt does not make the account excessively idealistic or weak. I want to finish those arguments by showing that I consider the alternative extreme from the realpolitische anti-liberalism equally unsavory, and for the same reason.

A bit of self-indulgent autobiography. Like most European countries, Finland, my native country, has conscription for men, and also like many European countries, it offers alternative forms of civilian national service for conscientious objectors. I chose this option in 1990. Although I was and remain ambivalent about the use of violence, it seemed obvious to me that my moral principles and political strategy made the refusal to serve in the military the right choice then. (I am slightly less certain of what choice I would make now.) My objection was conscientious, or at least conscientious enough.

During this period, I became marginally involved with the Finnish Union of Conscientious Objectors. In the organization, there were two types of people: young men like me who had chosen the alternative civilian service and promoted it and young men known as total objectors, people who would refuse their putative national duty entirely and go to prison for about a year instead. In their view, the alternative service still endorsed the legitimacy of armed national defense. They certainly were technically right: The statute that then governed the alternative service did describe it as being part of the national defense effort.

I greatly admired the total objectors' courage, even when I disagreed with them. I once asked one of them why he had decided to go to prison. "It's simple," he said. "If you are a pacifist, that's just what you do." I was, at best, a contingent pacifist, but there were many quite committed ones among the people who had "settled for" the alternative service. In some cases, this may have reflected disagreements with the total objectors on what the alternative service endorsed or didn't endorse. But my sense was, on the basis of many conversations, that that wasn't all. The option of prison was simply too frightening, a price too large to pay for even a strong conviction. I certainly felt that even if I had been a committed pacifist, I wouldn't have had the courage to go to prison.

The total objectors represent a common intuition about the truly committed political agent. In that view, the agent is willing to sacrifice greatly for her convictions. Obviously, many do. (And in that group, doing twelve months in a cozy Scandinavian prison with its weekend leaves isn't even particularly impressive.) Those people deserve great admiration for their courage. However, the intuition that they are the model of principled political action is wrong, and it has been the purpose of this book to show that.

Call this understanding of political action the "Jesus model." Despite the irreverent sound, I don't mean to give offense: The notion is based on an idealized, perhaps even caricatured conception of the theological Jesus, which itself is likely to be an idealization of the historical Jesus of Nazareth. According to the model, this idealized Jesus is the appropriate exemplar for political action: Political action is simply the uncompromising pursuit of one's political principles. It may be very difficult, in that it can involve great sacrifices, but it is theoretically straightforward: The agent's gotta do what the agent's gotta do, the Right Thing, even if heavens fall.

It is trivially true that the Jesus model is not an accurate empirical characterization of political action. Most people who engage in political action don't come anywhere near the model Jesus. But although it is trivially true, it isn't trivial. We should wonder about models that fit badly with empirical reality. Again, I don't mean to reject ideal theory—I have, after all, endorsed the legitimacy of ideal theorizing. But I do mean to suggest that it is reasonable to raise the empirical adequacy question I introduced in Chapter 1. The last part of this book has been to put the ideal theory I developed in the earlier parts to an empirical adequacy test.

More importantly, however, I want to raise skeptical questions about the Jesus model *as* a piece of ideal theory. If Kant thinks humans can't ever shed their animality and become angels, then it also seems folly to hope they become divine. And what I have said in the preceding chapters should indeed suggest that the Jesus model doesn't even present a desirable exemplar of political action. Because of the essential openness of political contexts and of the partial independence of the meanings of our actions of our intentions, no agent can have a complete set of absolute principles as a practical guide. To think that an agent has a ready and straightforward blueprint for what to do in pursuit of her principles is to ignore that (1) the principles need a social context for their realization, and that is always contingent, and (2) the meaning of the blueprint also depends on the social context. The liberal inference is that an agent needs to be committed to the contingent public justifiability of *both* her principles *and* her engagement. In other words, from a liberal perspective, there are no principles that fully predate actual justificatory practices. But as we have seen, this needn't turn liberals into cowards. Rather, it opens the door for *principled* willingness to compromise.

The position isn't, after all, so different from Machiavellianism. I have suggested in the preceding chapters that *if* Machiavellianism means that strategic-instrumental considerations exhaust the range of normative considerations, then my account significantly differs from it. It is an open question whether that is really the position Machiavelli takes in the *Prince,* but that is beyond the scope of this book. However, there is an element distinct from but related to Machiavellianism, namely, the idea that political action fundamentally involves compromises, that the Jesus model of uncompromising pursuit of one's principles isn't even a theoretically coherent idea. That aspect of Machiavellianism is, of course, the very position I have advocated here. What I have done is to show why it is reasonable even when one grants that politics is about the justifiable pursuit of one's principled conception of legitimate authority.

At the same time, liberal conclusions about legitimate political action do often look different from those drawn by self-proclaimed Machiavellians, as I discussed in the previous chapter. This is because the liberal commitment to the justifiability of one's engagement *usually* (but not always) generates reasons to refrain from practices that deny or disrespect others' agency and even foreclose the very project of justification. This is most obvious in the nonviolent reformism that liberals generally prefer to plans for revolutionary overhaul. So liberals don't fail to start revolutions because they don't have the argumentative or practical resources for them, but because they have good reasons not to.

In the end, Schmitt's position, on the one hand, and the Jesus model, on the other, are two sides of the same coin. The coin is that of dogmatism. One general virtue of liberalism is that it tries to avoid falling into dogmatic slumbers, or, to use George Orwell's stronger phrase, it tries to steer clear of "smelly little orthodoxies."[5] It hasn't, of course, always succeeded in this, but insofar it has, it has been a powerful force of human emancipation (despite Marx's claim to the contrary in "On the Jewish Question"). This book has tried to show that this liberal virtue also applies attractively to political action.

We'll end with a final observation about the Kantian metaphor of the scholar. One of the central principles of modern scholarly inquiry is the principle of "fallibilism," the commitment to the idea that whatever hypothesis I might be entertaining might turn out to be a wrong one. It is central not only as some kind of boundary condition, but one of the very reasons *for* inquiry: If I dogmatically hold that hypothesis x must be true, I have no reason to test it. Of course, I do have good reasons to think hypothesis x will turn out to be true; that's why I'm testing it, and not hypothesis y. The same principle of fallibilism applies to the liberal political agent: She pursues some line of action because she has good reasons to think that it is a good one, but, at the same time, she knows that she might be mistaken.

ENDNOTES

Chapter 1: Agency and Politics—Problems for Liberal Theory?

1. Carl Schmitt, *The Crisis of Parliamentary Democracy*, trans. Ellen Kennedy (Cambridge, MA: MIT Press, 1985), p. 35.
2. Ibid., p. 64.
3. Carl Schmitt, *Political Theology: Four Chapters on the Concept of Sovereignty*, trans. George Schwab (Cambridge, MA: MIT Press, 1985), pp. 61–62.
4. He discusses his "decisionism" also in ch. 2 of *Political Theology*.
5. Betty Friedan, *The Feminine Mystique* (New York: Norton, 1963).
6. The literature on "bounded rationality" is very diverse and rapidly growing in many different directions. For examples, without my endorsement, see Herbert Alexander Simon, "Human Nature in Politics: The Dialogue of Psychology with Political Science," *The American Political Science Review* 79, no. 2 (1985); Simon, *Models of Bounded Rationality* (Cambridge, MA: MIT Press, 1982); Robert M. Axelrod, *The Complexity of Cooperation: Agent-Based Models of Competition and Collaboration* (Princeton, NJ: Princeton University Press, 1997); Axelrod, *The Evolution of Cooperation* (New York: Basic Books, 1984); Daniel Kahneman, Paul Slovic, and Amos Tversky, *Judgment under Uncertainty: Heuristics and Biases* (Cambridge: Cambridge University Press, 1982); and the contributions in Jerome H. Barkow, Leda Cosmides, and John Tooby, eds., *The Adapted Mind: Evolutionary Psychology and the Generation of Culture* (New York: Oxford University Press, 1992), and Gerd Gigerenzer and Peter M. Todd, eds., *Simple Heuristics That Make Us Smart* (New York: Oxford University Press, 1999).
7. Hilary Putnam, *Reason, Truth and History* (Cambridge: Cambridge University Press, 1981), ch. 7.
8. I leave open the question of how useful thought experiments might be for other kinds of theoretical projects. For two very different critiques, see Kathleen V. Wilkes, *Real People: Personal Identity without Thought Experiments* (Oxford: Clarendon Press, 1988) (on the metaphysics of personal identity), and Don Herzog, *Happy Slaves* (Chicago: University of Chicago Press, 1989), ch. 5 (on debates on liberal neutrality).
9. My view on the relationship between normative theory and actual social practices resembles that in Bryan G. Norton, "Applied Philosophy versus Practical Philosophy: Toward an Environmental Policy Integrated According to Scale," in *Environmental Philosophy and Environmental Activism*, ed. Don E. Marietta and Lester Embree (Lanham, MD: Rowman & Littlefield, 1995). Also see Norman Daniels, *Justice and Justification: Reflective Equilibrium in Theory and Practice* (Cambridge: Cambridge University Press, 1996). At source for these views are versions of American pragmatism; see, e.g., John Dewey, *Experience and Nature*, 2nd ed. (New York: Dover, 1958), pp. 398ff.
10. Hannah Arendt offers a classic case against the market conception of politics; see her *The Human Condition* (Chicago: University of Chicago Press, 1958). For a succinct discussion of the alternative conceptions, see Jon Elster, "The Market and the Forum: Three Varieties of Political Theory," in *Foundations of Social Choice Theory*, ed. Jon Elster and Aanund Hylland (Cambridge: Cambridge University Press, 1986). Discus-

sions of democracy and democratic citizenship make up a burgeoning cottage industry; for examples, see the articles in Seyla Benhabib, ed., *Democracy and Difference: Contesting Boundaries of the Political* (Princeton, NJ: Princeton University Press, 1996); James Bohman and William Rehg, *Deliberative Democracy: Essays on Reason and Politics* (Cambridge, MA: MIT Press, 1997); Jon Elster, ed., *Deliberative Democracy* (Cambridge: Cambridge University Press, 1998); see also John S. Dryzek, *Deliberative Democracy and Beyond: Liberals, Critics, Contestations,* (Oxford: Oxford University Press, 2000); Emily Hauptman, "Deliberation = Legitimacy = Democracy," *Political Theory* 27, no. 6 (1999); Will Kymlicka and Wayne Norman, "Return of the Citizen: A Survey of Recent Work on Citizenship Theory," *Ethics* 104, no. 2 (1994); Robert Post, "Managing Deliberation: The Quandary of Democratic Dialogue," *Ethics* 103, no. 4 (1993); Lynn Sanders, "Against Deliberation," *Political Theory* 25, no. 3 (1997); Ian Shapiro, *Democratic Justice* (New Haven, CT: Yale University Press, 1999); Chantal Mouffe, "Deliberative Democracy or Agonistic Pluralism?" *Social Research* 66, no. 3 (1999); Seyla Benhabib, "Citizens, Residents, and Aliens in a Changing World: Political Membership in the Global Era," *Social Research* 66, no. 3 (1999). The aggregative or "pluralist" model of democracy is defended, e.g., in Robert A. Dahl, *Democracy in the United States: Promise and Performance,* 4th ed. (Boston: Houghton Mifflin Co., 1981), and *Dilemmas of Pluralist Democracy: Autonomy vs. Control* (New Haven, CT: Yale University Press, 1982).

11. I am grateful to Kitty Holland for helping me formulate this thought more clearly.

12. For the "fact of pluralism," see John Rawls, "The Idea of an Overlapping Consensus," *Oxford Journal of Legal Studies* 7, no. 1 (1987), p. 4; Rawls, "Justice as Fairness: A Restatement" (Cambridge, MA: Harvard University Press, 2001), p. 3; Rawls, *Political Liberalism* (New York: Columbia University Press, 1993), p. 36; also Joshua Cohen, "Procedure and Substance in Deliberative Democracy," in *Democracy and Difference: Contesting the Boundaries of the Political,* ed. Seyla Benhabib (Princeton, NJ: Princeton University Press, 1996). For the idea of individualism, see, e.g., Jeremy Waldron, *Liberal Rights: Collected Papers 1981–1991* (New York: Cambridge University Press, 1993), ch. 2.

13. The account closest to mine is in Mark Sagoff, *The Economy of the Earth* (Cambridge: Cambridge University Press, 1988), pp. 150–151. The "ideal type of a liberal theorist" in Stephen Holmes, *Passions and Constraint: On the Theory of Liberal Democracy* (Chicago: University of Chicago Press, 1995), ch. 1, also comes close, although Holmes's emphases are different. Brian Barry, *Political Argument* (New York: The Humanities Press, 1965), pp. 66–69, is also similar, although it doesn't dwell on the fact of pluralism.

14. Isaiah Berlin, *Four Essays on Liberty* (Oxford: Oxford University Press, 1969). For an interesting recent review of Berlin's position, see William A. Galston, "Value Pluralism and Liberal Political Theory," *American Political Science Review* 93, no. 4 (1999).

15. For related statements, see, e.g., Cohen, "Procedure and Substance in Deliberative Democracy"; T. M. Scanlon, "Contractualism and Utilitarianism," in *Utilitarianism and Beyond,* ed. A. Sen and B. Williams (Cambridge: Cambridge University Press, 1982); Jürgen Habermas, *The Inclusion of the Other: Studies in Political Theory* (Cambridge, MA: MIT Press, 1998), chs. 1–2.

16. For the now-classic piece on the "liberalism of fear," see Judith Shklar, "The Liberalism of Fear," in *Liberalism and the Moral Life,* ed. Nancy L. Rosenblum (Cambridge, MA: Harvard University Press, 1989). I call the Hobbes-influenced variety "stripped-down" because, as Shklar convincingly argues, the liberalism of fear need not be purely instrumental. In fact, her middle-brow liberalism comes close to mine, although our emphases are very different.

17. See, e.g., Jürgen Habermas, "Three Normative Models of Democracy," in *Democracy and Difference: Contesting the Boundaries of the Political,* ed. Seyla Benhabib (Princeton,

NJ: Princeton University Press, 1996), which is reprinted also in *The Inclusion of the Other*, ch. 9. See also Habermas, *Between Facts and Norms: Contributions to a Discourse Theory of Law and Democracy*, trans. William Rehg (Cambridge, MA: MIT Press, 1998), pp. 99–100, 269–270, 298.

18. For the debate, see Jürgen Habermas, "Reconciliation through the Public Use of Reason: Remarks on John Rawls's Political Liberalism," *Journal of Philosophy* 92, no. 3 (1995); John Rawls, "Political Liberalism: Reply to Habermas," *Journal of Philosophy* 92, no. 3 (1995). Habermas's contribution and further arguments are reprinted as chs. 2–3 in *The Inclusion of the Other*.

19. Jürgen Habermas, *The Theory of Communicative Action: Reason and the Rationalization of Society*, trans. Thomas McCarthy, vol. 1 (Boston: Beacon Press, 1984), and *The Theory of Communicative Action: Lifeworld and System*, trans. Thomas McCarthy, vol. 2 (Boston: Beacon Press, 1989).

20. Habermas, *Between Facts and Norms*. Some of the themes receive an early exploration in Habermas's *On the Logic of the Social Sciences*, ed. Thomas McCarthy, trans. Shierry Weber Nicholsen and Jerry A. Stark (Cambridge, MA: MIT Press, 1988).

21. Habermas, "Reconciliation through the Public Use of Reason," p. 110, and *The Inclusion of the Other*, p. 50.

22. See, e.g., Rawls, *Political Liberalism*, pp. 145ff.

23. See, e.g., Jürgen Habermas, *Legitimation Crisis*, trans. Thomas McCarthy (Boston: Beacon Press, 1975), pp. 102–110; Habermas, *The Theory of Communicative Action*, vol. 1: ch. 1 and pp. 328–337; Habermas, *Justification and Application: Remarks on Discourse Ethics* (Cambridge, MA: MIT Press, 1993), ch. 2; Habermas, *The Inclusion of the Other*, ch. 1; Habermas, *Between Facts and Norms*, pp. 1–9.

Chapter 2: The Scope of the Political

1. Carl Schmitt, *Political Theology: Four Chapters on the Concept of Sovereignty*, trans. George Schwab (Cambridge, MA: MIT Press, 1985), p. 59.

2. Carl Schmitt, *The Concept of the Political*, trans. George Schwab (New Brunswick, NJ: Rutgers University Press, 1976), p. 26.

3. Ibid., p. 27.

4. See, e.g., Chantal Mouffe, "Deliberative Democracy of Agonistic Pluralism?" in *The Return of the Political* (London: Verso, 1993); Iris Marion Young, "Communication and the Other: Beyond Deliberative Democracy," in *Democracy and Difference: Contesting Boundaries of the Political, Princeton Paperbacks*, ed. Seyla Benhabib (Princeton, NJ: Princeton University Press, 1996).

5. Anchee Min, *Red Azalea* (New York: Pantheon Books, 1994).

6. Don Herzog, *Poisoning the Minds of the Lower Orders* (Princeton, NJ: Princeton University Press, 1998), ch. 11.

7. See, e.g., Glyn Moody, *The Rebel Code: The Inside Story of Linux and the Open Source Revolution* (Cambridge, MA: Perseus Publishers, 2001); Linus Torvalds, *Just for Fun: The Story of an Accidental Revolutionary* (New York: HarperCollins, 2001).

8. Arne Naess, *Ecology, Community and Lifestyle: Outline of an Ecosophy*, trans. David Rothenberg (Cambridge: Cambridge University Press, 1989), p. 130.

9. Fred Pearce, *Green Warriors: The People and the Politics Behind the Environmental Revolution* (London: The Bodley Head, 1991), p. 248.

10. I owe the idea of controversial claims to legitimate authority to Don Herzog, although my conception differs in small details from his. See *Poisoning the Minds of the Lower Orders*, pp. 155–156.

11. For the distinction, see, e.g., Mark Dowie, *Losing Ground: American Environmentalism at the Close of the Twentieth Century* (Cambridge, MA: MIT Press, 1995), pp. 1–2;

Mark Sagoff, *The Economy of the Earth* (Cambridge: Cambridge University Press, 1988), p. 154; Robert C. Paehlke, *Environmentalism and the Future of Progressive Politics* (New Haven, CT: Yale University Press, 1989), pp. 14–22.

12. Rachel Carson, *The Silent Spring* (Boston: Houghton Mifflin, 1962) . Since this is not a historical project, I will glibly use Rachel Carson as a placeholder for the emergence of modern, preservationist environmentalism. To be sure, Aldo Leopold and John Muir, perhaps even Thoreau, can be seen as important critics of modern industrial society, but in terms of having generated both an important movement and affected many people's consciousness, *The Silent Spring* is sufficiently central.

13. See, e.g., Schmitt, *The Concept of the Political*, p. 23, and Max Weber, "Politics as a Vocation," in *From Max Weber: Essays in Sociology*, ed. Hans H. Gerth and C. Wright Mills (New York: Oxford University Press, 1958); also in *Selections in Translation*, ed. W. G. Runciman, trans. E. Matthews (Cambridge: Cambridge University Press, 1978).

14. On this, see Don Herzog, "Externalities and Other Parasites," *University of Chicago Law Review* 67, no. 3 (2000).

15. For the Humean circumstances of justice, see David Hume, *An Inquiry Concerning the Principles of Morals* (Indianapolis: Bobbs-Merrill, 1957), sec. II, pt. I, pp. 14–21, or Hume, *A Treatise of Human Nature*, Selby-Bigge & Nidditch 2nd ed. (Oxford: Clarendon Press, 1978), bk. III, pt. II, sec. II, pp. 484–501. I elaborate on the Kantian conception of the political in Chapter 4; here I simply have in mind the "ought implies can" postulate.

16. See, e.g., Catherine MacKinnon, *Toward a Feminist Theory of the State* (Cambridge, MA: Harvard University Press, 1989).

17. The politicization of toxic wastes originally in Love Canal, New York. See, e.g., Andrew Szasz, *Ecopopulism: Toxic Waste and the Movement for Environmental Justice* (Minneapolis: University of Minnesota Press, 1994), ch. 3.

18. See the discussion about Rio Tinto Zinc in Al Gedicks, *The New Resource Wars: Native and Environmental Struggles against Multinational Corporations* (Boston: South End Press, 1993), ch. 2, and Rick Whaley and Walter Bresette, *Walleye Warriors: An Effective Alliance against Racism and for the Earth* (Philadelphia: New Society Publishers, 1994), ch. 8.

19. Steven Yearley, "Standing in for Nature: The Practicalities of Environmental Organizations' Use of Science," in *Environmentalism: The View from Anthropology*, ed. Kay Milton (London: Routledge, 1993), p. 59.

20. Yearley has the latter in mind, but as we will see later, there need not be any sort of necessary connection between the kinds of descriptive and normative claims.

21. Pearce, *Green Warriors*, p. 18.

22. Gabriel Gutierréz, "Mothers of East Los Angeles Strike Back," and Cynthia Hamilton, "Concerned Citizens of South Central Los Angeles," both in *Unequal Protection*, ed. Robert D. Bullard (San Francisco: Sierra Club Books, 1994); Szasz, *Ecopopulism*; Jim Schwab, *Deeper Shades of Green: The Rise of Blue-Collar and Minority Environmentalism in America* (San Francisco: Sierra Club Books, 1994).

23. See, e.g., Robin Broad and John Cavanagh, *Plundering Paradise: The Struggle for the Environment in the Philippines* (Berkeley: University of California Press, 1993), ch. 2; Gedicks, *The New Resource Wars*, ch. 2 and pt. II.

24. Whaley and Bresette, *Walleye Warriors*, pp. 216–218.

25. See, e.g., Broad and Cavanagh, *Plundering Paradise*, ch. 3; Philip Shenon, "Isolated Papua New Guineans Fall Prey to Foreign Bulldozers," *New York Times*, June 5, 1994; Pearce, *Green Warriors*, passim.

26. Ulrich Beck, *Ecological Enlightenment: Essays on the Politics of Risk Society*, trans. Mark A. Ritter (Atlantic Highlands, NJ: Humanities Press, 1995), p. 10.

27. See, e.g., Herbert Marcuse, *One Dimensional Man* (London: Sphere Books, 1968), or Jürgen Habermas, "Technology and Science as 'Ideology,'" in *Toward a Rational Society* (Boston: Beacon Press, 1971); see also Václav Havel, "Politics and Conscience," in *Open*

Letters: Selected Writings 1965–1990, ed. Paul Wilson (New York: Alfred A. Knopf, 1991), pp. 249–256.

28. See, e.g., Havel, "Politics and Conscience," p. 252.

29. John Locke, *A Letter Concerning Toleration* (Indianapolis: Hackett, 1983).

30. See, e.g., Langdon Winner, *The Whale and the Reactor* (Chicago: The University of Chicago Press, 1986).

31. I am ignoring here the relatively rare monumental cases in which an individual's actions are directly significant in the aggregate. The political paradigm case is the assassination of Archduke Ferdinand by Gavril Prinzip in Sarajevo in 1914, which in popular imagination "started" World War I. A contemporary example is the terrorist attack on the United States on September 11, 2001.

32. For classic discussions of related questions, see Donald Davidson, *Essays on Actions & Events* (Oxford: Clarendon Press, 1980).

33. Max Weber, *Economy and Society*, ed. Guenther Roth and Claus Wittch (Berkeley: University of California Press, 1978), vol. I, pp. 24–26.

34. David Hume, "Of Parties in General," in *David Hume's Political Essays* (New York: The Liberal Arts Press, 1953).

35. For two interesting cases of solidarity that reverse conventional gender roles, see Hamilton, "Concerned Citizens of South Central Los Angeles," and Gutierréz, "Mothers of East Los Angeles Strike Back."

36. Schmitt, *The Concept of the Political*, chs. 2–3. See also Schmitt, *The Crisis of Parliamentary Democracy*, trans. Ellen Kennedy (Cambridge, MA: MIT Press, 1985), ch. 4.

37. See Whaley and Bresette, *Walleye Warriors*.

38. Thomas E. Hill, Jr., "Symbolic Protest and Calculated Silence," *Philosophy & Public Affairs* 9, no. 1 (1979), grapples with these issues in a related way.

39. For a discussion on the ambiguities involved in the "discourses of organic food," see Allison James, "Eating Green(s): Discourses of Organic Food," in *Environmentalism: The View from Anthropology*, ed. Milton.

40. Thanks to Liz Anderson for this example.

41. Schmitt, *The Crisis of Parliamentary Democracy*, p. 35.

42. See, e.g., the account offered in Charles Larmore, *The Morals of Modernity* (Cambridge: Cambridge University Press, 1996), ch. 8.

43. I have in mind much of the contemporary analytic political philosophy, the theories concerned about finding something far more theoretically robust to defend liberal principles than the mere fact of social order.

44. Weber, *Economy and Society*, p. 31.

45. Ibid., p. 33.

46. Ibid.

47. Friedrich Nietzsche, *Beyond Good and Evil: Prelude to a Philosophy of the Future*, trans. R. J. Hollingdale (Harmondsworth: Penguin, 1990), aphorism 226.

48. Bernard Yack, *The Problems of a Political Animal: Community, Justice, and Conflict in Aristotelian Political Thought* (Berkeley: University of California Press, 1993), is an intriguing argument for a *normative* conception of the political as something that can only happen between equals. This doesn't mean that Yack would agree with my view.

49. See, e.g., Jürgen Habermas, *Justification and Application; Moral Consciousness and Communicative Action* (Cambridge, MA: MIT Press, 1990).

50. But see Jürgen Habermas, "The European Nation-State and the Pressures of Globalization," *New Left Review* 235 (1999).

51. Simon Schama, *Citizens: A Chronicle of the French Revolution* (New York: Random House, 1989).

52. Herbert Marcuse, "Repressive Tolerance," in *A Critique of Pure Tolerance*, ed. Robert Paul Wolff, Barrington Moore, and Herbert Marcuse (Boston: Beacon Press, 1969).

53. On "pluralizing" the Enlightenment, see, e.g, James Schmidt, "What Enlightenment Project?" *Political Theory* 28, no. 6 (2000).

Part II: Passions and Reasons

1 . James Schmidt, "What Enlightenment Project?" *Political Theory* 28, no. 6 (2000).
2 . Stephen Holmes, "The Permanent Structure of Antiliberal Thought," in *Liberalism and the Moral Life*, ed. Nancy L. Rosenblum (Cambridge, MA: Harvard University Press, 1989).

Chapter 3: If All Are Wicked, How Can They Change?

1. This point stands in some contrast with the enthusiasm of Bk. I, ch. 1 in SL, but I believe we are best off not taking Montesquieu literally, especially since the chapter is in some tension with his own ideas elsewhere. Abbreviations are explained in the Bibliography. With the *Spirit of the Laws*, the Roman numeral refers to the book, the Arabic to the chapter.
2. Bernard Yack, *The Longing for Total Revolution: Philosophic Sources of Social Discontent from Rousseau to Marx and Nietzsche* (Berkeley: University of California Press, 1992), pp. 35–36.
3. Nannerl O. Keohane, *Philosophy and the State in France: The Renaissance to the Enlightenment* (Princeton, NJ: Princeton University Press, 1980), p. 418.
4. My account borrows from Keohane's, although my emphases differ.
5. See, e.g., "The Authority of Society and the Individual" in John Stuart Mill, *On Liberty* (Indianapolis: Hackett, 1978). Recall that Locke, in his *A Letter Concerning Toleration,* argues that atheists and Catholics, among others, need not be tolerated.
6. These are among the central and recurring themes throughout SL, but books XI and XII capture many of them. See also, e.g., II: 4; V: 5, 14–16.
7. "It is a paralogism to say, that the good of the individual should give way to that of the public; this can never take place, except when the government of the community, or, in other words, the liberty of the subject is concerned" (SL, XXVI: 15).
8. See also SL, XI: 6; XIX: 27.
9. See, e.g., Edmund Burke, "Speech to the Electors of Bristol," in *The Writings & Speeches of the Right Honourable Edmund Burke* (Boston: Little, Brown & Co., 1901), or the *Federalist Papers.*
10. "These parties being composed of freemen, if the one becomes too powerful for the other, as a consequence of liberty this other is depressed" (SL, XIX: 27).
11. Keohane, *Philosophy and the State in France*, p. 419.
12. Louis Althusser, *Politics and History: Montesquieu, Rousseau, Hegel and Marx*, trans. Ben Brewster (London: NLB, 1972), p. 61.
13. Yack, *The Longing for Total Revolution*, pp. 39–48.
14. Mark Hulliung, *Montesquieu and the Old Regime* (Berkeley: University of California Press, 1976), p. 220, makes the same point, albeit more politely.
15. Ibid., passim.
16. Althusser, *Politics and History*, pp. 37–38.
17. This is one of the places where the Nugent translation is annoyingly misleading and encourages the unnecessarily psychological reading. Nugent translates "un sentiment, et non une suit de connoissances" at V: 2 as "a *sensation*, and not a consequence of acquired knowledge."
18. I do argue elsewhere that, conventional wisdom aside, Montesquieu's way is of the less racist and culturally imperialist variety ("The Ironic Climate Theory: Montesquieu as an Anti-Racist," paper presented at the American Political Science Association meeting, Washington, DC, 2000).
19. The Roman numeral refers to the numbered letters in *Persian Letters*, the Arabic to the page.
20. We should note that since honor is a positional good—someone's having it depends on others having none or less—one might be inclined to think that the all-or-nothing

nature of duels tracks this by making it a zero-sum game. That's not correct, however; the two duelers' honor doesn't depend on each other's: Victory or defeat in the duel itself is irrelevant to their honor; both are honorable as long as they duel. I briefly return to duels and honor in the next chapter.

21. There are other important benefits, too: As Yack points out, one consequence of love of one's country is that it helps Montesquieu sidestep the Church as a social stabilizer. See *The Longing for Total Revolution*, p. 46. However, that is not central to my discussion here.

22. This seems to have been generally one of the most pressing problems in social situations where social action is based on a sense of honor. See Eiko Ikegami, *The Taming of the Samurai: Honorific Individualism and the Making of Modern Japan* (Cambridge, MA.: Harvard University Press, 1995), for an excellent treatment of this phenomenon in the context of Tokugawa Japan.

23. This does not mean that love of one's country always points to a simple course of correct action or that there can't be disagreements on what this love means.

24. In addition to the critiques in Schmitt's *The Crisis of Parliamentary Democracy* that I discussed in Chapter 1, see, e.g., Alasdair MacIntyre, *After Virtue*, 2nd ed. (Notre Dame, IN: Notre Dame University Press, 1984); Michael Sandel, "The Procedural Republic and the Unencumbered Self," *Political Theory* 12, no. 1 (1984).

25. This brief sketch of an argument is roughly the view defended in Don Herzog, *Happy Slaves* (Chicago: University of Chicago Press, 1989).

26. Georg Simmel, "The Web of Group Affiliations," in *Conflict and the Web of Group Affiliations* (New York: Free Press, 1955).

27. I want to emphasize the notion of essentialism about *identity* to leave open the possibility of some other kinds of essentialism. See, e.g., Martha Nussbaum, "Human Functioning and Social Justice: In Defense of Aristotelian Essentialism," *Political Theory* 20, no. 2 (1992), and Nussbaum, *Women and Human Development: The Capabilities Approach* (Cambridge: Cambridge University Press, 2000), for a plausible argument for essentialism that centers on human functioning.

28. On the use of fiction as a replacement for natural law arguments, see Hulliung, *Montesquieu and the Old Regime*, ch. 5.

29. Yack, *The Longing for Total Revolution*, p. 52. See also Althusser, *Politics and History*, p. 58.

30. Nussbaum's argument in "Human Functioning and Social Justice" is an example of this.

31. It is an enduring open question how selfish Hobbes thinks people are, but there is little question that he generally was taken to think that.

32. 1 Sam. 8: 11–18.

33. MacIntyre, *After Virtue*.

34. In the G. D. H. Cole translation, this is called the Appendix. It is actually the very long footnote (i) to a passage in Part I of D2.

35. My translation. N. J. H. Dent, in his *Rousseau: An Introduction to His Psychological, Social and Political Theory* (New York: Basil Blackwell, 1989), p. 124, points out that Rousseau is talking about Émile, whose isolation in his childhood may have pushed back the corruption of the natural sentiments more than in others. But the point is, according to Rousseau, that the sentiment of natural compassion can be found in people at some stage of their development.

36. Rousseau's note (o).

37. My following discussion has benefited from Jean Starobinski, *Jean-Jacques Rousseau: Transparency and Obstruction*, trans. Arthur Goldhammer (Chicago: University of Chicago Press, 1988); Dent, *Rousseau: An Introduction*; and Joshua Cohen, "Autonomy and Authority: Rousseau on Democracy" (unpublished manuscript, MIT, 1993).

38. Dent, *Rousseau: An Introduction*, p. 119.

39. Ibid., p. 121.

40. Ibid., p. 56.

41. See SC, ch. IX, pp. 178–181, for Rousseau's discussion of property.
42. Dent, *Rousseau: An Introduction*, p. 60.
43. Yack, *The Longing for Total Revolution*, pp. 63–72.
44. See, e.g., Carl Schmitt, *The Crisis of Parliamentary Democracy*, trans. Ellen Kennedy (Cambridge, MA: MIT Press, 1985), p. 13.
45. See Yack, *The Longing for Total Revolution*, p. 57.
46. Ibid., pp. 81–82.

Chapter 4: Liberalism Grown Pale and Königsbergian

1. The abbreviations to Kant's work are listed in the Bibliography. The volume and page numbers refer to the standard Berlin Akademie Ausgabe.
2. This refers to the running numbering of the *Reflexionen* in the handwritten *Nachlass*.
3. Barbara Herman, "Could It Be Worth Thinking about Kant on Sex and Marriage?" in *A Mind of One's Own: Feminist Essays on Reason & Objectivity*, ed. Louise M. Antony and Charlotte Witt (Boulder, CO: Westview Press, 1993); Christine M. Korsgaard, "The Right to Lie: Kant on Dealing with Evil," *Philosophy and Public Affairs* 15 (1986).
4. Putting the matter this way may seem to court trouble from the other side, namely, the Hegelian critique of the categorical imperative as an empty formula. I don't think my account is at all at risk of succumbing to that critique, although I don't have the space to show that here.
5. See, e.g., Jürgen Habermas, *The Philosophical Discourse of Modernity: Twelve Lectures*, trans. Frederick Lawrence (Cambridge, MA: MIT Press, 1987), especially lecture 11; *Justification and Application: Remarks on Discourse Ethics* (Cambridge, MA: MIT Press, 1993); and *Moral Consciousness and Communicative Action* (Cambridge, MA: MIT Press, 1993).
6. Korsgaard, "The Right to Lie," p. 347, n22. See G, IV: 422.
7. See, e.g., Robert Paul Wolff, *In Defense of Anarchism* (New York: Harper & Row, 1970).
8. I borrow the title phrase from Nietzsche's "history of an error" in the *Twilight of the Idols*, where he accounts for "how the real world became a myth." At one stage, we have "[f]undamentally the same old sun, but shining through mist and scepticism; the idea grown sublime, pale, northerly, Königsbergian"; in *Twilight of the Idols/the Anti-Christ* (London: Penguin, 1990), p. 50. What Nietzsche thinks of the Kantian metaphysics is not very different from what many others think of Kant's politics.
9. Kurt Joachim Grau, ed., *Kant-Anekdoten* (Berlin: Verlag von Georg Stilke, 1924), p. 72; Ernst Cassirer, *Rousseau, Kant, Goethe* (Hamburg: Felix Meiner Verlag, 1991), p. 3.
10. It may be more than a coincidence that the following paragraph in the *Remarks*, which begins "The third thought at which one only arrives with difficulty," is unfinished.
11. Richard L. Velkley, "The Crisis of the End of Reason in Kant's Philosophy and the *Remarks* of 1764–1765," in *Kant & Political Philosophy*, ed. Ronald Beiner and William James Booth (New Haven, CT: Yale University Press, 1993).
12. Frederick C. Beiser, *The Fate of Reason: German Philosophy from Kant to Fichte* (Cambridge, MA: Harvard University Press, 1987), p. 24.
13. It is also worth observing the conjecture that it was Hamann who introduced Rousseau to Kant (Ibid., pp. 33 and 333, n58).
14. See Chapter 3 and SC, Bk. I, ch. 5; Bk. II, chs. 2–3, and Bk. IV, ch. 2, p. 250.
15. We should be careful here. As Onora (Nell) O'Neill, *Acting on Principle* (New York: Columbia University Press, 1975) points out (p. 35), the term categorical is misleading. However, the kind of categoricity that categorical imperative does have can be seen in the general will in that the general will cannot be applied for a single, narrowly defined issue.

16. Particularly important is the theological influence of pietism.
17. Velkley, "The Crisis of the End of Reason" (p. 86), translates "*Mittelding*" slightly mis-
    leadingly when he says merely that humans are "between" angels and cattle, and not "a
    cross between." I think it is clear from other contexts that Kant thinks "rational animal-
    ity" is exactly what it means to be a human being: We have aspects of both.
18. There is a significant translation error for the essay's title in the Reiss volume of Kant's
    Political Writings (Cambridge: Cambridge University Press, 1991): "*die mutmaßlicher
    Anfang*" is translated mistakenly as "Conjectures on the Beginning" when it should be
    "The Conjectural Beginning."
19. It is important to keep in mind that for Kant, *any* state of society is better than the state
    of nature since society is a guarantee against the proverbial *bellum omnium contra omnes*.
    See Alexander Altmann, "Prinzipien politischer Theorie bei Mendelssohn und Kant," in
    *Die Trostvolle Aufklärung: Studien zur Metaphysik und politischen Theorie Moses Mendels-
    sohns* (Stuttgart: Friedrich Frommann Verlag, 1982), p. 211. I'll return to this later.
20. Marcia Baron, *Kantian Ethics Almost without Apology* (Ithaca: NY Cornell University
    Press, 1995), ch. 3, esp. §2. Specifically, Baron argues, Kant is a rigorist about the duty
    of moral self-improvement.
21. This echoes Korsgaard's hopes for developing a "double-level" Kantian theory, one for
    ideal and one for nonideal conditions (Korsgaard, "The Right to Lie," pp. 342–349),
    except that I think I am more optimistic than she is about how much help Kant's politi-
    cal texts give us in that respect (see her p. 349).
22. For a repudiation of the first caricature, see Onora O'Neill, *Constructions of Reason*
    (Cambridge: Cambridge University Press, 1989), ch. 8, and Barbara Herman, *The Prac-
    tice of Moral Judgment* (Cambridge, MA: Harvard University Press, 1993), chs. 5 and 9;
    of the second, Korsgaard, "The Right to Lie"; and of the third, Herman, *The Practice of
    Moral Judgment*, ch. 1. See also Baron, *Kantian Ethics Almost without Apology*, passim.
23. O'Neill, *Acting on Principle*; also John Rawls, "Themes in Kant's Moral Philosophy,"
    and Barbara Herman, "Justification and Objectivity: Comments on Rawls and Allison,"
    both in *Kant's Transcendental Deductions*, ed. Eckart Förster (Stanford, CA: Stanford
    University Press, 1989).
24. My discussion here owes much to O'Neill, *Acting on Principle*, pp. 34–39, although I
    put the issue somewhat differently. A brief but largely helpful account by Kant himself
    can be found in his attempt to correct Garve's misunderstanding of his position in
    "Theory and Practice" (TP, VIII: 278–289).
25. Thanks to Liz Anderson for this formulation.
26. See *Critique of Judgment* (hereafter CJ), especially the unpublished First Introduction
    (included in the Pluhar translation). The important point is that objectivity in Kant's
    sense implies nothing about moral realism: It stems from the particular way human
    beings cognize, not from some metaphysically robust features in the mind-independent
    world. I do not have time to explore Kant's epistemology and theory of cognition here
    further, but it is worth noting that imagination (Einbildungskraft), which plays a funda-
    mental role in judgment for Kant, also serves as the catalyst of moving humans onto
    higher levels of their moral development. See, e.g., CBH. Stuart Hampshire, "The
    Social Spirit of Mankind," in *Kant's Transcendental Deductions*, ed. Förster; and Dieter
    Henrich, *Aesthetic Judgment and the Moral Image of the World: Studies in Kant* (Stanford,
    CA: Stanford University Press, 1992), chs. 1–2, explore these themes in slightly similar
    ways.
27. In recent Kant scholarship, most roads lead to Rawls, whose lectures on Kant philo-
    sophical folklore credits for the idea of the "self-love test." The term doesn't occur in the
    recently published notes, although clearly the idea is there. See, e.g., John Rawls, *Lec-
    tures on the History of Moral Philosophy*, ed. Barbara Herman (Cambridge, MA: Harvard
    University Press, 2000), pp. 162–216; see also O'Neill, *Acting on Principle*. I owe the
    term more directly to conversations with David Hills. There is much more to be done

to get this area of Kantian moral psychology clear—for example, there are some reasons to think that Kant might have two different notions of self-love. However, I believe my discussion suffices for the purpose at hand.

28. Lewis White Beck's slightly unfaithful "forever checks self-conceit" does capture nicely what I take to be Kant's idea, namely, that the moral law is consistent with self-love and merely puts it in its place.

29. To be sure, in the precritical *Lectures on Ethics,* Kant distinguishes self-love from self-esteem and treats the former as similar to self-conceit and, thus, to inflamed *amour-propre* (LE, 135). I have not had access to the original German, but I believe the difference here might be one only in the translation. The general spirit of the discussion in the section on self-love in LE is consistent with what I am saying here.

30. I say more about the role of the *Rechtslehre* in the Kantian corpus later.

31. It is important to note that the production of citizens is not the only function for the institution of marriage: Its purpose is also to prevent the inherently instrumental (and thus immoral) use of other people through sex. See Herman, "Could It Be Worth Thinking about Kant on Sex and Marriage?"

32. John Christian Laursen, "The Subversive Kant: The Vocabulary of 'Public' and 'Publicity,'" in *What Is Enlightenment? Eighteenth-Century Answers and Twentieth-Century Questions*, ed. James Schmidt (Berkeley: University of California Press, 1996). Joseph M. Knippenberg, "The Politics of Kant's Philosophy," in *Kant & Political Philosophy*, ed. Beiner and Booth, makes a somewhat similar argument, although I am not particularly sympathetic to his Straussian analysis.

33. For these views, I am heavily indebted to O'Neill, *Constructions of Reason*, especially chs. 2 and 8.

34. This view can be found in Thomas E. Hill, Jr., *Dignity and Practical Reason in Kant's Moral Theory* (Ithaca: NY: Cornell University Press, 1992), ch. 8, and Baron, *Kantian Ethics Almost without Apology*, pp. 31, 89.

35. The historical context I am providing here comes from James Schmidt, "The Question of Enlightenment: Kant, Mendelsson, and the *Mittwochgesellschaft*," *Journal of the History of Ideas* 50 (1989), and Laursen, "The Subversive Kant: The Vocabulary of 'Public' and 'Publicity.'"

36. J. K. W. Möhsen, "What Is to Be Done toward the Enlightenment of the Citizenry?" in *What Is Enlightenment?* ed. Schmidt, p. 50.

37. Schmidt, "The Question of Enlightenment," p. 288. Laursen, "The Subversive Kant" (p. 258), claims that Kant's emphasis comes from the fear of Frederick's sensors, who were most tolerant in matters of religion. It should be noted that in finding special significance in Kant's focus on clergy, I am not engaging in some kind of Straussian enterprise of looking for a hidden message, carefully disguised only for other political philosophers to discover. Quite the contrary: I am claiming, with Schmidt and Laursen, that Kant is writing on a hot issue of the day, quite explicitly participating in a discussion. Whatever may seem "disguised" is only because he *need not* spell out the relevance of the discussion of clergy to his contemporaries, and what is "hidden" is hidden only from those commentators who see in the essay a "timeless" work and who have not done their history homework.

38. The discussion here owes, again, much to O'Neill, *Constructions of Reason*, ch. 2. See also Jürgen Habermas, *The Structural Transformation of the Public Sphere: An Inquiry into a Category of Bourgeois Society*, ed. Thomas McCarthy, trans. Thomas Burger (Cambridge, MA: MIT Press, 1989), ch. 13.

39. Altmann, "Prinzipien politischer Theorie bei Mendelssohn und Kant," p. 211.

40. Charles Taylor, *Philosophical Arguments* (Cambridge, MA: Harvard University Press, 1995), ch. 13, especially pp. 263–266. See also ch. 11.

41. Thanks to David Hills for helping me sharpen the point of contention with Taylor.

42. See also *Reflexion* 8077 (XIX: 603–612), parts of which are verbatim the passages in CF.

This *Reflexion* was written on a folded folio sheet, all pages tightly filled, sometime between October 1795 and November 1799.

43. Grau, ed., *Kant-Anekdoten*, p. 18.

44. Biester's letter to Kant, quoted in Werner Haensel, *Kants Lehre vom Widerstandsrecht*, vol. 60, *Kant-Studien Ergänzungshefte* (Berlin: Pan-Verlag, 1926), p. 74.

45. Laursen, "The Subversive Kant," p. 263. See also Dieter Henrich, "On the Meaning of Rational Action in the State," in *Kant & Political Philosophy*, ed. Beiner and Booth, pp. 99–100, and Henrich, *Aesthetic Judgment and the Moral Image of the World*, ch. 4.

46. Haensel, *Kants Lehre vom Widerstandsrecht*, pp. 7–32, 60.

47. This is not the same as constructing a *Kantian* doctrine of resistance. My claim is stronger in that I claim Kant *wants* to imply this. If my interpretation is correct, then the former possibility follows a fortiori.

48. Haensel, *Kants Lehre vom Widerstandsrecht*, pp. 56, 58–68.

49. Christine M. Korsgaard, "Taking the Law into Our Own Hands: Kant on the Right to Revolution," in *Reclaiming the History of Ethics: Essays for John Rawls*, ed. Andrews Reath, Barbara Herman, and Christine M. Korsgaard (Cambridge: Cambridge University Press, 1997), p. 327, n25, makes the same point.

50. Thomas Hobbes, *Leviathan*, ed. Edwin Curley (Indianapolis: Hackett, 1994), ch. 28, para. 2, pp. 203–204.

51. Ibid., ch. 28, para. 2, p. 204; ch. 14, para. 4, p. 80.

52. This connection was pointed out to me by Claire Finkelstein.

53. Haensel, while of course writing before Leo Strauss, offers versions of this; see *Kants Lehre vom Widerstandsrecht*, ch. 3. Laursen also makes similar suggestions in "The Subversive Kant."

54. Unlike his "enlightened" and relatively liberal predecessor Fredrick II, Fredrick William was a religious mystic who heavily cracked down on the religious toleration that had flourished under Fredrick II. See, e.g., Horst Möller, *Vernunft und Kritik: Deutsche Aufklärung im 17. und 18. Jahrhundert* (Frankfurt am Main: Suhrkamp, 1986); Richard van Dülmen, *The Society of Enlightenment: The Rise of the Middle Class and Enlightenment Culture in Germany*, trans. Anthony Williams (Cambridge: Polity Press, 1992).

55. Altmann, "Prinzipien politischer Theorie bei Mendelssohn und Kant," pp. 209–212. For an interesting contrast with Kant's answer to the question of Enlightenment, see Moses Mendelssohn, "On the Question: What Is Enlightenment?" in *What Is Enlightenment?* ed. Schmidt, which appeared in the *Berlinische Monatsschrift* a month before Kant's essay.

56. van Dülmen, *The Society of Enlightenment*.

57. Altmann, "Prinzipien politischer Theorie bei Mendelssohn und Kant," p. 213.

58. Henrich, in "On the Meaning of Rational Action in the State," notes (p. 111) that Kant only arrived at this particular reading through a somewhat suspect *legerdemain:* Louis XVI was the only revolutionary since he had abdicated; the Estates-General-turned-Legislative-Assembly merely proceeded according to the principles of legitimate contract theory (see R 8055, XIX: 595–596). This might not be persuasive, but it is intelligible.

59. See ibid., p. 98.

60. van Dülmen, *The Society of Enlightenment*, pp. 83–92.

61. Henrich, "On the Meaning of Rational Action in the State," p. 102.

62. van Dülmen, *The Society of Enlightenment*, p. 49.

63. From "The Composition and Constitution of the Republic of Scholars," quoted in van Dülmen, *The Society of Enlightenment*, p. 50.

64. Ibid., pp. 57 and 89, and Joan B. Landes, *Women and the Public Sphere in the Age of the French Revolution* (Ithaca, NY: Cornell University Press, 1988); see also the contributions by Mary Ryan and Keith Michael Baker in Craig J. Calhoun, *Habermas and the Public Sphere* (Cambridge, MA: MIT Press, 1992), as well as Nancy Fraser, *Justice Inter-*

ruptus: Critical Reflections on the "Postsocialist" Condition (New York: Routledge, 1997), ch. 3.

65. A letter from Johann Heinrich Voss, quoted in van Dülmen, *The Society of Enlightenment*, p. 95.

Part III: No Secret Agents

1. Cf. James Johnson, "Arguing for Deliberation: Some Skeptical Considerations," in *Deliberative Democracy*, ed. Jon Elster (Cambridge: Cambridge University Press, 1998), p. 165.
2. PL, LXXIII: 149. Montesquieu was also less than flattering about the value of the coffeehouse conversations, where intellectuals "fritter[ed] away their talents on puerilities." See PL, XXXVI: 89.
3. Jürgen Habermas, *The Inclusion of the Other: Studies in Political Theory* (Cambridge, MA: MIT Press, 1998), p. 68.
4. Jürgen Habermas, "The European Nation-State and the Pressures of Globalization," *New Left Review* 233 (1999).
5. For sympathetic critiques, see, e.g., Johnson, "Arguing for Deliberation"; Robert Post, "Managing Deliberation: The Quandary of Democratic Dialogue," *Ethics* 103, no. 4 (1993); Lynn Sanders, "Against Deliberation," *Political Theory* 25, no. 3 (1997); Iris Marion Young. "Communication and the Other: Beyond Deliberative Democracy," in *Democracy and Difference: Contesting the Boundaries of the Political*, ed. Seyla Benhabib (Princeton, NJ: Princeton University Press, 1996).
6. John Rawls, "Justice as Fairness: Political Not Metaphysical," *Philosophy and Public Affairs* 14 (1985), p. 229.
7. John Rawls, *A Theory of Justice* (Cambridge, MA: Harvard University Press, 1971), p. 20; "Kantian Constructivism in Moral Theory," *The Journal of Philosophy* LXXVII, no. 9 (1980); and *Political Liberalism* (New York: Columbia University Press, 1993), pp. 28, 95ff. See also Nelson Goodman, *Fact, Fiction and Forecast*, 4th ed. (Cambridge, MA: Harvard University Press, 1983), p. 64, and Norman Daniels, *Justice and Justification: Reflective Equilibrium in Theory and Practice* (Cambridge: Cambridge University Press, 1996), ch. 2.
8. Consider, for example, the European Union sanctions against Austria in 2000 after Austrians voted, in perfectly legitimate elections, the far-right ÖFP into power.
9. Robert Paul Wolff, *In Defense of Anarchism* (New York: Harper & Row, 1970).
10. Christopher Bertram, "Political Justification, Theoretical Complexity, and Democratic Community," *Ethics* 107 (1997), passim.
11. See Hobbes, *Leviathan*, ch. xxvi, para. 16, pp. 178–179.
12. G. A. Cohen, "Incentives, Inequality, and Community," in *Equal Freedom*, ed. Stephen Darwall (Ann Arbor: The University of Michigan Press, 1995), p. 342.

Chapter 5: Landfills and Justice

1. Kenneth Gould, Allan Schnaiberg, and Adam S. Weinberg, *Local Environmental Struggles: Citizen Activism in the Treadmill of Production* (Cambridge: Cambridge University Press, 1996), p. 3; see also Gregory E. McAvoy, "Partisan Probing and Democratic Decisionmaking: Rethinking the Nimby Syndrome," *Policy Studies Journal* 26, no. 2 (1998); Edward Walsh, Rex Warland, and D. Clayton Smith, "Backyards, Nimbys, and Incinerator Sitings: Implications for Social Movement Theory," *Social Problems* 40, no. 1 (1993); Herbert Inhaber, *Slaying the NIMBY Dragon* (New Brunswick, NJ: Transaction Publishers, 1998), ch. 1.

2. See, for example Gould et al., *Local Environmental Struggles*, p. 3.
3. Andrew Szasz, *Ecopopulism: Toxic Waste and the Movement for Environmental Justice* (Minneapolis: University of Minnesota Press, 1994), p. 77.
4. Maarten Wolsink, "Entanglement of Interests and Motives: Assumptions behind the Nimby-Theory on Facility Siting," *Urban Studies* 31, no. 6 (1994), pp. 853–854; see also Michael Dear, "Understanding and Overcoming the Nimby Syndrome," *Journal of the American Planning Association* 58, no. 3 (1992); M. E. Vittes, P. E. Pollock, and S. A. Lilie, "Factors Contributing to NIMBY Attitudes," *Waste Management* 13 (1993); Debra Stein, "The Ethics of Nimbyism," *Journal of Housing and Community Development* 53, no. 6 (1996); Lois M. Takahashi and Michael J. Dear, "The Changing Dynamics of Community Opposition to Human Service Facilities," *Journal of the American Planning Association* 63, no. 1 (1997).
5. Charles Piller, "Nimbymania," *Utne Reader*, July/August 1992; Szasz, *Ecopopulism*; Vittes et al., "Factors Contributing to Nimby Attitudes."
6. Ian Welsh, "The Nimby Syndrome: Its Significance in the History of the Nuclear Debate in Britain," *British Journal of the History of Science* 26 (1993).
7. Margot Hornblower, "Not in My Backyard, You Don't," *Time*, June 17, 1988.
8. Gould et al., *Local Environmental Struggles*, ch. 2; Colin Crawford, *Uproar at Dancing Rabbit Creek: Battling over Race, Class, and the Environment* (Reading, MA: Addison-Wesley, 1996), ch. 2.
9. Dear, "Understanding and Overcoming the Nimby Syndrome," p. 292; see also Israel Colon and Brett Marston, "Resistance to a Residential AIDS Home: An Empirical Test of Nimby," *Journal of Homosexuality* 37, no. 3 (1999).
10. Langdon Winner, "The Mice That Roared," *Technology Review*, August/September 1994.
11. William B. Meyer, "NIMBY Then and Now: Land-Use Conflict in Worcester, Massachusetts, 1876–1900," *Professional Geographer* 47, no. 3 (1995); see also the classic study of suburbanization by Kenneth T. Jackson, *Grabgrass Frontier: The Suburbanization of the United States* (New York: Oxford University Press, 1985).
12. Vittes et al., "Factors Contributing to NIMBY Attitudes," p. 126; Douglas J. Lober, "Why Protest? Public Behavioral and Attitudinal Response to Siting a Waste Disposal Facility," *Policy Studies Journal* 23, no. 3 (1995).
13. Stephen F. Wilcox, *The Nimby Factor* (New York: St. Martin's Press, 1992), p. 178.
14. Recall the discussion of environmental politicization by Rachel Carson and others in Chapter 2.
15. Wolsink, "Entanglement of Interests and Motives," pp. 858–859.
16. Lober, "Why Protest?"
17. Ibid., p. 507.
18. Wolsink, "Entanglement of Interests and Motives," pp. 860–861. For a general critique of the irrationality charge, see also William R. Freudenburg and Susan K. Pastor, "Nimbys and Lulus: Stalking the Syndromes," *Journal of Social Issues* 48, no. 4 (1992).
19. Lober, "Why Protest?" p. 500.
20. Ibid., p. 504.
21. Gould et al., *Local Environmental Struggles*, p. 45.
22. Crawford, *Uproar at Dancing Rabbit Creek*, pp. 54–55, 63.
23. Gould et al., *Local Environmental Struggles*, p. 45.
24. Lober, "Why Protest?" pp. 504, 513.
25. Vittes et al., "Factors Contributing to NIMBY Attitudes," p. 125; Lober, "Why Protest?" p. 506; Wolsink, "Entanglement of Interests and Motives," pp. 863–865.
26. Elaine Cogan, "Is Your Community Being Invaded by Nimbys?" and Perry Norton, "Some Observations on Nimby-Ism," in *Planning Commissioners Journal*, http://www.webcom.com/pcj/articles/epc23.html (1996); Dear, "Understanding and Overcoming the Nimby Syndrome," pp. 294–297.

27. Toni Cade Bambara, *The Salt Eaters* (New York: Vintage Books, 1992), p. 242.
28. Michael C. Dawson, *Behind the Mule: Race and Class in African-American Politics* (Princeton, NJ: Princeton University Press, 1994), p. 57.
29. Ibid.
30. Ibid.
31. Giovanna Di Chiro, "Nature as Community: The Convergence of Environment and Social Justice," in *Uncommon Ground: Rethinking the Human Place in Nature*, ed. William Cronon (New York: W. W. Norton, 1996), p. 304, citing the United Church of Christ Commision for Racial Justice report *Toxic Waste and Race in the United States: A National Report on the Racial and Socioeconomic Characteristics of Communities with Hazardous Waste Sites*. See also Charles Lee, "Beyond Toxic Wastes and Race," in *Confronting Environmental Racism: Voices from the Grassroots*, ed. Robert D. Bullard (Boston: South End Press, 1993), pp. 48–49.
32. Di Chiro, "Nature as Community," p. 304.
33. Dorceta E. Taylor, "Women of Color, Environmental Justice, and Ecofeminism," in *Ecofeminism: Women, Culture, Nature*, ed. Karen J. Warren (Bloomington: Indiana University Press, 1997), provides a summary of the most significant research and its findings with regard to toxic waste siting (pp. 45–46).
34. Jim Schwab, *Deeper Shades of Green: The Rise of Blue-Collar and Minority Environmentalism in America* (San Francisco: Sierra Club Books, 1994), p. 172.
35. Ibid., pp. 173–174.
36. Donald A. Grinde and Bruce E. Johansen, *Ecocide of Native America: Environmental Destruction of Indian Land and Peoples* (Santa Fe, NM: Clear Light Publishers, 1995), pp. 173–174.
37. The concept was, to my knowledge, first articulated by Thadis Box in *Rehabilitation Potential of Western Coal Lands: A Report to the Energy Policy Project of the Ford Foundation*, ed. National Academy of Sciences (Cambridge, MA: Ballinger Publishing Co., 1974). See also Grinde and Johansen, *Ecocide of Native America*, chs. 5 and 8; Ward Churchill, *Struggle for the Land: Indigenous Resistance to Genocide, Ecocide and Expropriation in Contemporary North America* (Monroe, ME: Common Courage Press, 1993), Part III, and also Al Gedicks, *The New Resource Wars: Native and Environmental Struggles against Multinational Corporations* (Boston: South End Press, 1993).
38. Grinde and Johansen, *Ecocide of Native America*, p. 247; Churchill, *Struggle for the Land*, pp. 23–26.
39. Gedicks, *The New Resource Wars*, ch. 1.
40. Gertrude Ezorsky, *Racism and Justice: The Case for Affirmative Action* (Ithaca, NY: Cornell University Press, 1991), p. 9.
41. Cerrell Associates and J. Stephen Powell, *Political Difficulties Facing Waste-to-Energy Conversion Plant Siting* (Sacramento: California Waste Management Board, 1984), p. 17.
42. Jon Elster, *Political Psychology* (Cambridge: Cambridge University Press, 1993), p. 17.
43. Schwab, *Deeper Shades of Green*, ch. 8; Grinde and Johansen, *Ecocide of Native America*, ch. 5.
44. For the mechanisms of urban housing discrimination in general, see Jackson, *Grabgrass Frontier*, ch. 11, and Douglas S. Massey and Nancy A. Denton, *American Apartheid: Segregation and the Making of the Underclass* (Cambridge, MA: Harvard University Press, 1993), ch. 4. For specific examples relating to the environmental hazards, see, e.g., Schwab, *Deeper Shades of Green*; Francis Calpotura and Rinku Sen, "Pueblo Fights Lead Poisoning," Gabriel Gutierréz, "Mothers of East Los Angeles Strike Back," and Cynthia Hamilton, "Concerned Citizens of South Central Los Angeles," all in *Unequal Protection*, ed. Robert D. Bullard (San Francisco: Sierra Club Books, 1994); and also Churchill, *Struggle for the Land*.
45. Massey and Denton, *American Apartheid*, pp. 109–114.

46. Grinde and Johansen, *Ecocide of Native America*, pp. 122–133; Schwab, *Deeper Shades of Green*, pp. 351–355; Crawford, *Uproar at Dancing Rabbit Creek*, ch. 4 and passim.

47. Robert D. Bullard, "Introduction," in *Confronting Environmental Racism*, p. 10.

48. Churchill, *Struggle for the Land*, pp. 50–54.

49. Schwab, *Deeper Shades of Green*, pp. 360–364.

50. Grinde and Johansen, *Ecocide of Native America*, ch. 4; Mark Dowie, *Losing Ground: American Environmentalism at the Close of the Twentieth Century* (Cambridge, MA: MIT Press, 1995), p. 148.

51. Grinde and Johansen, *Ecocide of Native America*; Rick Whaley and Walter Bresette, *Walleye Warriors: An Effective Alliance against Racism and for the Earth* (Philadelphia: New Society Publishers, 1994), ch. 6.

52. On "framing," see, e.g., David A. Snow et al., "Frame Alignment Processes, Micromobilization, and Movement Participation," *American Sociological Review* 51, no. 4 (1986), and William Gamson, "Constructing Social Protest," in *Social Movements: Perspectives and Issues*, ed. Steven M. Buechler and F. Curt Cylke (Mountain View, CA: Mayfield Publishing Co., 1997).

53. Reported in the *Economist*, February 8, 1992, p. 66.

54. Crawford, in *Uproar at Dancing Rabbit Creek*, offers a particularly gripping example of this.

55. *This* is what it means to say that "ethics needs history," even though Elster might disagree. See "Sour Grapes—Utilitarianism and the Genesis of Wants," in *Utilitarianism and Beyond*, ed. A. Sen and B. Williams (Cambridge: Cambridge University Press, 1982), p. 238.

56. See Schwab, *Deeper Shades of Green*, p. 383.

57. Ibid., p. 390.

58. Welsh, "The Nimby Syndrome," p. 16.

59. For a case of an international alliance that didn't track anything other than shared experience of mercury poisoning, consider the case of Canadian Ojibway and the Japanese Minamata victims' alliance. See George Hutchison and Dick Wallace, *Grassy Narrows* (Toronto: Van Nostrand Reinhold, 1977), chs. 7 and 8.

60. See, e.g., John Rawls, "Political Liberalism: Reply to Habermas," *Journal of Philosophy* 92, no. 3 (1995), 140ff. and Jürgen Habermas, *The Inclusion of the Other: Studies in Political Theory* (Cambridge, MA: MIT Press, 1998), p. 72.

61. The view is discussed at length in Christopher Bertram, "Political Justification, Theoretical Complexity, and Democratic Community," *Ethics* 107 (1997). I return to some of these issues later.

62. Brian Barry, *Justice as Impartiality* (Oxford: Clarendon Press, 1995), p. 5.

63. Louis Hartz, *The Liberal Tradition in America* (San Diego: Harcourt Brace Jovanovich, 1955). For explicit critiques, see, e.g., Rogers M. Smith, *Civic Ideals: Conflicting Visions of Citizenship in U.S. History* (New Haven, CT: Yale University Press, 1997), Mark E. Kann, *On the Man Question: Gender and Civic Virtue in America* (Philadelphia: Temple University Press, 1991), ch. 1, or Catherine A. Holland, *The Body Politic: Foundings, Citizenship, and Difference in the American Political Imagination* (New York: Routledge, 2001).

64. For this line of argument, see Judith N. Shklar, *American Citizenship: The Quest for Inclusion* (Cambridge, MA: Harvard University Press, 1991).

65. Dorceta E. Taylor, "Environmentalism and the Politics of Inclusion," in *Confronting Environmental Racism*, ed. Bullard, p. 54.

66. For simplicity, I am collapsing the difference between subjective and objective interests here.

67. A classic definition and discussion is in Mancur Olson, *The Logic of Collective Action: Public Goods and the Theory of Groups* (New York: Schocken Books, 1968).

68. I'm following Charles Taylor here; see ch. 7, "Irreducibly Social Goods," in *Philosophical Arguments* (Cambridge: MA: Harvard University Press, 1995), especially p. 137.
69. Ibid., ch. 7.
70. Ibid., p. 139.
71. For another interesting discussion of friendship along similar lines, see Elizabeth Anderson, *Value in Ethics and Economics* (Cambridge, MA: Harvard University Press, 1993), pp. 40–41. For related philosophical discussions on ontological priority and supervenience, see, e.g., Donald Davidson, *Essays on Actions & Events* (Oxford: Clarendon Press, 1980); Jaegwon Kim, "Concepts of Supervenience," *Philosophy and Phenomenological Research* 45, no. 2 (1984); Harold Kincaid, "Reduction, Explanation and Individualism," *Philosophy of Science* 53 (1986); D. M. Armstrong, *Universals: An Opinionated Introduction* (Boulder, CO: Westview Press, 1989); Stephen Yablo, "Mental Causation," *Philosophical Review* 101, no. 2 (1992).
72. Taylor, *Philosophical Arguments*, p. 140; see also pp. 191 and 246ff [the latter chapter is a reprint of *Multiculturalism and the Politics of Recognition* (Princeton, NJ: Princeton University Press, 1992)]. The contrast to the Philippines is mine.
73. The following comes from Anderson, *Value in Ethics and Economics*; Christine Korsgaard, "Two Distinctions in Goodness," *The Philosophical Review* XCII, no. 2 (1983), pp. 19–21.
74. Wilhelm von Humboldt, *The Limits of State Action*, ed. J. W. Burrow, trans. Joseph Coulthard (Indianapolis: Liberty Fund, 1993): "It may easily be foreseen, therefore, that the important inquiry into the proper limits of State agency must lead to a consideration of greater freedom for human energies, and a richer diversity of circumstances and situations" (p. 5); "The true end of Man . . . is the highest and most harmonious development of his powers to a complete and consistent whole. Freedom is the first and indispensable condition which the possibility of such a development presupposes; but there is besides another essential—intimately connected with freedom, it is true—a variety of situations" (p. 10); ". . . how, when every one was developing in his individuality, more varied and finer modifications of the beatiful human character would spring up, and one-sidedness would become more rare" (p. 33); "the chief point to be kept in view by the State is the development of the powers of its citizens in their full individuality" (p. 133).
75. I want to sidestep issues of protected group identities, cultural reification, "post-ethnicity" [see David Hollinger, *Postethnic America: Beyond Multiculturalism* (New York: Basic Books, 1995)], and the like here, not because I don't think of them as important, but because they are not central to the point I'm making here.
76. For the debate, see, e.g., William Connolly, "Speed, Concentric Cultures, and Cosmopolitanism," *Political Theory* 28, no. 5 (2000); Charles Jones, *Global Justice: Defending Cosmopolitanism* (Oxford: Oxford University Press, 1999); Avishai Margalit and Joseph Raz, "National Self-Determination," *Journal of Philosophy* 87, no. 9 (1990); Pratap Bhanu Mehta, "Cosmopolitanism and the Circle of Reason," *Political Theory* 28, no. 5 (2000); David Miller, *On Nationality* (Oxford: Oxford University Press, 1997); Kai Nielsen, "Cosmopolitan Nationalism," *The Monist* 82, no. 3 (1999); Martha Nussbaum and Joshua Cohen, *For Love of Country: Debating the Limits of Patriotism* (Boston: Beacon Press, 1996); Bernard Yack, "The Myth of the Civic Nation," *Critical Review* 10, no. 2 (1996).
77. My discussion in this paragraph follows ch. 2, "Right and Individual Well-Being," as well as ch. 6, "Free Expression," in Joseph Raz, *Ethics in the Public Domain: Essays in the Morality of Law and Politics* (Oxford: Clarendon Press, 1994).
78. Ibid., p. 31.
79. Ibid., p. 132.
80. Rawls, *Political Liberalism*, and "Political Liberalism: Reply to Habermas"; see also Joshua Cohen, "Procedure and Substance in Deliberative Democracy"; and T. M. Scan-

lon, "Contractualism and Utilitarianism," in *Utilitarianism and Beyond*, ed. A. Sen and B. Williams (Cambridge: Cambridge University Press, 1982), and *What We Owe to Each Other* (Cambridge, MA: Belknap Press of Harvard University Press, 1998).

81. Anderson, *Value in Ethics and Economics*, p. xiii; see also pp. 93–97.

82. E.g., Rawls, *Political Liberalism*, pp. 48–54 and lecture IV.

83. Waldron, *Liberal Rights: Collected Papers 1981–1991* (New York: Cambridge University Press, 1993), pp. 56–57. See also Johnson, "Arguing for Deliberation: Some Skeptical Considerations," in *Deliberative Democracy*, ed. Jon Elster (Cambridge: Cambridge University Press, 1998).

84. See, e.g., Seyla Benhabib, "The Generalized and the Concrete Other: The Kohlberg-Gilligan Controversy and Moral Theory," in *Women and Moral Theory*, ed. Eva Feder Kittay and Diana T. Meyers (Totowa, NJ: Rowman & Littlefield, 1987); Michael Sandel, *Liberalism and the Limits of Justice* (Cambridge: Cambridge University Press, 1982), and *Democracy's Discontent: America in Search of a Public Philosophy* (Cambridge, MA: Belknap Press of Harvard University Press, 1996).

Chapter 6: On Collective Agency

1. Mao Zedong, "Analysis of the Classes in Chinese Society," in *Selected Works of Mao Tse-Tung* (Peking: Foreign Language Press, 1975), p. 13.

2. Carl Schmitt, *The Concept of the Political*, trans. George Schwab (New Brunswick, NJ: Rutgers University Press, 1976). p. 27. For a typology of group formation, see Georg Simmel, *Conflict & the Web of Group Affiliations* (New York: Free Press, 1955).

3. For Aristotle's treatment of friendship, see *Nicomachean Ethics*, Bk. VIII.

4. David Hume, "Of Parties in General," in *David Hume's Political Essays* (New York: The Liberal Arts Press, 1953), p. 80.

5. The typology is discussed on pp. 80–84 in ibid.

6. See, e.g., Robert A. Dahl, *Democracy in the United States: Promise and Performance*, 4th ed. (Boston: Houghton Mifflin Co., 1981), and *Dilemmas of Pluralist Democracy: Autonomy vs. Control* (New Haven, CT: Yale University Press, 1982).

7. See, e.g., T. H. Aston and C. H. E. Philpin, eds., *The Brenner Debate: Agrarian Class Structure and Economic Development in Pre-Industrial Europe* (Cambridge: Cambridge University Press, 1985); Allen Buchanan, "Revolutionary Motivation and Rationality," *Philosophy and Public Affairs* 9 (1979); G. A. Cohen, *Karl Marx's Theory of History: A Defense* (Princeton, NJ: Princeton University Press, 1978); Jon Elster, *Making Sense of Marx* (Cambridge: Cambridge University Press, 1985); Andrew Levine, *Arguing for Socialism: Theoretical Considerations*, rev. ed. (London: Verso, 1988); Andrew Levine and Erik Olin Wright, "Rationality and Class Struggle," in *Marxist Theory*, ed. Alex Callinicos (Oxford: Oxford University Press, 1989); Daniel Little, "Microfoundations of Marxism," in *Readings in the Philosophy of Social Science*, ed. Michael Martin and Lee C. McIntyre (Cambridge, MA: MIT Press, 1994).

8. Mancur Olson, *The Logic of Collective Action: Public Goods and the Theory of Groups* (New York: Schocken Books, 1968).

9. Colin Crawford, *Uproar at Dancing Rabbit Creek: Battling over Race, Class, and the Environment* (Reading, MA: Addison-Wesley, 1996), offers a case study of these issues.

10. Rick Whaley and Walter Bresette, *Walleye Warriors: An Effective Alliance against Racism and for the Earth* (Philadelphia: New Society Publishers, 1994).

11. Ibid., ch. 3.

12. Pearce, *Green Warriors: The People and the Politics Behind the Environmental Revolution* (London: The Bodley Head, 1991), p. 19.

13. Hume, "Of Parties in General."

14. For a discussion of roles, see Martin Hollis, *The Cunning of Reason* (Cambridge: Cam-

bridge University Press, 1987), and *Reason in Action: Essays in the Philosophy of Social Science* (Cambridge: Cambridge University Press, 1996).

15. See Georg Simmel, "The Web of Group Affiliations," in *Conflict & the Web of Group Affiliations.* The discussion in Hollis, *Reason in Action,* especially in ch. 7, has also been instructive for me here.

16. Gabriel Gutiérréz, "Mothers of East Los Angeles Strike Back," p. 231, and Cynthia Hamilton, "Concerned Citizens of South Central Los Angeles," p. 216, both in *Unequal Protection,* ed. Robert D. Bullard (San Francisco: Sierra Club Books, 1994).

17. For two reviews, see Jean L. Cohen, "Strategy or Identity: New Theoretical Paradigms and Contemporary Social Movements," *Social Research* 52, no. 4 (1985), and Charles Tilly, "Models and Realities of Popular Collective Action," *Social Research* 52, no. 4 (1985). The account in the following paragraphs condenses discussions from Carl Boggs, *Social Movements and Political Power: Emerging Forms of Radicalism in the West* (Philadelphia: Temple University Press, 1986); Ron Eyerman and Andrew Jamison, *Social Movements: A Cognitive Approach* (Cambridge: Polity Press, 1991); Boris Frankel, *The Post-Industrial Utopias* (Madison, WI: The University of Wisconsin Press, 1987); William Gamson, "Constructing Social Protest" and "The Social Psychology of Collective Action," both in *Social Movements,* ed. Steven M. Buechler and F. Curt Cylke (Mountain View, CA: Mayfield, 1997); Andrew Jamison et al., *The Making of the New Environmental Consciousness: A Comparative Study of the Environmental Movements in Sweden, Denmark and the Netherlands* (Edinburgh: Edinburgh University Press, 1990); James M. Jasper, *The Art of Moral Protest: Culture, Biography, and Creativity in Social Movements* (Chicago: University of Chicago Press, 1997); Doug McAdam, "Culture and Social Movements," in *Social Movements,* ed. Buechler and Cylke, and *Political Process and the Development of Black Insurgency* (Chicago: University of Chicago Press, 1982); and David A. Snow et al., "Frame Alignment Processes, Micromobilization, and Movement Participation," *American Sociological Review* 51, no. 4 (1986).

18. For "postmaterial," see, e.g., the classic Ronald Inglehart, *The Silent Revolution: Changing Values and Political Styles among Western Publics* (Princeton, NJ: Princeton University Press, 1977).

19. See Michael W. McCann, *Rights at Work: Pay Equity Reform and the Politics of Legal Mobilization* (Chicago: University of Chicago Press, 1994).

20. See Mitchell Thomashow, *Ecological Identity: Becoming a Reflective Environmentalist* (Cambridge, MA: MIT Press, 1995).

21. The position that I attribute to him can be found in Jon Elster, "The Market and the Forum: Three Varieties of Political Theory," *Foundations of Social Choice Theory,* ed. J. Elster and A. Hylland (Cambridge: Cambridge University Press, 1986).

22. Hannah Arendt is famously the twentieth-century advocate for this conception. See, e.g., *The Human Condition* (Chicago: University of Chicago Press, 1958).

23. For further accounts, see Margaret Levi and David Olson, "The Battles in Seattle," *Politics & Society* 28, no. 3 (2000), and Jeffrey St. Clair, "Seattle Diary: It's a Gas, Gas, Gas," *New Left Review,* November–December, no. 238 (1999). For an excellent on-line resource, see Center for Labor Studies, *WTO History Project* [2000 (cited November 2000)]; available from http://depts.washington.edu/pcls/ WTO_History_Project.htm.

24. See, e.g., Anarchist Action Collective, "The World Is Not Enough," *Seattle Weekly,* November 25–December 1, 1999; Kim Murphy, "A Revolutionary Movement Hits Small-Town America: Eugene, Ore., Has Become a Test Kitchen for Anarchists Who Have Taken Their Message Mainstream," *Los Angeles Times,* August 3, 1999; Sam Howe Verhovek and Joseph Kahn, "Talks and Turmoil: Street Rage; Dark Parallels with Anarchist Outbreak in Oregon," *New York Times,* December 3, 1999; Associated Press, "Anarchists' Guru Says He's Proud," *Seattle Times,* December 3, 1999; Associated Press, "Anarchists Long for Simpler World," *Seattle Times,* December 13, 1999.

25. See, e.g., Patrick Harrington, "Steelworkers Rally against WTO, 'Dumping,'" *Seattle*

Times, December 2, 1999. For more interviews of participants, see Center for Labor Studies, *WTO History Project*.

26. Associated Press, "Anarchists' Guru Says He's Proud."

27. USWA, *Steelworkers Blast China Trade Agreement* [United Steel Workers of America, 1999 (cited March 15 2000)]; available from http://www.fixitornixit.com/ press/BeckerChinareact.html.

28. The evidence here is anecdotal, from my own marginal involvement with the movements in Finland in 1991.

Chapter 7: Who Is an Agent?

1. Philippa Foot, "Approval and Disapproval," in *Virtues and Vices and Other Essays in Moral Philosophy* (Berkeley: University of California Press, 1978).

2. Ibid., pp. 194–195.

3. Jeremy Waldron, *Liberal Rights: Collected Papers 1981–1991* (New York: Cambridge University Press, 1993), p. 58; see also his entire ch. 2.

4. John Rawls, *A Theory of Justice* (Cambridge, MA: Harvard University Press, 1971), p. 139.

5. Brian Barry, *Liberty and Justice*, vol. 2, *Essays in Political Theory* (Oxford: Clarendon Press, 1991), p. 254.

6. Thomas Hobbes, *Leviathan*, ed. Edwin Curley (Indianapolis: Hackett, 1994), ch. XIII, para. 14, p. 78.

7. Brian Barry, *Theories of Justice* (Berkeley: University of California Press, 1989), pp. 194–196; see also Barry, *Liberty and Justice*, ch. 11.

8. Barry, *Theories of Justice*, p. 205.

9. Originally published in *Southern California Law Review* 45 (1972); references here are to Christopher D. Stone, *Should Trees Have Standing? Toward Legal Rights for Natural Objects* (Los Altos, CA: William Kaufman, Inc., 1974).

10. See the dissenting opinions in *Sierra Club v. Morton, Secretary of the Interior, et al.*, 70 U.S. 34 (1972).

11. Stone, *Should Trees Have Standing?* p. 11.

12. Ibid., p. 17.

13. Ibid.

14. For a variety of statements, see, e.g., Bill Devall and George Sessions, *Deep Ecology: Living as If Nature Mattered* (Salt Lake City, UT: Peregrine Smith Books, 1985); Christopher Manes, *Green Rage: Radical Environmentalism and the Unmaking of Civilization* (Boston: Little, Brown & Co., 1990); Arne Naess, *Ecology, Community and Lifestyle: Outline of an Ecosophy*, trans. D. Rothenberg (Cambridge: Cambridge University Press, 1989); Dave Foreman's parts of the dialogue in Steve Chase, ed., *Defending the Earth: A Dialogue between Murray Bookchin and Dave Foreman* (Boston: South End Press, 1991); Martha F. Lee, *Earth First! Environmental Apocalypse* (Syracuse, NY: Syracuse University Press, 1995), pp. 37–38.

15. These are just two recent conceptions of rights. For the first one, see Robert Nozick, *Anarchy, State, and Utopia* (New York: Basic Books, 1974), pp. 28–29; for the second, Joseph Raz, *Ethics in the Public Domain: Essays in the Morality of Law and Politics* (Oxford: Clarendon Press, 1994), ch. 2. For an interesting discussion on these, see also Waldron, *Liberal Rights*, ch. 9.

16. Waldron makes a similar point about a slightly different issue in his discussion of neutrality. See *Liberal Rights*, p. 153.

17. Consider the *Outside* magazine cover headline: "Ted Nugent Can Save Nature—But Only If He Gets to Kill Something First." Daniel Coyle, "Better Environmentalism through Killing," *Outside*, March 1998.

18. Stone, *Should Trees Have Standing?* pp. 22–23.
19. Barry, *Theories of Justice*, §§ 24–25. See also chs. 10–11 in *Liberty and Justice*.
20. Keith Thomas, *Man and the Natural World: Changing Attitudes in England 1500–1800* (New York: Oxford University Press, 1983), pp. 97–99.
21. James Oakes, *Slavery and Freedom: An Interpretation of the Old South* (New York: Alfred A. Knopf, 1990), ch. 4; see also ch. 2.
22. For the example, see Bryan G. Norton, "Applied Philosophy versus Practical Philosophy: Toward an Environmental Policy Integrated According to Scale," in *Environmental Philosophy and Environmental Activism*, ed. Don E. Jr. Marietta and Lester Embree (Lanham, MD: Rowman & Littlefield, 1995).
23. See, e.g., Joni Seager, "'Hysterical Housewives' and Other Mad Women: Grassroots Environmental Organizing in the United States," in *Feminist Political Ecology: Global Issues and Local Experiences*, ed. Dianne Rocheleau, Barbara Thomas-Slayter, and Esther Wangari (London: Routledge, 1996).
24. These concerns fuel some of the critiques of deliberative democracy I have mentioned in the earlier chapters. See, e.g., Lynn Sanders, "Against Deliberation." *Political Theory* 25, no. 3 (1997); Iris Marion Young, "Communication and the Other," in *Democracy and Difference*, ed. Seyla Benhabib (Princeton, NJ: Princeton University Press, 1996); James Johnson, "Arguing for Deliberation," in *Deliberative Democracy*, ed. Jon Elster (Cambridge: Cambridge University Press, 1998).
25. Don Herzog, *Poisoning the Minds of the Lower Orders* (Princeton, NJ: Princeton University Press, 1998).
26. Abbreviations for Kant's works are given in the Bibliography.
27. I am mixing the White, Beck, and Gregor translations here.
28. Gregor translates *affektive* here as "passionate," but as I note later, this seems inappropriate.
29. My reading differs here from that by Jane Keller, "The Failure of Kant's Imagination," in *What Is Enlightenment?* ed. James Schmidt (Berkeley: University of California Press, 196).
30. I am using Gregor's translation, but changing her "enthusiasm" to "fanaticism."
31. James Schmidt, "Introduction" in *What Is Enlightenment?* See also Hartmut Böhme and Gernot Böhme, "The Battle of Reason with the Imagination," in the same volume.
32. Hannah Ginsborg, *The Role of Taste in Kant's Theory of Cognition* (New York: Garland, 1990), p. 37.
33. Naomi Scheman, *Engenderings: Constructions of Knowledge, Authority, and Privilege* (New York: Routledge, 1993), p. 25.
34. Ibid., pp. 27–29; see also Foot, "Approval and Disapproval."
35. Ibid., pp. 192–195.
36. Those who think this isn't a Kantian point should consult ch. 9 in Barbara Herman, *The Practice of Moral Judgment* (Cambridge, MA: Harvard University Press, 1993), and related discussion in ch. 10 in Brian Barry, *Justice as Impartiality*, vol. 2, *A Treatise on Social Justice* (Oxford: Clarendon Press, 1995).
37. See Chapter 3.

Chapter 8: Agency and Liberal Legitimacy

1. For example, Christopher Manes, *Green Rage: Radical Environmentalism and the Unmaking of Civilization* (Boston: Little, Brown & Co., 1990), both concedes and defends the narrow misanthropy of some Earth First! positions: "Malthus may have been incorrect, famine may be based on social inequalities, plagues may be an undesirable way to control population—but the point remains that unless something is done to slow and reverse human population growth these contentions will soon become moot" (pp. 233–234).

For a history of Earth First!, see Martha F. Lee, *Earth First! Environmental Apocalypse* (Syracuse, NY: Syracuse University Press, 1995).

2. Edward Abbey, *The Monkey Wrench Gang*, 10th anniversary ed. (Salt Lake City, UT: Dream Garden Press, 1985). For his participation in the debates, see, e.g., Lee, *Earth First!*

3. The Sea Shepherd Society website is http://www.seashepherd.org/.

4. See Heida Diefenderfer, "Makah under Surveillance," *News from Indian Country*, January 1997, for an example of the Sea Shepherd Society's idiosyncratic politics: The Makah Indians are urged to "eat Big Macs" instead of whales. The rhetoric grows somewhat more sophisticated as the issue develops, however; see Earth First! Media, *Controversy over Makah Whale Hunt* [Sea Shepherd Society, 2000 (cited October 2000)]; available from http://www.efmedia.org/makah.html.

5. Max Weber, "Politics as a Vocation," in *From Max Weber: Essays in Sociology*, ed. Hans H. Gerth and C. Wright Mills (New York: Oxford University Press, 1958); also in *Selections in Translation*, trans. E. Matthews, ed. W. G. Runciman (Cambridge: Cambridge University Press, 1978).

6. See, e.g., the argument in John Rawls, *A Theory of Justice* (Cambridge, MA: Harvard University Press, 1971), §§57–59.

7. See my discussion in Chapter 3.

8. My earliest recollection of this is from the 1982 presidential election in Finland when a fellow ninth-grader said of the SDP front-runner: "Just wait and see: He'll nationalize all industries overnight."

9. I am somewhat suspicious of how long the coherence between Kant's liberalism and the teleology of the *Perpetual Peace* can be maintained and thus took care in Chapter 3 not to make the liberalism depend on the particular teleology. Lisa Ellis's work in progress on Kant's teleology provides a reconciliation I have found compelling.

10. Quoted in Andrew Jamison et al., *The Making of the New Environmental Consciousness* (Edinburgh: Edinburgh University Press, 1990), p. 66.

11. I use lowercase "g" to talk about those who identify with some version of green politics, capital "G" for the official organizations and their members.

12. Pauli Välimäki and Anne Brax, *Vihreä ABC-Kirja* (Helsinki: Vihreä liitto, 1991), pp. 21–22. In Pentti Linkola and Osmo Soininvaara, *Kirjeitä Linkolan Ohjelmasta* (Porvoo: WSOY, 1987), he debates his program with a Finnish *Realo* Green, Osmo Soininvaara, and outlines the details of his proposed "great leap backward." These details include getting rid of what in Linkola's view is an excessive respect for individual human life, as opposed to "Life."

13. Maurice Merleau-Ponty, *Humanism and Terror* (Boston: Beacon Press, 1969), is a classic statement; for a discussion that combines it with Williams-style considerations of "moral luck," see Peter Breiner, "Democratic Autonomy, Political Ethics, and Moral Luck," *Political Theory* 17 (1989).

14. Antonio Gramsci, *Selections from the Prison Notebooks*, trans. Quintin Hoare and Geoffrey Nowell Smith (New York: International Publishers, 1971); see the notes on the "modern Prince" (pp. 123–205). For a further development of the "two revolutions" idea, see Carl Boggs, *The Two Revolutions: Gramsci and the Dilemmas of Western Marxism* (Boston: South End Press, 1984).

15. For his own discussion, see Gramsci, *Prison Notebooks*, pp. 275–276. See also Václav Havel, *Open Letters: Selected Writings 1965–1990*, ed. Paul Wilson (New York: Alfred A. Knopf, 1991), and *Toward a Civil Society: Selected Speeches and Writings, 1990–1994*, trans. Paul Wilson et al. (Prague: Lidové Noviny, 1994).

16. Gramsci, *Prison Notebooks*, pp. 245–246. For the applications and criticisms of Gramsci's concept in contemporary social movement theory, see William A. Gamson, "The Social Psychology of Collective Action," and Doug McAdam, "Culture and Social

Movements," both in *Social Movements*, ed. Steven M. Buechler and F. Kurt Cylke, Jr. (Mountain View, CA: Mayfield, 1997).

17. Fred Pearce, *Green Warriors: The People and the Politics Behind the Environmental Revolution* (London: The Bodley Head, 1991), p. 19.

18. Todd Jefferson Moore's play "In the Heart of the Wood" (Seattle: Rain City Projects, 1994) about logging conflicts in the Pacific Northwest offers an excellent repertoire of these different perspectives. See also David Helvarg, *The War against the Greens: The "Wise-Use" Movement, the New Right, and Anti-Environmental Violence* (San Francisco: Sierra Club Books, 1994); Andrew Rowell, *Green Backlash: Global Subversion of the Environmental Movement* (London: Routledge, 1996), chs. 2 and 7; and Mark Dowie, *Losing Ground: American Environmentalism at the Close of the Twentieth Century* (Cambridge, MA: MIT Press, 1995), ch. 4, for a discussion of the anti-green perspectives.

19. Friedrich Nietzsche, *Beyond Good and Evil*, trans. R. J. Hollingdale (Harmondsworth: Penguin, 1990), pp. 68–69.

20. Quoted in Mark Sagoff, *The Economy of the Earth* (Cambridge: Cambridge University Press, 1988), p. 200.

21. Max Weber, *Economy and Society*, ed. Guenther Roth and Claus Wittch (Berkeley: University of California Press, 1978), p. 32.

22. Jon Elster, "The Market and the Forum: Three Varieties of Political Theory," in *Foundations of Social Choice Theory*, ed. Jon Elster and A. Hylland (Cambridge: Cambridge University Press, 1993).

Conclusion

1. George Orwell, "Reflections on Gandhi," in *A Collection of Essays* (San Diego: Harvest Books/HBJ, 1970), p. 176.

2. Max Weber, *Selections in Translation*, trans. E. Matthews, ed. W. G. Runciman (Cambridge: Cambridge University Press, 1978), p. 212; also in Weber, "Politics as a Vocation," in *From Max Weber: Essays in Sociology*, ed. Hans H. Gerth and C. Wright Mills (New York: Oxford University Press, 1958).

3. Cf. T. M. Scanlon, "The Significance of Choice," in *The Tanner Lectures on Human Values VIII*, ed. S. McMurrin (Salt Lake City, UT: The University of Utah Press, 1988), and Marion Smiley, *Moral Responsibility and the Boundaries of Community: Power and Accountability from a Pragmatic Point of View* (Chicago: The University of Chicago Press, 1992), especially chs. 8–10.

4. Mao Zedong, "Combat Liberalism," in *Selected Works of Mao Tse-Tung* (Peking: Foreign Language Press, 1975), p. 31.

5. See, e.g., George Orwell, *A Collection of Essays* (San Diego: Harvest Books/HBJ, 1970), p. 104.

BIBLIOGRAPHY

Abbreviations Used in the Text

Abbr.	Work	Original Year
MONTESQUIEU		
PL	*Persian Letters*	1721
SL	*The Spirit of Laws*	1748
ROUSSEAU		
LD	*Letter to M. D'Alembert on the Theatre*	1758
C3	*Correspondance III*	1765–1767
D	*Rousseau, Judge of Jean-Jacques: Dialogues*	1772
D1	*Discourse on Arts and Sciences*	1750
D2	*Discourse on the Origin and Foundations of Inequality among Men*	1755
E	*Émile, ou de l'education*	1762
GP	*Considérations sur le Gouvernement de Pologne*	1772
SC	*The Social Contract*	1762
KANT*		
A	*Anthropologie in pragmatischen Hinsicht* (*Anthropology from a Practical Point of View*)	1798
B	"Bemerkungen zu den Beobachtungen über das Gefühl des Schönen und Erhabenen" ("Remarks to the *Observations on the Feeling of the Beautiful and Sublime*") (vol. VII of *Kants handschriftlicher Nachlass*)	1764
CBH	"Conjectures on the Beginning of Human History"	1786
CF	*The Conflict of the Faculties*	1798
CJ	*Critique of Judgment*	1790
CPR	*Critique of Pure Reason*	1781(A); 1787(B)
DV	*Doctrine of Virtue* (part II of *The Metaphysics of Morals*)	1797
CPrR	*Critique of Practical Reason*	1788
G	*Foundations of the Metaphysics of Morals*	1785
LE	*Lectures on Ethics*	1775–1780
MM	*The Metaphysics of Morals*	1797
PP	*Perpetual Peace*	1795

*In cases where a translation is not listed in the Bibliography, I have used the standard Berlin Akademie Ausgabe.

R	"Reflexionen" (handwritten remarks on Kant's and others' works)	1753–1804
RL	*Rechtslehre* (Part I of *The Metaphysics of Morals*)	1797
RR	*Religion within the Limits of Reason Alone*	1793
RS	"Review of Schulz's Attempt at an Introduction to a Doctrine of Morals for All Human Beings Regardless of Religions"	1783
TP	"On the Common Saying: 'This May Be True in Theory, but It Does Not Apply in Practice'"	1793
UH	"Idea for a Universal History with a Cosmopolitan Purpose"	1784
VRL	"Über ein vermeintes Recht aus Menschenliebe zu lügen" ("On the Supposed Right to Lie from Altruistic Motives")	1797
WE	"Answer to the Question: What Is Enlightenment?"	1784
WOT	"What is Orientation in Thinking?"	1786

Works Cited

Abbey, Edward. *The Monkey Wrench Gang.* 10th anniversary ed. Salt Lake City, UT: Dream Garden Press, 1985.

Althusser, Louis. *Politics and History: Montesquieu, Rousseau, Hegel and Marx.* Translated by Ben Brewster. London: NLB, 1972.

Altmann, Alexander. "Prinzipien politischer Theorie bei Mendelssohn und Kant." In *Die Trostvolle Aufklärung: Studien zur Metaphysik und politischen Theorie Moses Mendelssohns,* 192–216. Stuttgart: Friedrich Frommann Verlag, 1982.

Anarchist Action Collective. "The World Is Not Enough." *Seattle Weekly,* November 25—December 1, 1999.

Anderson, Elizabeth. *Value in Ethics and Economics.* Cambridge, MA: Harvard University Press, 1993.

Arendt, Hannah. *The Human Condition.* Chicago: University of Chicago Press, 1958.

Aristotle. *Nicomachean Ethics.* Translated by Terence Irwin. 2nd ed. Indianapolis: Hackett Publishing Company, 1999.

Armstrong, D.M. *Universals: An Opinionated Introduction.* Boulder, CO: Westview Press, 1989.

Associated Press. "Anarchists' Guru Says He's Proud." *Seattle Times,* December 3, 1999.

———. "Anarchists Long for Simpler World." *Seattle Times,* December 13, 1999.

Aston, T. H., and C. H. E. Philpin, eds. *The Brenner Debate: Agrarian Class Structure and Economic Development in Pre-Industrial Europe.* Cambridge: Cambridge University Press, 1985.

Axelrod, Robert M. *The Complexity of Cooperation: Agent-Based Models of Competition and Collaboration, Princeton Studies in Complexity.* Princeton, NJ: Princeton University Press, 1997.

———. *The Evolution of Cooperation.* New York: Basic Books, 1984.

Bambara, Toni Cade. *The Salt Eaters.* First Vintage Contemporaries ed. New York: Vintage Books, 1992.

Barkow, Jerome H., Leda Cosmides, and John Tooby. *The Adapted Mind: Evolutionary Psychology and the Generation of Culture.* New York: Oxford University Press, 1992.

Baron, Marcia. *Kantian Ethics Almost without Apology.* Ithaca, NY: Cornell University Press, 1995.

Barry, Bryan. *Political Argument.* New York: The Humanities Press, 1965.

———. *Theories of Justice.* Vol. I, *Treatise on Social Justice.* Berkeley: University of California Press, 1989.

———. *Liberty and Justice.* Vol. 2, *Essays in Political Theory.* Oxford: Clarendon Press, 1991.

———. *Justice as Impartiality.* Vol. 2, *A Treatise on Social Justice.* Oxford: Clarendon Press, 1995.

Beck, Ulrich. *Ecological Enlightenment: Essays on the Politics of Risk Society.* Translated by Mark A. Ritter. Atlantic Highlands, NJ: Humanities Press, 1995.

Beiser, Frederick C. *The Fate of Reason: German Philosophy from Kant to Fichte.* Cambridge, MA: Harvard University Press, 1987.

Benhabib, Seyla. "The Generalized and the Concrete Other: The Kohlberg-Gilligan Controversy and Moral Theory." In *Women and Moral Theory*, edited by Eva Feder Kittay and Diana T. Meyers, 154–177. Totowa, NJ: Rowman & Littlefield, 1987.

———. "Citizens, Residents, and Aliens in a Changing World: Political Membership in the Global Era." *Social Research* 66, no. 3 (1999): 709–744.

———, ed. *Democracy and Difference: Contesting Boundaries of the Political.* Princeton, NJ: Princeton University Press, 1996.

Berlin, Isaiah. *Four Essays on Liberty.* Oxford: Oxford University Press, 1969.

Bertram, Christopher. "Political Justification, Theoretical Complexity, and Democratic Community." *Ethics* 107 (1997): 563–583.

Boggs, Carl. *The Two Revolutions: Gramsci and the Dilemmas of Western Marxism.* Boston: South End Press, 1984.

———. *Social Movements and Political Power: Emerging Forms of Radicalism in the West.* Philadelphia: Temple University Press, 1986.

Bohman, James, and William Rehg. *Deliberative Democracy: Essays on Reason and Politics.* Cambridge, MA: MIT Press, 1997.

Böhme, Hartmut, and Gernot Böhme. "The Battle of Reason with the Imagination." In *What Is Enlightenment? Eighteenth-Century Answers and Twentieth-Century Questions*, edited by James Schmidt, 426–452. Berkeley: University of California Press, 1996.

Box, Thadis. *Rehabilitation Potential of Western Coal Lands: A Report to the Energy Policy Project of the Ford Foundation.* Edited by National Academy of Sciences. Cambridge, MA: Ballinger Publishing Co., 1974.

Breiner, Peter. "Democratic Autonomy, Political Ethics, and Moral Luck." *Political Theory* 17 (1989): 550–574.

Broad, Robin, and John Cavanagh. *Plundering Paradise: The Struggle for the Environment in the Philippines.* Berkeley: University of California Press, 1993.

Buchanan, Allen. "Revolutionary Motivation and Rationality." *Philosophy and Public Affairs* 9, no. 1 (1979).

Bullard, Robert D. "Introduction." In *Confronting Environmental Racism: Voices from the Grassroots*, edited by Robert D. Bullard, 7–14. Boston: South End Press, 1993.

Burke, Edmund. "Speech to the Electors of Bristol." In *The Writings & Speeches of the Right Honourable Edmund Burke*, 89–98. Boston: Little, Brown & Co., 1901.

Calhoun, Craig J. *Habermas and the Public Sphere.* Cambridge, MA: MIT Press, 1992.

Calpotura, Francis, and Rinku Sen. "Pueblo Fights Lead Poisoning." In *Unequal Protection*, edited by Robert D. Bullard, 234–255. San Francisco: Sierra Club Books, 1994.

Carson, Rachel. *The Silent Spring.* Boston: Houghton Mifflin, 1962.

Cassirer, Ernst. *Rousseau, Kant, Goethe.* Hamburg: Felix Meiner Verlag, 1991.

Center for Labor Studies. *WTO History Project* (cited November 2000). Available from http://depts.washington.edu/pcls/WTO_History_Project.htm.

Cerrell Associates and J. Stephen Powell. *Political Difficulties Facing Waste-to-Energy Conversion Plant Siting.* Sacramento: California Waste Management Board, 1984.

Chase, Steve, ed. *Defending the Earth: A Dialogue between Murray Bookchin and Dave Foreman.* Boston: South End Press, 1991.

Churchill, Ward. *Struggle for the Land: Indigenous Resistance to Genocide, Ecocide and Expropriation in Contemporary North America.* Monroe, ME: Common Courage Press, 1993.

Cogan, Elaine. "Is Your Community Being Invaded by Nimbys?" In *Planning Commissioners Journal*, 1996.

Cohen, G. A. *Karl Marx's Theory of History: A Defense*. Princeton, NJ: Princeton University Press, 1978.

————. "Incentives, Inequality, and Community." In *Equal Freedom*, edited by Stephen Darwall, 331–397. Ann Arbor: The University of Michigan Press, 1995.

Cohen, Jean L. "Strategy or Identity: New Theoretical Paradigms and Contemporary Social Movements." *Social Research* 52, no. 4 (1985): 663–716.

Cohen, Joshua. "Autonomy and Authority: Rousseau on Democracy." Unpublished MS, MIT, 1993.

————. "Procedure and Substance in Deliberative Democracy." In *Democracy and Difference: Contesting the Boundaries of the Political*, edited by Seyla Benhabib. Princeton, NJ: Princeton University Press, 1996.

Colon, Israel, and Brett Marston. "Resistance to a Residential AIDS Home: An Empirical Test of Nimby." *Journal of Homosexuality* 37, no. 3 (1999): 135.

Connolly, William. "Speed, Concentric Cultures, and Cosmopolitanism." *Political Theory* 28, no. 5 (2000): 596.

Coyle, Daniel. "Better Environmentalism through Killing." *Outside*, March 1998, 58–66; 138–39.

Crawford, Colin. *Uproar at Dancing Rabbit Creek: Battling over Race, Class, and the Environment*. Reading, MA: Addison-Wesley, 1996.

Dahl, Robert A. *Democracy in the United States: Promise and Performance*. 4th ed. Boston: Houghton Mifflin Co., 1981.

————. *Dilemmas of Pluralist Democracy: Autonomy vs. Control*. New Haven, CT: Yale University Press, 1982.

Daniels, Norman. *Justice and Justification: Reflective Equilibrium in Theory and Practice*. Cambridge: Cambridge University Press, 1996.

Davidson, Donald. *Essays on Actions & Events*. Oxford: Clarendon Press, 1980.

Dawson, Michael C. *Behind the Mule: Race and Class in African-American Politics*. Princeton, NJ: Princeton University Press, 1994.

Dear, Michael. "Understanding and Overcoming the Nimby Syndrome." *Journal of the American Planning Association* 58, no. 3 (1992): 288–300.

Dent, N. J. H. *Rousseau: An Introduction to His Psychological, Social and Political Theory*. New York: Basil Blackwell, 1989.

Devall, Bill, and George Sessions. *Deep Ecology: Living as If Nature Mattered*. Salt Lake City, UT: Peregrine Smith Books, 1985.

Dewey, John. *Experience and Nature*. 2nd ed. New York: Dover, 1958.

Di Chiro, Giovanna. "Nature as Community: The Convergence of Environment and Social Justice." In *Uncommon Ground: Rethinking the Human Place in Nature*, edited by William Cronon, 298–320. New York: W. W. Norton, 1996.

Diefenderfer, Heida. "Makah under Surveillance." *News from Indian Country*, January 1997, 13A.

Dowie, Mark. *Losing Ground: American Environmentalism at the Close of the Twentieth Century*. Cambridge, MA: MIT Press, 1995.

Dryzek, John S. *Deliberative Democracy and Beyond: Liberals, Critics, Contestations*. Oxford: Oxford University Press, 2000.

Earth First! Media. *Controversy over Makah Whale Hunt* Sea Shepherd Society, 2000 cited October 2000. Available from http://www.efmedia.org/makah.html.

Elster, Jon. *Making Sense of Marx, Studies in Marxism and Social Theory*. Cambridge: Cambridge University Press, 1985.

————. "The Market and the Forum: Three Varieties of Political Theory." In *Foundations of*

Social Choice Theory, edited by Jon Elster and Aanund Hylland, 103–132. Cambridge: Cambridge University Press, 1986.

———. *Political Psychology*. Cambridge: Cambridge University Press, 1993.

———. "Sour Grapes—Utilitarianism and the Genesis of Wants." In *Utilitarianism and Beyond*, edited by A. Sen and B. Williams, 219–238. Cambridge: Cambridge University Press, 1982.

———, ed. *Deliberative Democracy, Cambridge Studies in the Theory of Democracy*. Cambridge: Cambridge University Press, 1998.

Eyerman, Ron, and Andrew Jamison. *Social Movements: A Cognitive Approach*. Cambridge: Polity Press, 1991.

Ezorsky, Gertrude. *Racism and Justice: The Case for Affirmative Action*. Ithaca, NY: Cornell University Press, 1991.

Foot, Philippa. "Approval and Disapproval." In *Virtues and Vices and Other Essays in Moral Philosophy*, 189–207. Berkeley: University of California Press, 1978.

Frankel, Boris. *The Post-Industrial Utopias*. Madison, WI: The University of Wisconsin Press, 1987.

Fraser, Nancy. *Justice Interruptus: Critical Reflections on the "Postsocialist" Condition*. New York: Routledge, 1997.

Freudenburg, William R., and Susan K. Pastor. "Nimbys and Lulus: Stalking the Syndromes." *Journal of Social Issues* 48, no. 4 (1992): 39–63.

Friedan, Betty. *The Feminine Mystique*. New York,: Norton, 1963.

Galston, William A. "Value Pluralism and Liberal Political Theory." *American Political Science Review* 93, no. 4 (1999): 769–778.

Gamson, William. "Constructing Social Protest." In *Social Movements: Perspectives and Issues*, edited by Steven M. Buechler and F. Curt Cylke, 228–244. Mountain View, CA: Mayfield, 1997.

———. "The Social Psychology of Collective Action." In *Social Movements: Perspectives and Issues*, edited by Steven M. Buechler and F. Kurt Cylke, Jr., 487–504. Mountain View, CA: Mayfield, 1997.

Gedicks, Al. *The New Resource Wars: Native and Environmental Struggles against Multinational Corporations*. Boston: South End Press, 1993.

Gigerenzer, Gerd, and Peter M. Todd, eds. *Simple Heuristics That Make Us Smart*. New York: Oxford University Press, 1999.

Ginsborg, Hannah. *The Role of Taste in Kant's Theory of Cognition*. New York: Garland, 1990.

Goodman, Nelson. *Fact, Fiction and Forecast*. 4th ed. Cambridge, MA: Harvard University Press, 1983.

Gould, Kenneth, Allan Schnaiberg, and Adam S. Weinberg. *Local Environmental Struggles: Citizen Activism in the Treadmill of Production*. Cambridge: Cambridge University Press, 1996.

Gramsci, Antonio. *Selections from the Prison Notebooks*. Translated by Quintin Hoare and Geoffrey Nowell Smith. New York: International Publishers, 1971.

Grau, Kurt Joachim, ed. *Kant-Anekdoten*. Berlin: Verlag von Georg Stilke, 1924.

Grinde, Donald A., and Bruce E. Johansen. *Ecocide of Native America: Environmental Destruction of Indian Land and Peoples*. Santa Fe, NM: Clear Light Publishers, 1995.

Gutierréz, Gabriel. "Mothers of East Los Angeles Strike Back." In *Unequal Protection*, edited by Robert D. Bullard, 220–233. San Francisco: Sierra Club Books, 1994.

Habermas, Jürgen. "Technology and Science as 'Ideology.'" In *Toward a Rational Society*, 81–122. Boston: Beacon Press, 1971.

———. *Legitimation Crisis*. Translated by Thomas McCarthy. Boston: Beacon Press, 1975.

———. *The Theory of Communicative Action: Reason and the Rationalization of Society*. Translated by Thomas McCarthy. 2 vols. Vol. 1. Boston: Beacon Press, 1984.

———. *The Philosophical Discourse of Modernity: Twelve Lectures.* Translated by Frederick Lawrence. Cambridge, MA: MIT Press, 1987.

———. *On the Logic of the Social Sciences.* Translated by Shierry Weber Nicholsen and Jerry A. Stark. Cambridge, MA: MIT Press, 1988.

———. *The Theory of Communicative Action: Lifeworld and System.* Translated by Thomas McCarthy. 2 vols. Vol. 2. Boston: Beacon Press, 1989.

———. *The Structural Transformation of the Public Sphere: An Inquiry into a Category of Bourgeois Society.* Translated by Thomas Burger. Edited by Thomas McCarthy, *Studies in Contemporary German Social Thought.* Cambridge, MA: MIT Press, 1989.

———. *Moral Consciousness and Communicative Action.* Cambridge, MA: MIT Press, 1990.

———. *Justification and Application: Remarks on Discourse Ethics.* Cambridge, MA: MIT Press, 1993.

———. "Reconciliation through the Public Use of Reason: Remarks on John Rawls's Political Liberalism." *Journal of Philosophy* 92, no. 3 (1995): 109–131.

———. "Three Normative Models of Democracy." In *Democracy and Difference: Contesting the Boundaries of the Political,* edited by Seyla Benhabib, 67–94. Princeton, NJ: Princeton University Press, 1996.

———. *Between Facts and Norms: Contributions to a Discourse Theory of Law and Democracy.* Translated by William Rehg. Cambridge, MA: MIT Press, 1998.

———. *The Inclusion of the Other: Studies in Political Theory.* Cambridge, MA: MIT Press, 1998.

———. "The European Nation-State and the Pressures of Globalization." *New Left Review* 235 (1999): 46–59.

Haensel, Werner. *Kants Lehre vom Widerstandsrecht.* Vol. 60, *Kant-Studien Ergänzungshefte.* Berlin: Pan-Verlag, 1926.

Hamilton, Cynthia. "Concerned Citizens of South Central Los Angeles." In *Unequal Protection,* edited by Robert D. Bullard, 207–219. San Francisco: Sierra Club Books, 1994.

Hampshire, Stuart. "The Social Spirit of Mankind." In *Kant's Transcendental Deductions,* edited by Eckart Förster, 145–156. Stanford: Stanford University Press, 1989.

Harrington, Patrick. "Steelworkers Rally against WTO, 'Dumping.'" *Seattle Times,* December 2, 1999.

Hartz, Louis. *The Liberal Tradition in America.* San Diego: Harcourt Brace Jovanovich, 1955.

Hauptman, Emily. "Deliberation = Legitimacy = Democracy." *Political Theory* 27, no. 6 (1999): 857–872.

Havel, Václav. *Open Letters: Selected Writings 1965–1990.* Edited by Paul Wilson. New York: Alfred A. Knopf, 1991.

———. *Toward a Civil Society: Selected Speeches and Writings, 1990–1994.* Translated by Paul Wilson et al. Prague: Lidové Noviny, 1994.

Helvarg, David. *The War against the Greens: The "Wise-Use" Movement, the New Right, and Anti-Environmental Violence.* San Francisco: Sierra Club Books, 1994.

Henrich, Dieter. *Aesthetic Judgment and the Moral Image of the World: Studies in Kant.* Edited by Eckart Förster. Stanford: Stanford University Press, 1992.

———. "On the Meaning of Rational Action in the State." In *Kant & Political Philosophy: The Contemporary Legacy,* edited by Ronald Beiner and William James Booth, 97–116. New Haven, CT: Yale University Press, 1993.

Herman, Barbara. "Justification and Objectivity: Comments on Rawls and Allison." In *Kant's Transcendental Deductions,* edited by Eckart Förster, 131–141. Stanford: Stanford University Press, 1989.

———. "Could It Be Worth Thinking about Kant on Sex and Marriage?" In *A Mind of One's Own: Feminist Essays on Reason & Objectivity,* edited by Louise M. Antony and Charlotte Witt, 49–68. Boulder: Westview Press, 1993.

———. *The Practice of Moral Judgment.* Cambridge, MA: Harvard University Press, 1993.

Herzog, Don. *Happy Slaves.* Chicago: University of Chicago Press, 1989.

———. *Poisoning the Minds of the Lower Orders.* Princeton, NJ: Princeton University Press, 1998.

———. "Externalities and Other Parasites." *University of Chicago Law Review* 67, no. 3 (2000): 895–923.

Hill, Thomas E. Jr. "Symbolic Protest and Calculated Silence." *Philosophy & Public Affairs* 9, no. 1 (1979): 83–102.

———. *Dignity and Practical Reason in Kant's Moral Theory.* Ithaca, NY: Cornell University Press, 1992.

Hobbes, Thomas. *Leviathan.* Edited by Edwin Curley. Indianapolis: Hackett, 1994.

Hollinger, David. *Postethnic America: Beyond Multiculturalism.* New York: Basic Books, 1995.

Hollis, Martin. *The Cunning of Reason.* Cambridge: Cambridge University Press, 1987.

———. *Reason in Action: Essays in the Philosophy of Social Science.* Cambridge: Cambridge University Press, 1996.

Holmes, Stephen. "The Permanent Structure of Antiliberal Thought." In *Liberalism and the Moral Life,* edited by Nancy L. Rosenblum, 227–253. Cambridge, MA: Harvard University Press, 1989.

———. *Passions and Constraint: On the Theory of Liberal Democracy.* Chicago: University of Chicago Press, 1995.

Hornblower, Margot. "Not in My Backyard, You Don't." *Time,* June 17, 1988 1988, 44–45.

Hulliung, Mark. *Montesquieu and the Old Regime.* Berkeley: University of California Press, 1976.

Hume, David. "Of Parties in General." In *David Hume's Political Essays,* 77–84. New York: The Liberal Arts Press, 1953.

———. *An Inquiry Concerning the Principles of Morals.* Indianapolis: Bobbs-Merrill, 1957.

———. *A Treatise of Human Nature.* Revised and annotated, Selby-Bigge & Nidditch 2nd ed. Oxford: Clarendon Press, 1978.

Hutchison, George, and Dick Wallace. *Grassy Narrows.* Toronto: Van Nostrand Reinhold, 1977.

Ikegami, Eiko. *The Taming of the Samurai: Honorific Individualism and the Making of Modern Japan.* Cambridge, MA: Harvard University Press, 1995.

Inglehart, Ronald. *The Silent Revolution: Changing Values and Political Styles among Western Publics.* Princeton, NJ: Princeton University Press, 1977.

Inhaber, Herbert. *Slaying the Nimby Dragon.* New Brunswick and London: Transaction Publishers, 1998.

Jackson, Kenneth T. *Grabgrass Frontier: The Suburbanization of the United States.* New York: Oxford University Press, 1985.

James, Allison. "Eating Green(s): Discourses of Organic Food." In *Environmentalism: The View from Anthropology,* edited by Kay Milton, 205–218. London: Routledge, 1993.

Jamison, Andrew, Ron Eyerman, Jacqueline Cramer, and Jeppe Læssøe. *The Making of the New Environmental Consciousness: A Comparative Study of the Environmental Movements in Sweden, Denmark and the Netherlands.* 216 ed. Edinburgh: Edinburgh University Press, 1990.

Jasper, James M. *The Art of Moral Protest: Culture, Biography, and Creativity in Social Movements.* Chicago: University of Chicago Press, 1997.

Johnson, James. "Arguing for Deliberation: Some Skeptical Considerations." In *Deliberative Democracy,* edited by Jon Elster, 161–184. Cambridge: Cambridge University Press, 1998.

Jones, Charles. *Global Justice: Defending Cosmopolitanism.* Oxford: Oxford University Press, 1999.

Kahneman, Daniel, Paul Slovic, and Amos Tversky. *Judgment under Uncertainty: Heuristics and Biases.* Cambridge: Cambridge University Press, 1982.

Kann, Mark E. *On the Man Question: Gender and Civic Virtue in America*. Philadelphia: Temple University Press, 1991.

Kant, Immanuel. *Critique of Pure Reason*. Translated by Norman Kemp Smith. New York: Macmillan, 1929.

———. *Critique of Practical Reason*. Translated by Lewis White Beck. New York: Macmillan, 1956.

———. *Religion within the Limits of Reason Alone*. Translated by Theodore M. Greene and Hoyt H. Hudson. New York: Harper & Row, 1960.

———. *Lectures on Ethics*. Translated by Louis Infield. Indianapolis: Hackett, 1979.

———. *Grounding for the Metaphysics of Morals*. Translated by James W. Ellington. Indianapolis: Hackett, 1981.

———. *Critique of Judgment*. Translated by Werner Pluhar. Indianapolis: Hackett, 1987.

———. *Foundations of the Metaphysics of Morals*. Translated by Lewis White Beck. 2nd ed. New York: Macmillan, 1985.

———. *The Metaphysics of Morals*. Translated by Mary Gregor. Cambridge: Cambridge University Press, 1991.

———. *Political Writings*. Edited by Hans Reiss. Cambridge: Cambridge University Press, 1991.

———. *Practical Philosophy*. Translated by Mary Gregor. Edited by Paul Guyer and Allen W. Wood. *The Cambridge Edition of the Works of Immanuel Kant*. Cambridge: Cambridge University Press, 1996.

Keller, Jane. "The Failure of Kant's Imagination." In *What Is Enlightenment? Eighteenth-Century Answers and Twentieth-Century Questions*, edited by James Schmidt, 453–470. Berkeley: University of California Press, 1996.

Keohane, Nannerl O. *Philosophy and the State in France: The Renaissance to the Enlightenment*. Princeton, NJ: Princeton University Press, 1980.

Kim, Jaegwon. "Concepts of Supervenience." *Philosophy and Phenomenological Research* 45, no. 2 (1984): 153–176.

Kincaid, Harold. "Reduction, Explanation and Individualism." *Philosophy of Science* 53 (1986): 492–513.

Knippenberg, Joseph M. "The Politics of Kant's Philosophy." In *Kant & Political Philosophy*, edited by Ronald Beiner and William James Booth, 155–172. New Haven, CT: Yale University Press, 1993.

Korsgaard, Christine. "Two Distinctions in Goodness." *The Philosophical Review* XCII, no. 2 (1983): 169–195.

———. "The Right to Lie: Kant on Dealing with Evil." *Philosophy and Public Affairs* 15 (1986): 325–349.

———. "Taking the Law into Our Own Hands: Kant on the Right to Revolution." In *Reclaiming the History of Ethics: Essays for John Rawls*, edited by Andrews Reath, Barbara Herman and Christine M. Korsgaard, 297–328. Cambridge: Cambridge University Press, 1997.

Kymlicka, Will, and Wayne Norman. "Return of the Citizen: A Survey of Recent Work on Citizenship Theory." *Ethics* 104 (1994): 352–381.

Landes, Joan B. *Women and the Public Sphere in the Age of the French Revolution*. Ithaca: Cornell University Press, 1988.

Larmore, Charles. *The Morals of Modernity*. Cambridge: Cambridge University Press, 1996.

Laursen, John Christian. "The Subversive Kant: The Vocabulary of 'Public' and 'Publicity.'" In *What Is Enlightenment? Eighteenth-Century Answers and Twentieth-Century Questions*, edited by James Schmidt, 253–269. Berkeley: University of California Press, 1996.

Lee, Charles. "Beyond Toxic Wastes and Race." In *Confronting Environmental Racism: Voices from the Grassroots*, edited by Robert D. Bullard, 41–52. Boston: South End Press, 1993.

Lee, Martha F. *Earth First! Environmental Apocalypse*. Syracuse, NY: Syracuse University Press, 1995.

Levi, Margaret, and David Olson. "The Battles in Seattle." *Politics & Society* 28, no. 3 (2000): 309–329.

Levine, Andrew. *Arguing for Socialism: Theoretical Considerations*. rev. ed. London: Verso, 1988.

Levine, Andrew, and Erik Olin Wright. "Rationality and Class Struggle." In *Marxist Theory*, edited by Alex Callinicos, 17–47. Oxford: Oxford University Press, 1989.

Linkola, Pentti, and Osmo Soininvaara. *Kirjeitä Linkolan ohjelmasta*. Porvoo: WSOY, 1987.

Little, Daniel. "Microfoundations of Marxism." In *Readings in the Philosophy of Social Science*, edited by Michael Martin and Lee C. McIntyre, 479–496. Cambridge, MA: MIT Press, 1994.

Lober, Douglas J. "Why Protest? Public Behavioral and Attitudinal Response to Siting a Waste Disposal Facility." *Policy Studies Journal* 23, no. 3 (1995): 488–518.

Locke, John. *A Letter Concerning Toleration*. Indianapolis: Hackett, 1983.

MacIntyre, Alasdair. *After Virtue*. 2nd ed. Notre Dame, IN.: Notre Dame University Press, 1984.

MacKinnon, Catherine. *Toward a Feminist Theory of the State*. Cambridge, MA: Harvard University Press, 1989.

Manes, Christopher. *Green Rage: Radical Environmentalism and the Unmaking of Civilization*. Boston: Little, Brown & Co., 1990.

Mao Zedong. "Analysis of the Classes in Chinese Society." In *Selected Works of Mao Tse-Tung*, 13–21. Peking: Foreign Language Press, 1975.

———. "Combat Liberalism." In *Selected Works of Mao Tse-Tung*, 31–33. Peking: Foreign Language Press, 1975.

Marcuse, Herbert. *One Dimensional Man*. London: Sphere Books, 1968.

———. "Repressive Tolerance." In *A Critique of Pure Tolerance*, edited by Robert Paul Wolff, Barrington Moore,and Herbert Marcuse. Boston: Beacon Press, 1969.

Margalit, Avishai, and Joseph Raz. "National Self-Determination." *Journal of Philosophy* 87, no. 9 (1990): 439–461.

Massey, Douglas S., and Nancy A. Denton. *American Apartheid: Segregation and the Making of the Underclass*. Cambridge, MA: Harvard University Press, 1993.

McAdam, Doug. *Political Process and the Development of Black Insurgency*. Chicago: University of Chicago Press, 1982.

———. "Culture and Social Movements." In *Social Movements: Perspectives and Issues*, edited by Steven M. Buechler and F. Kurt Cylke, Jr., 473–487. Mountain View, CA: Mayfield, 1997.

McAvoy, Gregory E. "Partisan Probing and Democratic Decisionmaking: Rethinking the Nimby Syndrome." *Policy Studies Journal* 26, no. 2 (1998): 274–93.

McCann, Michael W. *Rights at Work: Pay Equity Reform and the Politics of Legal Mobilization*. Chicago: University of Chicago Press, 1994.

Mehta, Pratap Bhanu. "Cosmopolitanism and the Circle of Reason." *Political Theory* 28, no. 5 (2000): 619.

Mendelssohn, Moses. "On the Question: What Is Enlightenment?" In *What Is Enlightenment? Eighteenth-Century Answers and Twentieth-Century Questions*, edited by James Schmidt, 53–57. Berkeley: University of California Press, 1996.

Merleau-Ponty, Maurice. *Humanism and Terror*. Boston: Beacon Press, 1969.

Meyer, William B. "NIMBY Then and Now: Land-Use Conflict in Worcester, Massachusetts, 1876–1900." *Professional Geographer* 47, no. 3 (1995): 298–308.

Mill, John Stuart. *On Liberty*. Indianapolis: Hackett, 1978.

Miller, David. *On Nationality*. Oxford: Oxford University Press, 1997.

Min, Anchee. *Red Azalea*. New York: Pantheon Books, 1994.

Möhsen, J. K. W. "What Is to Be Done toward the Enlightenment of the Citizenry?" In *What Is Enlightenment? Eighteenth-Century Answers and Twentieth-Century Questions*, edited by James Schmidt, 49–52. Berkeley: University of California Press, 1996.

Möller, Horst. *Vernunft und Kritik: Deutsche Aufklärung im 17. und 18. Jahrhundert.* Frankfurt am Main: Suhrkamp, 1986.

Montesquieu, Charles Louis de Secondat, Baron. *The Spirit of the Laws.* Translated by Thomas Nugent. II vols. New York: Hafner Press, 1949.

———. *Persian Letters.* Translated by C. J. Betts. London: Penguin Books, 1973.

Moody, Glyn. *The Rebel Code: The Inside Story of Linux and the Open Source Revolution.* Cambridge, MA: Perseus Publishers, 2001.

Moore, Todd Jefferson. *In the Heart of the Wood.* Seattle: Rain City Projects, 1994.

Mouffe, Chantal. *The Return of the Political.* London: Verso, 1993.

———. "Deliberative Democracy of Agonistic Pluralism?" *Social Research* 66, no. 3 (1999): 745–758.

Murphy, Kim. "A Revolutionary Movement Hits Small-Town America: Eugene, Ore., Has Become a Test Kitchen for Anarchists Who Have Taken Their Message Mainstream." *Los Angeles Times*, August 3, 1999, A1.

Naess, Arne. *Ecology, Community and Lifestyle: Outline of an Ecosophy.* Translated by David Rothenberg. Cambridge: Cambridge University Press, 1989.

Nielsen, Kai. "Cosmopolitan Nationalism." *The Monist* 82, no. 3 (1999): 446.

Nietzsche, Friedrich. *Beyond Good and Evil: Prelude to a Philosophy of the Future.* Translated by R. J. Hollingdale. Harmondsworth: Penguin, 1990.

———. "Twilight of the Idols." In *Twilight of the Idols/the Anti-Christ*, 30–122. London: Penguin, 1990.

Norton, Bryan G. "Applied Philosophy Versus Practical Philosophy: Toward an Environmental Policy Integrated According to Scale." In *Environmental Philosophy and Environmental Activism*, edited by Don E. Jr. Marietta and Lester Embree, 125–148. Lanham, MD: Rowman & Littlefield, 1995.

Norton, Perry. "Some Observations on Nimby-ism." In *Planning Commissioners Journal*, 1996.

Nozick, Robert. *Anarchy, State, and Utopia.* New York: Basic Books, 1974.

Nussbaum, Martha. "Human Functioning and Social Justice: In Defense of Aristotelian Essentialism." *Political Theory* 20, no. 2 (1992): 202–246.

———. *Women and Human Development: The Capabilities Approach.* Cambridge: Cambridge University Press, 2000.

Nussbaum, Martha, and Joshua Cohen. *For Love of Country: Debating the Limits of Patriotism.* Boston: Beacon Press, 1996.

———. *Constructions of Reason.* Cambridge: Cambridge University Press, 1989.

Oakes, James. *Slavery and Freedom: An Interpretation of the Old South.* New York: Alfred A. Knopf, 1990.

Olson, Mancur. *The Logic of Collective Action: Public Goods and the Theory of Groups.* New York: Schocken Books, 1968.

O'Neill, Onora (Nell). *Acting on Principle.* New York: Columbia University Press, 1975.

Orwell, George. *A Collection of Essays.* San Diego: Harvest Books/HBJ, 1970.

Paehlke, Robert C. *Environmentalism and the Future of Progressive Politics.* New Haven, CT: Yale University Press, 1989.

Pearce, Fred. *Green Warriors: The People and the Politics behind the Environmental Revolution.* London: The Bodley Head, 1991.

Piller, Charles. "Nimbymania." *Utne Reader*, July/August 1992, 114–115.

Post, Robert. "Managing Deliberation: The Quandary of Democratic Dialogue." *Ethics* 103, no. 4 (1993): 654–678.

Putnam, Hilary. *Reason, Truth and History*. Cambridge, MA: Cambridge University Press, 1981.

Rawls, John. *A Theory of Justice*. Cambridge, MA: Harvard University Press, 1971.

———. "Kantian Constructivism in Moral Theory." *The Journal of Philosophy* LXXVII, no. 9 (1980): 515–572.

———. "Justice as Fairness: Political Not Metaphysical." *Philosophy and Public Affairs* 14 (1985): 223–251.

———. "The Idea of an Overlapping Consensus." *Oxford Journal of Legal Studies* 7, no. 1 (1987): 1–25.

———. "Themes in Kant's Moral Philosophy." In *Kant's Transcendental Deductions*, edited by Eckart Förster, 81–113. Stanford, CA: Stanford University Press, 1989.

———. *Political Liberalism*. New York: Columbia University Press, 1993.

———. "Political Liberalism: Reply to Habermas." *Journal of Philosophy* 92, no. 3 (1995): 132–180.

———. *Lectures on the History of Moral Philosophy*. Edited by Barbara Herman. Cambridge, Mass., and London: Harvard University Press, 2000.

———. *Justice as Fairness: A Restatement*. Cambridge, MA: Harvard University Press, 2001.

Raz, Joseph. *Ethics in the Public Domain: Essays in the Morality of Law and Politics*. Oxford: Clarendon Press, 1994.

Rousseau, Jean-Jacques. *Correspondance III*. Vol. XIX, *Oeuvres De J. J. Rousseau*. Paris: Werdet et Lequien fils, 1826.

———. "Considérations sur le Gouvernement de Pologne et sur sa Réformation Projetée En Avril 1772." In *Du Contrat Social*, 337–417. Paris: Garnier Frères, 1962.

———. *Émile, ou de L'éducation*. Paris: Garnier-Flammarion, 1966.

———. "Letter to M. D'alembert on the Theatre." In *Politics and the Arts*, 1–137. Ithaca, NY: Cornell University Press, 1968.

———. *Social Contract and Discourses*. Translated by G. D. H. Cole. London: Dent, 1973.

———. *Rousseau, Judge of Jean-Jacques: Dialogues*. Translated by Christopher Kelly and Roger D. Masters Judith R. Bush. Vol. 1, *The Collected Writings of Rousseau*. Hanover and London: University Press of New England, 1990.

Rowell, Andrew. *Green Backlash: Global Subversion of the Environmental Movement*. London: Routledge, 1996.

Sagoff, Mark. *The Economy of the Earth*. Cambridge: Cambridge University Press, 1988.

Sandel, Michael. *Liberalism and the Limits of Justice*. Cambridge: Cambridge University Press, 1982.

———. "The Procedural Republic and the Unencumbered Self." *Political Theory* 12, no. 1 (1984): 81–96.

———. *Democracy's Discontent: America in Search of a Public Philosophy*. Cambridge, MA: Belknap Press of Harvard University Press, 1996.

Sanders, Lynn. "Against Deliberation." *Political Theory* 25, no. 3 (1997): 347–376.

Scanlon, T. M. "Contractualism and Utilitarianism." In *Utilitarianism and Beyond*, edited by A. Sen and B. Williams, 103–128. Cambridge: Cambridge University Press, 1982.

———. "The Significance of Choice." In *The Tanner Lectures on Human Values VIII*, edited by S. McMurrin, 149–216. Salt Lake City: The University of Utah Press, 1988.

———. *What We Owe to Each Other*. Cambridge, MA: Belknap Press of Harvard University Press, 1998.

Schama, Simon. *Citizens: A Chronicle of the French Revolution*. New York: Random House, 1989.

Scheman, Naomi. *Engenderings: Constructions of Knowledge, Authority, and Privilege.* New York: Routledge, 1993.

Schmidt, James. "The Question of Enlightenment: Kant, Mendelsson, and the *Mittwochge-sellschaft.*" *Journal of the History of Ideas* 50 (1989): 269–291.

———. "Introduction: What Is Enlightenment? A Question, Its Context, and Some Consequences." In *What Is Enlightenment? Eighteenth-Century Answers and Twentieth-Century Questions,* edited by James Schmidt, 1–44. Berkeley: University of California Press, 1996.

———. "What Enlightenment Project?" *Political Theory* 28, no. 6 (2000): 734–757.

Schmitt, Carl. *The Concept of the Political.* Translated by George Scwab. New Brunswick, NJ: Rutgers University Press, 1976.

———. *The Crisis of Parliamentary Democracy.* Translated by Ellen Kennedy. Cambridge, MA: MIT Press, 1985.

———. *Political Theology: Four Chapters on the Concept of Sovereignty.* Translated by George Schwab. Cambridge, MA: MIT Press, 1985.

Schwab, Jim. *Deeper Shades of Green: The Rise of Blue-Collar and Minority Environmentalism in America.* San Francisco: Sierra Club Books, 1994.

Seager, Joni. "Hysterical Housewives and Other Mad Women: Grassroots Environmental Organizing in the United States." In *Feminist Political Ecology: Global Issues and Local Experiences,* edited by Dianne Rocheleau, Barbara Thomas-Slayter and Esther Wangari, 271–283. London: Routledge, 1996.

Shapiro, Ian. *Democratic Justice.* New Haven, CT: Yale University Press, 1999.

Shenon, Philip. "Isolated Papua New Guineans Fall Prey to Foreign Bulldozers." *The New York Times,* June 5, 1994 1994, A1, A6.

Shklar, Judith. "The Liberalism of Fear." In *Liberalism and the Moral Life,* edited by Nancy L. Rosenblum, 21–38. Cambridge, MA: Harvard University Press, 1989.

———. *American Citizenship: The Quest for Inclusion.* 3 vols. Cambridge, MA: Harvard University Press, 1991.

Simmel, Georg. "Conflict." In *Conflict & the Web of Group Affiliations,* 11–123. New York: Free Press, 1955.

———. "The Web of Group Affiliations." In *Conflict & the Web of Group Affiliations,* 125–195. New York: Free Press, 1955.

Simon, Herbert Alexander. *Models of Bounded Rationality.* Cambridge, MA: MIT Press, 1982, 1984, 1997.

———. "Human Nature in Politics: The Dialogue of Psychology with Political Science." *The American Political Science Review* 79, no. 2 (1985): 293–304.

Smiley, Marion. *Moral Responsibility and the Boundaries of Community: Power and Accountability from a Pragmatic Point of View.* Chicago: University of Chicago Press, 1992.

Smith, Rogers M. *Civic Ideals: Conflicting Visions of Citizenship in U.S. History.* New Haven, CT: Yale University Press, 1997.

Snow, David A., E. Burke Rochford, Steven K. Worden, and Robert D. Benford. "Frame Alignment Processes, Micromobilization, and Movement Participation." *American Sociological Review* 51, no. 4 (1986): 464–481.

St. Clair, Jeffrey. "Seattle Diary: It's a Gas, Gas, Gas." *New Left Review,* November–December 238 (1999).

Starobinski, Jean. *Jean-Jacques Rousseau: Transparency and Obstruction.* Translated by Arthur Goldhammer. Chicago: University of Chicago Press, 1988.

Stein, Debra. "The Ethics of Nimbyism." *Journal of Housing and Community Development* 53, no. 6 (1996): 34.

Stone, Christopher D. *Should Trees Have Standing? Toward Legal Rights for Natural Objects.* Los Altos, CA: William Kaufman, Inc., 1974.

Szasz, Andrew. *Ecopopulism: Toxic Waste and the Movement for Environmental Justice.* Minneapolis: University of Minnesota Press, 1994.

Takahashi, Lois M., and Michael J. Dear. "The Changing Dynamics of Community Opposition to Human Service Facilities." *Journal of the American Planning Association* 63, no. 1 (1997): 79–94.

Taylor, Charles. *Multiculturalism and the Politics of Recognition.* Princeton, NJ: Princeton University Press, 1992.

———. *Philosophical Arguments.* Cambridge, MA: Harvard University Press, 1995.

Taylor, Dorceta E. "Environmentalism and the Politics of Inclusion." In *Confronting Environmental Racism: Voices from the Grassroots*, edited by Robert D. Bullard, 53–61. Boston: South End Press, 1993.

———. "Women of Color, Environmental Justice, and Ecofeminism." In *Ecofeminism: Women, Culture, Nature*, edited by Karen J. Warren, 38–81. Bloomington: Indiana University Press, 1997.

Thomas, Keith. *Man and the Natural World: Changing Attitudes in England 1500–1800.* New York: Oxford University Press, 1983.

Thomashow, Mitchell. *Ecological Identity: Becoming a Reflective Environmentalist.* Cambridge, MA: MIT Press, 1995.

Tilly, Charles. "Models and Realities of Popular Collective Action." *Social Research* 52, no. 4 (1985): 717–747.

Torvalds, Linus. *Just for Fun: The Story of an Accidental Revolutionary.* New York: Harper Collins, 2001.

USWA. *Steelworkers Blast China Trade Agreement*. United Steel Workers of America, 1999 [cited March 15 2000]. Available from http://www.fixitornixit.com/press/ BeckerChinareact.html.

Välimäki, Pauli, and Anne Brax. *Vihreä ABC-Kirja.* Helsinki: Vihreä liitto, 1991.

van Dülmen, Richard. *The Society of Enlightenment: The Rise of the Middle Class and Enlightenment Culture in Germany.* Translated by Anthony Williams. Cambridge: Polity Press, 1992.

Velkley, Richard L. "The Crisis of the End of Reason in Kant's Philosophy and the *Remarks* of 1764–1765." In *Kant & Political Philosophy*, edited by Ronald Beiner and William James Booth, 76–94. New Haven, CT: Yale University Press, 1993.

Verhovek, Sam Howe, and Joseph Kahn. "Talks and Turmoil: Street Rage; Dark Parallels with Anarchist Outbreak in Oregon." *New York Times*, December 3, 1999, A12.

Vittes, M. E., P. E. Pollock, and S. A. Lilie. "Factors Contributing to NIMBY Attitudes." *Waste Management* 13 (1993): 125–129.

von Humboldt, Wilhelm. *The Limits of State Action.* Translated by Joseph Coulthard. Edited by J. W. Burrow. Indianapolis: Liberty Fund, 1993.

Waldron, Jeremy. *Liberal Rights: Collected Papers 1981–1991.* New York: Cambridge University Press, 1993.

Walsh, Edward, Rex Warland, and D. Clayton Smith. "Backyards, Nimbys, and Incinerator Sitings: Implications for Social Movement Theory." *Social Problems* 40, no. 1 (1993): 25–39.

Weber, Max. "Politics as a Vocation." In *From Max Weber: Essays in Sociology*, edited by Hans H. Gerth and C. Wright Mills, 77–128. New York: Oxford University Press, 1958.

———. *Economy and Society.* Edited by Guenther Roth and Claus Wittch. Berkeley: University of California Press, 1978.

———. *Selections in Translation.* Translated by E. Matthews. Edited by W. G. Runciman. Cambridge: Cambridge University Press, 1978.

Welsh, Ian. "The Nimby Syndrome: Its Significance in the History of the Nuclear Debate in Britain." *British Journal of the History of Science* 26 (1993): 15–32.

Whaley, Rick, and Walter Bresette. *Walleye Warriors: An Effective Alliance against Racism and for the Earth.* Philadelphia: New Society Publishers, 1994.

Wilcox, Stephen F. *The Nimby Factor.* New York: St. Martin's Press, 1992.

Wilkes, Kathleen V. *Real People: Personal Identity without Thought Experiments.* Oxford: Clarendon Press, 1988.

Winner, Langdon. *The Whale and the Reactor.* Chicago: The University of Chicago Press, 1986.

———. "The Mice That Roared." *Technology Review,* August/September 1994, 72.

Wolff, Robert Paul. *In Defense of Anarchism.* New York: Harper & Row, 1970.

Wolsink, Maarten. "Entanglement of Interests and Motives: Assumptions behind the Nimby-Theory on Facility Siting." *Urban Studies* 31, no. 6 (1994): 851–866.

Yablo, Stephen. "Mental Causation." *Philosophical Review* 101, no. 2 (1992): 245–280.

Yack, Bernard. *The Longing for Total Revolution: Philosophic Sources of Social Discontent from Rousseau to Marx and Nietzsche.* Berkeley: University of California Press, 1992.

———. *The Problems of a Political Animal: Community, Justice, and Conflict in Aristotelian Political Thought.* Berkeley: University of California Press, 1993.

———. "The Myth of the Civic Nation." *Critical Review* 10, no. 2 (1996): 193–211.

Yearley, Steven. "Standing in for Nature: The Practicalities of Environmental Organizations' Use of Science." In *Environmentalism: The View from Anthropology,* edited by Kay Milton, 59–72. London: Routledge, 1993.

Young, Iris Marion. "Communication and the Other: Beyond Deliberative Democracy." In *Democracy and Difference: Contesting the Boundaries of the Political,* edited by Seyla Benhabib. Princeton, NJ: Princeton University Press, 1996.

INDEX

For Product Safety Concerns and Information please contact our EU
representative GPSR@taylorandfrancis.com
Taylor & Francis Verlag GmbH, Kaufingerstraße 24, 80331 München, Germany

www.ingramcontent.com/pod-product-compliance
Lightning Source LLC
Chambersburg PA
CBHW072120020426
42334CB00018B/1665

*9 7 8 0 4 1 5 9 3 1 9 9 1 *